Finally Free
My Escapes from Behind the Big Black Fences

Copyright 2005
by
Gisela Sterling
Cover art by Jack Moncure

ISBN 1-932196-78-1

WordWright.biz, Inc.
WordWright Business Park
46561 State Highway 118
Alpine, TX 79830

Printed in the United States of America

For Andrew, James, and Marcus, my three sons.

Acknowledgments

I acknowledge and thank my good friends with whom I taught for many years at Austin High School, Mary Adkins and Warner Dahlberg. They encouraged me to write this book and advised me on the manuscript. I thank my friends from Covenant United Methodist Church who studied with me in the Disciple I Bible class and urged me to write my story. I also express my appreciation to my three sons, Andrew, James, and Marcus, for their patience and encouragement as I have struggled with my computer and my memories, often reminding and correcting me about our experiences together. And I thank all of those friends who have listened to my stories and read them and urged me from time to time to go on with the project.

Introduction

So, who am I? Well, I'm Gisela Sterling a true American living in Texas, no longer Gisela Koch, the little girl born and raised in Berlin. At 80-years-old, but still young at heart I want to share my life experiences through this book. As a teacher, a preacher's wife, a mother and, now, a grandmother, I lived through a war, the bombing of my home, and the destruction of my country. I became a stranger in a new land, married a Methodist preacher and raised three boys. Over the years, I preached, cooked, cleaned, organized, suffered, and found happiness in my family and my Lord. In this book, I share all of these things with you, my readers, with joy and the desire that my life offers hope and promise to others.

Chapter 1

My Question

By September 1937, the German political climate filled the very air with a sense of danger. Everyone everywhere talked of war. People grew increasingly frightened. Jewish people left the country very suddenly, like the two Jewish girls in our class. One day they just stopped coming to school. We never saw them again.

Then, in November 1938, came the *Kristallnacht,* the night of the broken glass. During the night, the brown shirts and the SS (*Schutzstaffel*) broke the windows of Jewish businesses in Berlin into a thousand pieces, ruining everything. They destroyed desks, chairs, typewriters, cash registers, and goods of all kinds. They set fire to many synagogues. We in Zehlendorf, our large suburb southwest of Berlin, didn't know of this until we read about it in the newspaper the next morning. I don't know whether we had Jewish businesses in Zehlendorf or not, for at the age of thirteen, I didn't think very much about such things. I can't even remember my parent's reactions the next morning.

I'm not really sure how my father felt about the Jews, but I know that he helped a Jewish neighbor of ours by shoveling coal into her cellar and later she spoke of him as a Nazi. My mother had great sympathy for the Jewish people. In fact, she had Jewish friends who had to leave Germany. To me, however, as a thirteen-year-old, such things held little importance.

That is until things affected my friend Karl Ulrich, a Jewish boy who lived in the apartment house across the street. Karl's father practiced medicine in Zehlendorf and had, after the death of Karl's mother, remarried a non-Jewish woman before he himself died. Karl, a very nice person, came by my house every morning and we walked to school together, although he went to a school for boys and I to a nearby school for girls. One morning he didn't show up at our meeting place; nor did he the next morning, nor the next. I wondered what the matter was. There were two girls in our school who did not come any more either. We asked about them, and we were told that the school did not allow Jews anymore.

Worried about Karl, I talked to his stepmother who trusted me as a friend of Karl's. She told me that one day when she came home from the factory where she worked, she found Karl gone. The authorities had drafted him for "essential service." When she inquired, the Nazi watchman told her the Gestapo had picked Karl up and put him in a camp. Mrs. Ulrich didn't know what to do. When she found out the location of the camp near Berlin, she went there by train and took along some sandwiches. She told the man at the gate to take half of the sandwiches and give the other half to Karl Ulrich. The man gave her a stern look but took the sandwiches without saying a thing.

Three days later, she took two packages of cigarettes and the man at the gate said, "You're not a Jew."

She explained about being Karl's stepmother and how she loved the boy very much. The man told her to come back the next morning, and no matter what happened, not to open her mouth.

The next morning, she did as the man had told her. Suddenly she saw Karl coming out of one of the barracks. He came straight towards the gate, opened it, and walked out of the camp. Stepmother and stepson did not utter a word until they reached home. The man at the gate saved Karl Ulrich' life at his own risk.

6

Mrs. Ulrich kept Karl hidden well. Later, a former patient and very true friend of Karl's father came and took Karl to his big farm in the country where he remained safe until the war ended. On the eighth of May 1945, Karl Ulrich came back to Berlin to his beloved stepmother. In the meantime, I missed him very much and had lost a good friend.

Starting in 1941 the Nazi's required all Jews to wear a yellow Star of David. This made them easy to recognize. Some fanatical Nazis spit at people wearing this star.

I must've been about 16 years old when my mother and I rode the bus to town. An elderly lady who looked very tired and wore a yellow star stood by my seat. I got up and offered it to her. The lady looked around and did not show any signs of wanting to sit down. My mother motioned to me to keep my seat. I did not understand. My parents had told me always to offer my seat to elderly people. Why not now? What a sudden change!

Later at home my mother tried to explain to me why I had to keep my seat in the bus. Clearly, we had to treat people who wore the yellow Star of David as inferior and as outcasts. My mother also explained the brown shirts, or SA as we knew them, and SS in civilian clothes watched everybody. They took away people friendly to Jews and no one knew where. This frightened me greatly.

My grandparents Loebel had many Jewish friends who patronized their restaurant regularly. Suddenly, they did not show up any more. Mother and *Omi,* my grandmother, said they did not mention going somewhere. They hadn't said good-bye. They simply left and no one knew where.

Now, I understood why my friend, an American lady, did not come to the big old fence anymore to talk to me, and why she had not said good-bye. She probably had to leave as quickly as she could. Who wanted to live in a country where everyone watched everyone else and where brown shirts and the secret police walked around and suddenly took people away? Our beautiful Germany seemed to have changed into the devil's kitchen.

I remember the story Mother told me of Sara and Martin, very good Jewish friends of my parents and grandparents. Sara taught kindergarten in a Jewish school and Martin wrote books. Fine young people about 35 years old, they had no children. Sara greatly feared the Nazis. She wanted to leave the country, but Martin, a very proud individual, didn't want to leave the Fatherland. He also did not want to give in to the Nazis. After his marriage to Sara, he wrote a novel the general public praised and acknowledged. Unfortunately, the Nazis destroyed it during the book burning in May 1933. In 1934 the office of the cultural ministry forbade Martin to write any more books. He then found a job at a newspaper and wrote articles about sports events. He also did other odd jobs such as cleaning people's homes. At least he earned a little money.

One evening, Martin's father came to visit his son and daughter-in-law. Very upset, he told them he'd received a letter from the Gestapo informing him they planned to take him to the *Konzentrationslager* or concentration camp in Buchenwald. A fragile old man, he didn't want to hide, but he wasn't strong enough to leave the country.

A few days later, Sara received a letter from her mother. The letter told Sara that she should leave the country and go to her cousin in America. The cousin lived in Oklahoma and had offered all the family members refuge. Sara wanted to go, but Martin did not want to leave.

When, on the sixth of September, 1941, the Jews received the order to wear the yellow Star of David, Sara cried as she sewed the star on Martin's overcoat, and then her own coat. Martin sat beside her. He waited for her to throw accusations at him because he would not leave the country with her. She only looked at him with a very sad expression on her face.

When the siren sounded for another air raid, Sara and Martin took the bags they'd prepared for the shelter. Others took their belongings into the cellar too. When Sara and Martin looked for a place to sit down, Mrs. Keller, the head of the shelter committee, pushed Sara and Martin out because Jews weren't allowed in the shelter. Sara, very much afraid, sat with Martin on the cellar steps.

A few days later, Martin received a letter from the Gestapo. The letter informed him that his father had died suddenly from heart failure. He probably died from the harsh conditions in the camp. Saddened, Sara again begged Martin to leave Germany with her, but he still refused although he knew it was dangerous for them to stay.

A few days later, after Martin cleaned house for Felicitas, a very rich lady and a very good friend, he asked if she'd hide Sara and him in the cellar of her house. Felicitas agreed gladly, because she had known Sara since childhood. She asked Martin to stay in the house while she drove to pick up Sara from the apartment. She found Sara very depressed because of a letter from the Gestapo stating they would come for her and Martin in the morning. Felicitas told Sara to go to the car so she could take her to join Martin. Sara wanted to pack some more and refused to go with Felicitas at that time.

About an hour later the Gestapo arrived and took Sara with them. No one ever heard from Sara again. She most likely died in a *Konzentrationslager*. Because of Martin's pride and very strong will, he had sacrificed his wife by refusing to leave Germany earlier.

Martin stayed in Felicitas' house where he lived in the cellar and came up during the day. When the doorbell rang, he hurried to the cellar and covered up. He lived in this manner throughout the war, a very hard life. He and other Jews lived like that behind a big black fence.

After the war ended he left his hiding place. When he saw the destruction of Berlin, he finally made up his mind to leave the country, but putting off his decision had cost him his wife.

In 2001 while visiting Berlin I went to a concentration camp named *Sachsenhausen*. My grandson wanted to see one. There, we saw the small cells barely large enough for one person into which the Nazis put 50 or 60 people. I also saw a cement platform where some Jewish men received deadly shots in the neck. We saw the places where the Jewish men and women where killed with gas. It seemed we could still smell the burned flesh. When I saw all that, I asked myself how could this have happened right under our noses. The Nazis around Hitler knew about these horrors, but the average citizen did not.

I also saw the place where the Gypsy's had their gas chambers. They were separated from the Jews. I did not know that the Gypsies had been treated like the Jews. I was surprised when I found out. I guess they were killed because of their dark skin color. Hitler wanted an Aryan race. He wanted blond and blue-eyed people. I wonder if he ever looked in the mirror. He had dark eyes and hair and looked so ugly. He probably hated himself and all people who had dark color. There will never be, probably, a true answer for these horrifying deeds.

I guess we knew things happened to the Jews, but felt it best not to ask too many questions. Amazing what horrible things a dictator can get away with. But, at the time, as a child and largely unaware of most of these things, I found family and school most important to me.

Chapter 2

Where Did I Come From?

On February 21, 1925, a cold day in Berlin, Germany, I came into the world, a miracle baby. My parents called me their miracle because my mother had four pregnancies and four miscarriages before me. My father had his heart set on a boy and promised my mother a golden bracelet if she gave him a son, so when I was born, he gave her a dozen red roses.

Mother wanted to name me Karen, but Father insisted on Gisela, an old Germanic name meaning honored one, because he said, "Our last name is so short, she needs a musical name." So, my parents named me Gisela Koch. My mother, Gertrud Loebel came from Nordhausen, in the Harz Mountains, in the middle-eastern part of Germany.

Grandmother Berta Loebel, *Omi*, came from Saxony, Germany, and Grandpa Anton Loebel, *Opi*, came from Lobosicze, Bohemia, which belonged at that time to the great Austrian Empire. His parents had a large farm called a *Gut* in German. A *Gut* usually had at least thirty cows, many sheep, horses, pigs and chickens, while smaller farms called *Bauernhöfe*, had only one or two cows, a pig, a few chickens and some rabbits. Quite well to do because they owned a *gut*, my great-grandparents lived some distance from town. While the other children had to walk one or two kilometers to school no matter the weather, my grandfather rode in a horse and buggy year-round.

In Germany, as in most of Europe, a man chose his trade by the age of fourteen, and then spent the next ten years learning it. Thus, at fourteen, Grandfather Loebel left the *Gut* and apprenticed to a carpenter where he learned cabinetmaking. He trained in this trade in the mornings, and after lunch attended the *Berufsshule, a* school where he studied math, reading, and writing. At the age of eighteen, he completed this part of his education and began the next phase, that of a journeyman.

A journeyman traveled away from home for several years to work under a master craftsman to perfect his craft. After this, he created a work to submit to a board of masters. Only when they approved his work did they accept him as a master craftsman who could open his own business, a long process, still practiced in Germany.

As a journeyman, Grandfather Loebel moved to Saxony to continue his training. There, he became a master craftsman and opened his own business. In Saxony, he also met his future wife, my grandmother, Berta Dilsner. Grandmother and Grandfather Loebel had three children, a boy and two girls. Unfortunately, the happy couple had two terrible tragedies.

The first happened one day as my grandmother prepared to host her friends for what they called *Kraenzchen*. In a *Kraenzchen,* women came together in the afternoon once a month to make hand-made articles with needlework, knitting, or crocheting. They met each month in a different home to do this handwork, drink coffee and eat cake, gossip, and have a very good time. Grandmother had just placed a big pitcher of boiling coffee on the table when the first guest rang the doorbell. As she went to open the door, Liesbeth, her little three-year old daughter, pulled on the tablecloth. The pitcher fell over and spilled the boiling hot coffee over her, badly scalding her little body. Unfortunately, with little medical help available at that time, she died a week later in grandmother's arms.

A few years later, another tragedy happened. At that time, my grandparents lived in an apartment building on the second floor. Several stone steps went up to the front of the building. One day as six-year-old Bruno walked down to play with his friends, he stumbled, fell, and hit his head on one of the steps. He had an open wound and contracted meningitis, a fatal disease at the time. My grandparents suffered great pain losing their two older children. My mother, the youngest, then grew up as an only child.

At the time of these tragedies, my mother's parents lived in Saxony around Leipzig, a very large industrial city, heavily polluted and extremely ugly. Instead of green parks and open areas, the city had long stretches of gray colored apartment blocks. The whole city appeared dark and uninviting.

Seeing his sister's suffering over losing her children, grandmother's brother, a district supervisor of chimney sweeps in Berlin, offered to lend my grandparents money to buy a restaurant there. He thought Grandmother's getting away from Leipzig might help her get over her depression.

So, Grandfather gave up his cabinetmaking and my grandparents went into the restaurant business in Berlin. Grandmother, a very good cook, prepared the food, and Grandfather managed. Her brother knew all sorts of people in the soccer clubs in Zehlendorf, a suburb of southwestern Berlin. In order to drum up business, he suggested the players come into the city to try Grandmother's cooking.

The soccer players loved Grandmother's cooking so much they traveled all the way from Zehlendorf to the center of Berlin after every game. These players helped make the restaurant successful, so my grandparents decided to move it to Zehlendorf. The new restaurant grew so popular the cash registers couldn't hold all the money and my grandparents kept the cash in big wicker wash baskets. Though not professionals, they built a very good and profitable business.

Grandfather Loebel didn't want to fool with investments and instead put all of his money in the bank. When the banks crashed during the Great Depression, he lost it all. My mother always said we could've owned all of Winfried Strasse, the next street over from where we lived. Most of the neighbors on that street had wanted to mortgage their homes, and grandfather refused to loan them the money, my mother said.

The houses survived World War I in good condition and even had great value after World War II. My grandparents Loebel lost two fortunes, one after World War I and another after World War II, and they suffered the loss of two of their three children. Yet, they managed. Married for 65 years, they both lived to a ripe old age: Grandfather 89 and Grandmother 90.

I never heard them fuss. When my grandmother, *Omi,* sometimes got a little irritated, my grandfather *Opi* patted her on the shoulder and said *"O Berte, das ist nicht so schlimm,"* or "It's not so bad," and they hugged and made up. They were always so sweet to each other.

A real character, Grandfather Loebel enjoyed having fun with people and especially with me. He had a nickname for everybody. Around my family, he referred to my Uncle Carl as the baron and his wife as the baroness. A lady friend of my grandparents he called *Schnell-laufer*, or fast walker. Me, he called *Giesse* or *Wiesenhase* meaning meadow rabbit. I can never remember his calling me by my real name. My tall father he called *der Lange Kerl* meaning the long fellow.

My mother liked an open house where people always felt free to come to visit, but my grandfather didn't like a lot of company at our house. He and Grandmother lived in the small house on the same property as we. He enjoyed expressing his dislike for company by appearing at our house in his worst clothes, old and spattered with paint, wrinkled and with tears in the pant legs. Whenever the Kochs visited, grandfather Loebel showed up in this outfit. If their visit lasted until 10:00 p.m., he said, "It is time to go

home. If I were visiting in someone's home, I would leave now."
He'd then loudly place the house keys on the table. He waited for a
while to see if anyone left, and then, soon, went home himself.

Often Mother refused to let him come to a party, telling him,
"You're not coming upstairs unless you dress properly."

Sometimes he would come up, but then he dressed well. He
and I got along well, usually. Later, he'd dress in those old clothes
when he knew my boyfriends would visit. He loved to embarrass
me and kid me. Thankfully when my boyfriends came, Mother
usually refused to let him in the house. No telling what he might
have said or done.

Often, I ran next door to Grandmother Loebel to cry on her
shoulder when I wanted to get around my parents. She always
made it right for me. She'd talk to my parents or find me a little
gift or do something special for me. My *Omi* Loebel and I were
very close.

Many times she cooked for me one of my favorite dishes, big
yeast dumplings covered with thick, sweet, fruit compote. Mother
and *Omi* preserved the compote in the spring when the fruit trees in
our yard and those in Grandfather Koch's garden grew heavy with
peaches and pears and plums. They also added strawberries and
currents from the garden. Sometimes, *Omi* also made me thick,
fluffy cheese omelets or very delicate potato pancakes.

I often had lunch with her. When I didn't like Mother's
cooking, then I went down to *Omi*. When I appeared, Grandmother
often said, "Well, I guess you don't like *Mutti's* cooking."
Sometimes she took me to town with her on little shopping sprees.
She usually let me buy something, and we normally ended in a
Konditorei or coffee shop for ice cream and cake. I did not
regularly get ice cream and cake at home, so I really enjoyed these
trips with Grandmother.

Because my grandparents owned the restaurant, my mother
grew up in well-to-do circumstances. As a young woman she
traveled quite a bit in Germany, and went to the theatre, operas,

and concerts. She learned to play the piano well and loved it. Sometimes she gave small house concerts. Several times she played the piano in small public concerts. My grandfather, very proud of her, gave her a beautiful diamond ring that I now own. After she graduated from business school, my mother really didn't have to work for money, but her job gave her independence from her parents. She always liked banking, so she entered that business and worked several years as a teller and bookkeeper.

The bank brought my father and mother together. My father headed the loan department. Not only did my parents work in the same bank, but they saw each other every morning and afternoon on the train from and to Zehlendorf. After about a year of courtship, they married. My mother wanted to keep working after they married because she enjoyed it, but at that time men felt inadequate if their wives worked. My father saw to it my mother left her job.

My father, Ernst Koch, came from Boizenburg, Uckermark in the northeastern part of Germany. My father's parents also came from Boizenburg but by the time of my birth, they had moved to Berlin. I think they moved to Berlin because of my grandfather's job as a postal inspector.

Helene and Karl Koch, like the Loebels, had a good marriage. Once a week on Friday, Grandmother Koch, an excellent cook also, invited the rest of their family for fish dinner in her home. I enjoyed going there.

Grandparents Koch had a very big garden in Dueppel, a farming and gardening community a few kilometers outside of Zehlendorf. Their garden had a variety of vegetables, lots of fruit trees (peach, plum, pear, and both sweet and sour cherries), and many bushes of currants and gooseberries. They also had lots of strawberry and asparagus beds. I hated those old gooseberries because the thorns of the bushes stung and I had to pick them. Grandfather Koch always rode his bicycle to our house and brought me the first strawberries of the season. We always had enough fruit and vegetables from the garden to share with all of the neighbors and friends.

Grandfather Koch belonged to several different clubs and, consequently, we always went to parties and different events with him. I believe I developed a strong liking for partying from him. Even today, I like family parties, movies, theatres, operas, concerts and balls. I like to have people around, a trait I think I also gained from Grandfather Koch. When we buried Grandfather, a popular member of the war veterans of the First World War, a band of his buddies came marching up with music and a flag. As an eight-year old, this impressed me.

Thus, I grew up with Grandparents Loebel and Grandparents Koch all living in Zehlendorf. I have fond memories of large family gatherings for meals and parties.

We always enjoyed vegetables and fruits from Grandfather Koch's garden in Duepppel and from my *Omi's* and *Opi's* garden in our backyard. I also enjoyed having *Omi* and *Opi* living next to us and helping to spoil me. I felt very blessed to have such good grandparents who played such a large part in so much of my life.

Chapter 3

Childhood Behind the Big Old Fence

As an only child with grandparents close, I lived a very sheltered and protected life. In addition, I lived in a house with a yard behind a big old black chain-link fence. The fence stood at least six feet tall with two layers of barbed wire on top of it. My grandfather painted the entire fence black. The fence extended across the front of the yard, while stone walls enclosed the sides and the back of the yard. The fence had two doors, one for a motorcycle or car and one for the main entrance, and both doors had locks on them. Visitors rang the bell outside the fence. We had an automatic door opener, but during the winter it always froze up, so we had to go down and open the gate. Most of the houses in our neighborhood had gate openers, and most had the same trouble in winter.

Behind the fence sat three houses. My parents and I lived in the big three-story house. We belonged to the upper middle class, and fortunately owned our own home. My mother received it from her parents as a gift. The first level had an entrance room, the toilet, the kitchen, the living and dining rooms, and a closed-in sunroom. On the second level we had three bedrooms, a sitting room, a bathroom, and a balcony with large French doors. We stored some of the fruits and vegetables from the garden in the attic on the third level. In bad weather we hung the laundry up there too. In the back of the house there was a walled courtyard where we all ate our meals during the summer months of June, July and August.

Our very heavy living and dining room furniture consisted of a handcrafted and hand-carved buffet, a sideboard, a sofa, and a table with chairs. It took three men to move the table. My parents' bedroom set, ivory in color with a trim of ebony wood, had a very fashionable design for the time. I had a nice, cozy room with a big bed couch decorated with many soft cuddly pillows, a desk, and a comfortable armchair.

As a teenager, I had a large radio which I enjoyed listening to very much. Also, as a teen, I had lots of pictures on the walls. I liked sculpture very much and, for a while, most of the pictures were of Italian sculptured pieces. Later, I liked Durer's paintings, the "Mother's Hands" and the "Akelei," a beautiful flowery plant. Another time I had prints of pictures by Spitzweg, including "The Book Worm."

We had a very open house and enjoyed a lot of company. Almost daily we had friends visit. The mother of my girlfriend often came for lunch. She liked my grandmother's cooking, and she did not have a lot of money for groceries. My mother and my grandmother enjoyed her company even though my grandfather didn't like her coming over. He was rather stingy, but Grandmother usually overruled him.

Grandfather and Grandmother Loebel lived in the smaller, one-story house next to us. On the back of the property, we had another small house with a washroom, two one-room apartments and a garage. A man with a motorcycle rented the garage and parked it there. My grandparents rented out the two one-room apartments.

With one set of parents, two sets of grandparents, and the big black fence all guarding me, I couldn't get away with anything very naughty.

Until I first entered school, every so often I disobeyed, talked back, or had a temper tantrum. Mother never spanked me but she did punish me. I always wanted to look nice and wear pretty clothes. When I disobeyed or misbehaved, Mother made me wear an old, ugly dress every day for several days. I really hated it when I had to wear high-top shoes in the middle of July or August.

When I visited my grandparents Koch in these clothes, my grandfather always said, "Na, Fritze, what did you do to wear this outfit?"

Grandfather Koch called me Fritze, a boy's name, because I didn't look like a pretty little girl at those times. He'd laugh and joke about it. This made me furious. As a result, my mother's punishments proved very effective. I often begged mother to lift my punishment, but no matter how much I begged the punishment remained. My mother appeared a pushover, but she meant what she said. She was a strong person but she did not look it.

At age three, my mother took me to the nearby kindergarten. By then I had overcome my baby illnesses and grown into a very lively and imaginative child. I suppose my mother thought I needed a life outside the big old fence and she took me to Aunt Ilse's kindergarten. In Germany, at that time, parents had to pay for kindergarten separately as it wasn't part of the public schools and wasn't required. I was a year or two younger than most of the kindergarten children who were four or five. I think maybe Mother just wanted some peace from a talkative, boisterous three-year-old. After all, Mother was older than most new parents.

As an only child, I needed playmates. In kindergarten, I made friends, learned many different songs and games, looked at books, and listened to stories and fairy tales. All in all I had a very good time. Kindergarten proved a wonderful experience for me and gave me a chance to experience the real world outside the fence. When mother took me home from kindergarten, once again behind the big old fence, I played my imaginary games alone.

At that age, whenever the weather permitted, I played outside in the yard. I called my favorite game the market place. The leaves and berries of the different bushes became my vegetables, and little pebbles served as the money. I had a lot of imagination and kept myself busy with all sorts of games. With my dolls and teddy bear, I often played school using the steps of our veranda as school benches. My pupils sat on the veranda steps while I taught them the alphabet and simple math. I showed them things I had learned in my kindergarten class. I also had a desk with a blackboard on which I wrote the lessons. I had a good time playing school and sometimes thought about being a teacher when I grew up.

Often an American lady from across the street came to the fence and talked to me. Always around grown people, I talked like them. She got a kick out of the way I talked, and I liked her American accent. It sounded so nice and sometimes even funny that I longed to have an accent too. I stood there by the big old black fence and listened to her. I could have listened all day long. Then she didn't come anymore. Only later would I understand why she left without even saying good-bye. At the time it made me very sad.

At the age of six I started school. We had no coeducation in our schools in Germany at that time so I went to a girl's school. I never played with boys. I lived in a girl's world till age 16. So as a little girl, I grew up afraid of boys. To me they seemed mean and threw things at girls.

Excitement filled the air on that first wonderful day of school. Relatives gave every girl a big cone called a *Zuckertuete*. Mine, filled to the brim with different kinds of chocolates, came from *Omi* and *Opi* my grandmother and grandfather. I imagine they intended the chocolates to make the first school days a little sweeter. My mother and grandparents went with me and gave me the *Zuckertuete* after we arrived at class. We girls sat there with our cones full of candies, and the bigger the better. Later the custom moved to outside of school because some of the poor children did not get the *Zuckertuete*.

My class consisted of about twenty-five girls in a huge room. The classroom had two big blackboards on the wall, one on the front and one on the side. A large picture of Paul von Hindenburg, president of Germany, hung above the front blackboard. Rows of two-seater benches painted green had black tops. The desks had a slot for pencils, and in the middle, an inkpot, not a good thing for someone like me with long pigtails. My pigtails reached my waist, and girls do things too, not just boys. Sometimes, the girl who sat behind me dipped my pigtails into the inkpot with blue or black ink, which, of course, got my good dress very dirty. I got mad at the child and turned around and said "Blaa." and stuck my tongue out at her. Sometimes, the girl said aloud, "Gisela is sticking her tongue out at me." And I'd say, "And she stuck my pigtails in the ink." Then, *Fraulein* Flachshar said, "You go in this corner and you go in that corner." We stayed in the corner at least ten minutes or until the end of class. When I got home, Mother said, "If this happens again, I am going to see *Fraulein* Flachshar." But she never did.

Fraulein Flachshar, my elementary school teacher, had a big, long, pointed nose. I'd never seen such a long and ugly nose before in my life. A tall and very serious woman she always sat on top of the first school bench. Sometimes her dress did not cover all her legs and one could not help but see her undergarments. I felt she also had an unpleasant odor about her. I saw her as a very strict teacher, an ancient old spinster who never seemed to have any fun. She might have been twenty or thirty, but to me, she was always old.

I also did not like her because she laughed at me. This happened around Christmas time. Germans and Austrians celebrate Saint Nicholas Day on December 6th. All boys and girls put their shoes in front of their beds before they go to sleep, hoping that Saint Nicholas will come to them during the night and put candy and small presents into their shoes. Well, one Saint Nicholas Day I woke up to find my shoes not filled with sweets and small presents, but with a switch and a letter. This surprised me! The letter explained I didn't deserve presents since I'd been a naughty girl. I didn't cry and I didn't say anything to my parents. I acted as if nothing had happened.

When I went to school that day, *Fraulein* Flachshar, who taught us through the four grades of elementary school, asked each of us to tell what Saint Nicholas had brought us. When my turn came to talk about it, though a little ashamed, I told the truth. Of course everybody laughed, and *Fraulein* Flachshar laughed too. I hadn't liked her before, but now I really didn't like her because she laughed at me. I felt she should have handled this Saint Nicholas affair differently.

In good weather, we could go out onto the *Schulhof,* or schoolyard for recess. School began at 8:00 a.m. and ended at noon for the little children, so recess came about 10:00 a.m. We brought our own sandwiches and we could buy milk at the school: strawberry fruit milk or chocolate milk. I usually took chocolate. After we had eaten our sandwiches, we could play ball or tag or walk around with our friends. During rainy days, we had to walk two by two in a circle inside the school, usually in the *Turnhalle* or gym. We couldn't run or play; we had to walk in a circle. I hated the restriction. It felt like the restrictions behind the big black fence.

During those first four years of elementary school, I remember especially another day in the fourth grade. I remember running home from school crying bitterly. Mother, very concerned, didn't know what to make of it.

Finally, I shouted, "Things will fall from the sky. They'll explode, they'll burn, and they'll kill us. They'll destroy all the houses and we won't know where to go. We need to go to Lake Wannsee where we'll be safe in the water." This happened in 1935 long before the war began.

It took quite a while to calm me down. Finally, I told Mother that *Fraulein* Flachshar had told us about the things falling from the sky. She frightened us telling us things would burn and we would be killed. I don't know where she got her information. Maybe she listened to the short wave from another country. Anyway, it scared all of us.

The school, a three-story building, had a railing on the side of the stairs. We loved to sit on the railing and slide down, but getting caught meant a serious reprimand and standing in the corner. Everyone who saw us there knew we'd done something wrong. Teachers didn't make us stay after school because they didn't want to have to notify our parents. If we wanted to go on to high school, we needed the principal's recommendation, which wouldn't happen if we behaved badly.

In high school, when we didn't do well, the administration sent home a *Blaue Brief*, or blue letter, shortly before Christmas. These stated you had bad grades and might not go into the next grade. Next the letter explained you might have to go back to the *Volkschule* or public school, which only went through the eighth grade. From the public school you went to a trade school or business school. You couldn't go to a university from the public school. So naturally my parents and I wanted me to stay in the *Gymnasium* or high school covering grades five through twelve.

My father, always strict with me, definitely ruled the household. When he whistled, my mother and I jumped. I think I wanted to please my father more out of fear than out of love. He had wanted a boy and got me. I don't think he ever forgave me for that. I remember my whippings even today. In school, I never did well in math, and whenever I brought home a C, I cried, my mother cried, and my grandmother cried. We all feared I'd get another whipping. While my grandmother didn't fear my father, she cried out of sympathy for my mother and me.

I admired my father, a strong, intelligent man, but I don't know that I loved him. He showed little patience with me. The impatience I have, I think I got from my father. Yet, my mother and I always felt secure with him at home. Everything went well as long as we did not go against his will. The typical German father and husband from the old school, he controlled the household.

My father, however, spent quite a bit of time with me. He loved me, I think, in his own way. I remember going with him on long walks that always turned into learning experiences I didn't enjoy very much. We often walked around the *Krumme Lanke* a small, beautiful lake with big pine trees and colorful bushes. Some bushes bloomed during spring and others blossomed during the summer. As we walked around the lake, Father quizzed me on the names of various trees and plants. When I didn't know the name of the plant, flower, or tree, he scolded me with "Didn't you learn anything in Biology?" That always hurt my feelings.

We also found many mushrooms in this area, especially *Fefferlinge*, small yellow mushrooms with short stems and tops that look like upside down hats with fringes. They grow well in this sandy ground. During the mushroom season, many people go there and gather *Fefferlinge*. We did this sometimes too. My mother usually fried the mushrooms in bacon grease and they tasted heavenly with the left over bacon bits scattered among them.

In winter we ice skated on the lake. When the music played, my father and I often danced together on the ice. I enjoyed that very much because my father skated very well. I especially liked skating in the evening under a clear sky. One could see the stars and the moon above the water of the lake; the trees surrounding the *Krumme Lanke* made it very beautiful and romantic. I liked the full moon and I always looked at it. I'd heard stories told about the man in the moon and sometimes I thought I saw him. My father did not like it at all when I stared at the moon. He always reprimanded me. Maybe he feared I'd become a lunatic or moonstruck.

They held car and horse races as well as soccer games at a place called Avus Rennen. Every time my father took me to Avus Rennen, it became clear I wasn't the boy he had wanted. Although I enjoyed time with my father, I didn't enjoy some of the activities to which he took me, and I often did not want to go.

My father also took me to Grandmother and Grandfather Koch's garden in Dueppel within bicycling distance. Grandparents Koch had a little weekend house where one could cook and sleep over night. It had a small kitchen, a bedroom, a living area, and a small bathroom with toilet and shower. Often on weekends, the whole family went there, Grandmother and Grandfather, Mother and Father, and Uncle Karl and Aunt Ilse. Grandmother Koch always had a good cake or tart there for all of us. *Mutti* and *Tante* Ilse usually brought potato salad and sausages for supper, and we stayed there all day. I enjoyed that very much and have fond memories of it.

When *Vati*, as I called my father, and I rode out there, I played around the gardens while my father worked. As I grew older, I had to help weed the garden. My memories of that aren't so fond because I did not like to get myself dirty. *Vati*, however, enjoyed working in the garden. He liked to pick the fruit, harvest the vegetables, cut the fresh flowers for home, and put new beds into the garden. He enjoyed taking the harvest to my grandparents and to his brother's family. When he took fruit with long stems, such as cherries, he always cut the stems a little and packed everything so-so and in order. He said everything had to look nice! Mother and I thought that silly.

My mother didn't mind working in the garden and sharing with my grandparents, but often fussed at *Vati* about working and furnishing everything for his brother's family. She felt like they were the "barons" and *Mutti* and *Vati* the "peons."

My father had many other interests such as reading, studying languages, and listening to and performing music. Trilingual, he spoke French, Polish, and, of course, German. My father played the violin very well and my mother the piano. Very often for their own entertainment, my parents played music in the evenings. Every so often, my parents gave small house concerts. They invited family friends: the Erdmanns, the Worbs, and the Schulzes.

26

They played and then we had refreshments.

Very often on Sundays these families gathered at one of the homes. The men played a card game called Skat, while the women knitted or crocheted. We children played in another room so as not to disturb our parents. At that time in Germany, children were seen but not heard.

The Worbs had one daughter, Traude. She and I were very close as we grew up, both of us being only children. We enjoyed playing together and having fun.

We always went to each other's birthday parties and often visited one another. Traude lived in another district, and we did not go to school together, but we went together with our parents to picnics, for swimming in Lake Wannsee, and on trips. Until we both finished high school, we did a lot together.

My family often went to the Erdmanns for afternoon coffee because mother and Mrs. Erdmann grew up childhood friends. The Erdmanns lived in a large three-bedroom apartment on the sixth floor of an apartment house near by. They had no elevator in the building and I remember climbing a lot of steps. They had a nice living and dining area, beautifully furnished and carpeted. They had new furniture and new carpets three different times in their lives. I'm sure they could have owned their own home, but during the 1930s very few people owned their own home. The apartment also had a large balcony overlooking much of the district of Zehlendorf. We lived fifteen minutes walking distance from the Erdmanns.

Germans consider friendships very important and not easily formed. German people usually don't take friendship for granted. Friendship meant sharing sadness as well as happiness. I considered Werner Erdmann a good friend despite a five-year age difference. Later, I became a bit infatuated with him.

At sixteen, Werner went to the Olympic games as one of the interpreters. I knew a lot about him, but he knew very little about me. At eleven years old, he saw me as a kid.

On birthdays or other celebrations the families always got together and Werner and I saw each other. His father gave him a car on his eighteenth birthday and he invited me for a ride. What girl wouldn't be infatuated with a tall handsome young man with blond hair, blue eyes, and a very nice smile? Later, Werner did not want to go to a University. Instead, he wanted to go into his father's carpet and furniture business until he was drafted.

During summer evenings, we practically lived outside in the yard. My parents and I played ball in the yard or rode the steamer down the Havel River. I played *Triesel*, a game with a top that I had to hit with a string on a stick so that it danced on the pavement. I also played with my yo-yo. My parents and I also rode our bicycles to Lake Wannsee, a large lake about thirty minutes from our home where we went swimming.

Several times when *Mutti*, *Vati* and I bicycled to Lake Wannsee, we heard the clicking of hooves and happy shouting from little children. We'd see Propaganda Minister Joseph Goebbels with his seven children in a horse drawn buggy. The minister, a short, rather thin and unattractive man, sat up on top and drove.

As he drove the coach, he wore, of course, his Nazi uniform with the swastika armband. Usually they waved, and we waved back. Naturally we waved with a stretched out hand and we shouted "Heil Hitler, Heil Hitler!" I feel my mother thought, "Hell Hitler" more appropriate.

Since she did not care to go behind the black fence of the concentration camp, she said it quietly to herself. Sometimes Goebbels stopped his coach and talked to us commoners for a moment. The SS with him listened to every word we said. "Where are you heading? To Lake Wannsee?" he asked. Only small talk, of course, but it made good propaganda. He had seven cute children. The boys dressed in short leather pants and white shirts and the girls wore pretty *Dirndl* dresses, and they smiled so sweetly. After the Minister talked kindly to us common people, he drove on.

Once, as a teenager about fifteen years old I think, I almost drowned in Lake Wannsee. One day I swam out beyond the shallow waters beyond the swimming buoys. I wanted to go to the other side of the lake. I had swum there before with my father and thought I could do it alone. All of a sudden, when I found myself in the passage where the steamers went, I got a cramp in my leg. Someone in a boat saw me struggling. The young man came and helped me. Since then, I have always feared deep water.

My parents loved the opera, the symphony, and the theatre. They always had season tickets. When I reached the age to enjoy the concerts, theatres, and operas, they took me with them. Of course, I had to prepare for such occasions. My father bought the sheet music for the famous arias, and he and my mother played them, she on the piano and he on the violin. I listened and enjoyed those evenings very much. Then we read the texts of the operas or plays in different parts. Sometimes my parents railroaded grandfather and grandmother Loebel into the occasion.

When I grew old enough to have boyfriends, my parents sometimes invited them to the theatre, the opera, or concerts with us. All my friends enjoyed this kind of entertainment, but we always had to walk in front of my parents. We hated this because we couldn't embrace or even smooch a little. And when we rode on the train, my father watched us very closely, my boyfriends and me.

Zehlendorf had no taxis and we had no car, so we traveled to the theaters in downtown Berlin by S-Bahn, the local fast train that went around and through the city of Berlin. The S stood for *schnell*, which means fast. We lived about five minutes from an S-Bahn station. The U-Bahn, another form of train, traveled underground. If we rode the U-Bahn we had to walk thirty minutes to the station. We could catch the S-Bahn and change to the U-Bahn if we wanted to go somewhere near an U-Bahn station. The S-Bahn even went to Lake Wannsee though we usually went by bicycle.

In 1933, when I was eight years old, Hitler came into power. These guys called Nazis meant things very seriously. They came marching on the 30th of January 1933 with their tar torches through the Brandenburg gate. Soon, his brown shirts, the *Sociallistische Arbeiter Partei* or Socialistic Worker's Party, were all over Berlin. President Hindenburg, the former Chancellor, was in his dotage, and the new man, Hitler, excited people. People joined the Nazi Party right and left. They saw it as something new, and "new brooms sweep clean."

The KDF or *Kraft Durch Freude,* meaning strength through pleasure, represented the new cultural organization of the work force. The Nazi labor union would make it possible for laborers to enjoy everything the elite had enjoyed previously. Hitler, at first, did a lot for the people, and they liked his ideas. He wanted to lift the lower classes. The union had steamboats and busses that transported workers to their places of vacation. They also transported artists to their different places of performance. Only laborers with at least four children could join the KDF.

One night at the opera, my parents and I sat in front of a family attending through the KDF program. We had paid for our tickets and expected to enjoy the opera. Suddenly, in the middle of the opera, behind us, we heard rustling as the family took out their sandwiches. They enjoyed them more than the opera performance. The people around tried to quiet them with "Shssss." We found it amazing someone brought food into the opera.

Being still a child, I didn't know much about the Nazi Party at that time. Sometimes, I heard my father say he might have to join the Nazi Party or lose his job. One day it happened. He either had a job and joined the Nazi party, or if he refused, he'd have no job. My father felt terrible, but my mother felt happy since he kept his job. We could read in his face things were more dangerous than we imagined. Friends no longer trusted each other. The situation pitted sons against fathers, brothers against brothers. It disrupted life and tore close-knit families apart.

My father later left the church because the Nazi Party pressured him. He believed in God and he called himself, *Gottglaubig* or "believer in God.

He said, "God is everywhere, not just in the church."

He saw God in nature and we always prayed at the dinner table. My mother, however, continued to attend the Lutheran church regularly. Mother never said, "Heil Hitler" either. She always said "Good morning." She never had anything to do with the Nazi Party. She opposed the regime and didn't want the Nazis to take over.

When Hitler talked on the radio, we had to turn it on, and we opened the windows so that the secret police could tell we listened, but neither my mother nor I really listened to Hitler, with his raspy and horrible shouting voice. I never thought of my mother as a particularly strong-willed person because she always did what my father said. But, I suppose in hindsight, she had greater inner strength than I knew. In her quiet way she showed her animosity against the regime. I always feared she might disappear one day. I didn't know where people went when the Nazis took them, but I knew they disappeared.

Over time, life grew increasingly difficult. The Nazis forbade everything foreign. People with English names had to change them. The Nazis allowed only German plays, music, musicals, and dances. They closed all the borders and no one could legally leave the country. Those who did, left secretly and with great difficulty. I felt like a big black fence surrounded us all.

The educated Germans of the upper and middle classes couldn't understand how this proletarian paperhanger, certainly unfit for the job, could become the leader of Germany. They wondered, but nobody did a thing about it. If they had, they could've prevented Hitler's rise to power.

Quite late one evening, the bell in our house rang. We all wondered who was coming to visit at such a late hour. Two young people appeared at the big old fence and *Vati* let them in. About twenty years old, the girl had long blonde pigtails and wore a dark blue skirt, a white blouse, an ugly, short brown jacket, and white socks with clunky brown shoes. The boy, about the same age, wore short pants, a white shirt, and an identical brown jacket. He also wore big brown shoes and white knee socks. Not allowed in the room, my mind raced with questions: Why are they here? What do they want? Who are they? Why so secretive? Why couldn't I come into the room?

They spoke a long time to my parents. I could hear questions asked by my father; sometimes his voice seemed louder than usual. My mother said very little. I couldn't hear what they said, but I had a strange feeling creeping into my body. I finally fell asleep before they left.

The next evening I asked my parents about those young people. Curious, I asked what they wanted. My father and mother told me they came from the Hitler Youth and they wanted me to join.

"Do I have to join?" I asked.

"Yes, you have to if you want to go to high school and the University," my parents answered.

During the year that I turned ten years old, three events happened. First, the principal of our elementary school recommended me and several other students for the *Gymnasium* or high school. Second, I had to take a very difficult examination for a ten-year old, but I passed and could enter the high school! Third, I joined the *Jungmaedel*, the young girls' organization of the Hitler Youth! The two young people hadn't forgotten me, and I had to join to enter high school. As all my friends had joined, I did too.

Admitted to high school, I enjoyed the next eight years. I really liked school! Some of my girlfriends considered me nuts for liking school, but I liked learning. I also enjoyed much of what we did in the Hitler Youth. It had, however, some things I never enjoyed.

We had to wear this awful, ugly uniform. It consisted of a

32

short-sleeved white blouse, a dark blue skirt, and white knee socks with ugly clunky brown shoes. We wore an ugly yellowish-brown, flimsy, short jacket or *Kletterweste*. We wore the same uniform winter and summer. In hot weather, we took the jacket off, but when it turned cold, we froze. We had nothing on our heads to protect us from the cold. The blouse had buttons on the bottom and the skirt had buttonholes in the waistband, and we buttoned the blouse to the skirt. They couldn't have designed anything uglier! I hated it! Often I went to meetings without the uniform and told the leaders it needed washing.

Our meetings took place every Thursday afternoon and every Sunday morning during church time. That, of course, prevented us from going to church, and that's the way the Nazis wanted it. Consequently, we did not know anything about God and His goodness, and we became indifferent toward religion and not bothered we couldn't go to church. My mother always went to church and would've have taken me with her, but we feared the consequences if I missed the Hitler Youth meetings.

Later, confirmed into the Lutheran Church and taking Communion for the first time at age fifteen meant nothing to me. I didn't realize in the act, I joined the church at that moment. I hadn't trained in the church, but in the Hitler Youth! In fact, I found it surprising the regime allowed the church to confirm us.

My *Jungschaft*, or youth group, met in the basement of the home of one of my friends. Her parents let the organization use it free of charge. Normally, the Hitler Youth had to rent a space, but this family offered theirs. I went home and said that we had no place to sit.

My grandfather, a cabinet-maker, said, "I build the tables and chairs. You can't sit on the floor. It's too cold."

He made one long, big table and long benches for the sides, just right for the twelve ten-year-old girls in the *Schaft* or group. Our leader, about five years older than the rest of us, also went to our high school. We had to greet each other with "Heil Hitler" and not with "Hello," or "Good day."

During the meeting we went into the yard and played games like soccer and *Schlagball*, a game similar to baseball. After the games, we went into the basement and sang songs. We sang a lot of folk songs and also learned some Hitler Youth songs about the fatherland and comradeship. Then we had refreshments and played some table games. Sometimes we even did crafts, but I didn't enjoy the crafts because I wasn't very good at it. I found it easier to learn the lives of all the Nazi leaders than to fold paper. We didn't work in small groups, but rather, everybody worked together to show comradeship. Germany had been a country of classes and the Nazis wanted to wipe out the class differences dominant in Germany at the time and make us all alike, one big group. They made a big deal out of this. The whole meeting lasted about two hours. I enjoyed it a great deal more than being alone at home. In that basement, my friends and I had a really good time.

During the following years we studied about the lives of Hitler and the other Nazi leaders. We had oral and written examinations about them, which we had to pass or be humiliated in front of everybody. The youth leaders learned very quickly how to make us feel worthless. They didn't care about anybody or anything. They cared only for the Fatherland. "We're learning for the Fatherland! We're working for the Fatherland! We're fighting for the Fatherland! We're dying for the Fatherland." We did everything for the Fatherland!

Later, when everyone shouted, "We're dying for the Fatherland," I thought, "How stupid. If everybody dies for the Fatherland, who is left in the Fatherland? What is a Fatherland without people?"

The next year we learned to march like soldiers. Every week we marched at least two hours, winter and summer. We nearly froze in our flimsy brownish jackets and white knee socks during the winter, but we dared not complain. Our leader said the more we froze the tougher it made us. And our leaders wanted us tough.

That was no fun. Our leaders treated us roughly and often kicked and slapped us. If we cried they kicked and slapped even more. Often one of them pushed us to the floor. We marched on Thursdays; but not on Sundays, so obviously we liked Sundays more. The Nazis wanted strong, masculine women able to bear many strong, healthy children. Because I wanted to be feminine and look pretty, I hated the marching and the regimentation, but I went along. Later, when I met my future husband in the United States, he said I had the Nazi walk, a very masculine, forceful walk.

Every summer, we had to go to camp for six weeks. I hated that too. It took place far from Berlin in southeastern Germany in a camp patterned after the life of the Spartans in Greece. It consisted of lots of sports, very simple food, and hard living conditions. We learned discipline and that life is rough and tough. We slept on bunk beds on sacks of straw through which the straw pricked all night long. We cleaned the barracks in which we slept by sweeping and mopping the floors and washing the windows. As we made our beds and as we shook the straw mattresses, dust went everywhere making it hard to keep the barracks clean. Instructors lectured us on the greatness of Germany and Hitler. We played sports and sang songs. In our rest periods, we could do what we wanted such as writing letters or sleeping, but we really didn't have free time. The regimentation felt like being behind the big old black fence.

During this camp we received our black neckerchief, meaning we had proven ourselves. The ceremony took place in the evening by the campfire. We stood in a circle around the fire and held hands with our arms crossed and sang songs of the Fatherland and the greatness of Germany. The crossed arms meant faithfulness to the Fatherland and to each other. During this serious and solemn event we were not allowed to speak. It was impressive to an eleven-year-old. In order to show our comradeship we all had to eat from one apple. I thought the idea of biting into everybody's spit disgusting.

Whenever Hitler came to town during school hours the teachers dismissed us, and we had to go to the *Reichskanclei* and wait for hours for him to appear. He loved having everybody wait for him. When he finally showed up, everybody yelled and screamed, "*Heil Hitler*" and "*Es lebe der Fuehrer!*" (Long live the leader).

Loud march music played, and with the yelling and screaming it created a crazy and hysterical affair. Not just the Hitler Youth had to attend, but all the members of organizations such as the SS, the SA, and the NSDAP. All Berlin came to see the great Fuehrer. Our only newspaper, *der Voelkische Beobachter* (*People's Observer*) said it showed the people's love of Hitler

I stayed in the Hitler youth until I turned eighteen. Although I didn't like the uniform and the regimentation, I tolerated it. Then, when I turned fourteen, I joined the BDM or *Bund Deutscher Maedchen* (Union of Young Girls). The term "Hitler Youth" is an inclusive term for the youth of Germany. Both the boys' and the girls' organizations were included, but each was separate. Boys and girls were always carefully segregated in Germany in school and in all the youth organizations.

In the *BDM* they continued to brainwash us with propaganda such as "Germans are the best and smartest people" and "Germany's the best country in the world." They told us that, "Everything German is the most fantastic. Everything else in the world means nothing," and "Germans are the super race."

I hated these latter years of the Hitler Youth. I could not stand the uniform and found the terrible regimentation awful. We had to think as our leaders thought, could not speak freely, and could not leave Germany. The Nazis fenced in our thoughts and our whole being. All of Germany sat behind a big black fence.

Yet, the year, 1936 was wonderful for Germany. After only three years in power, Hitler had improved the economy and everyone who needed a job had one because he had created jobs by building highways all over the country. Mothers who had at least four children could go on vacation because the government sent a helper to take care of the family while the mother enjoyed her vacation. Workers who never could afford taking off from their jobs could do it now through *Kraft durch Freude.*

People, especially the laborers, praised Hitler for these socialistic institutions. They shouted, "Hitler knows what he is doing. He's for the people and the fatherland. He does things right! Germany is the greatest country in the world. What glory and fame has it reached after the devastating dictate of Versailles."

The Olympic games took place in our country, and Berlin celebrated its seven-hundred-year centennial. People came from all over the world to celebrate Germany, our beloved Fatherland. We Germans felt pleased and proud of the Fatherland. Yet, butter was already being rationed.

Chapter 4

The War

More and more the political horizon darkened. More and more people looked scared and very serious. One heard more and more rumors of war.

The political incidents came fast and furious. Some people talked about war; others rejected the idea. Foreign Minister Joachim von Ribbentrop signed a peace treaty with Moscow. Poland then made agreements with England and France. The agreements called for England and France to provide military assistance if Germany attacked Poland.

On September 1, 1939, at 5:45 in the morning, German artillery fired over the Polish border. The Polish soldiers shot back and German soldiers marched into Poland.

Prime Minister Neville Chamberlain of England tried to change the horrible course towards war two days later. He had the English Ambassador in Berlin give the German government an ultimatum. All fighting in Poland had to stop right away or else. Nobody paid attention. The war was on. War! Something I'd read about in books, but I did not know it in reality.

Radio Berlin announced that the Poles had nailed German children's tongues to their desks in school. Many German families had lived a century among the Poles, and had gotten along fine. We asked ourselves, now, why such a drastic change? Most of the

Germans could not believe that the Poles suddenly nailed German children's tongues to their desks, but Hitler told us that Germany had to respond. So German troops marched into Poland, and in seven days Germany controlled the country.

German propaganda preached that Germany was *ein Volk ohne Raum* or a people without room. The propaganda said we needed to make war to unify Germany and to take back the areas surrendered by the *Diktat* of Versailles at the end of World War I. Germans lived in those lost provinces and they needed to return to the Fatherland.

Since Germany is located in the center of Europe, Hitler and the whole Nazi propaganda organization told everybody constantly the country could come under attack at any moment. Therefore, he needed to build a war machine that also helped the economy and created jobs. Factories built tanks, planes, ships, guns and munitions. Many women started working in those war factories. The propaganda constantly stressed the need for readiness.

It was easy to believe Hitler's propaganda. Goebbles, Hitler's propaganda minister, did his job extremely well. The German people, content and happy to have jobs, lived in a strong economy. The promised highways, a fantastic project, connected the main areas of the country. The bread lines disappeared, and in spite of fear, we accepted the propaganda about the need for war.

With all of this preparation for war, the Army began drafting both young and older men. I feared for my father. Naturally, I didn't want him to go to war. My mother feared for him but didn't say very much. I could see fear and anxiety written all over her face.

Soon after the so-called conquest of Poland, my mother's childhood friend Anni Erdmann called all upset and crying. Normally a woman of self-control who did not show emotions, Mrs. Erdmann soon had Mother crying too. The Nazis had drafted Werner, their only child. How terrible! Of course, since he was my friend, I was also very concerned, and I feared for his life. I should have prayed for his well-being and safety, but since I didn't know the Lord, I just worried.

Around this time, a friend introduced me to a very nice young man in his twenties. A soldier, the military moved him into her place because Frau Bartsch had a large apartment. I did not have a boyfriend at this time. He was very nice and charming, and it didn't take long before he charmed me into dating him. Somewhat older and experienced, he knew how to treat a young woman. With my former boyfriends I had a good time and I loved them dearly in a childlike way. This man kissed differently. He held me close to him when we danced. He took me to the nicest restaurants and most elegant places. This puzzled me because most of us couldn't afford such unlimited food, much less the luxuries of life, yet with him I went to places where everything seemed plentiful.

I asked him many questions about this but he only answered, "One must know the right people and places."

At one of our outings he advised me not to ask so many questions.

I liked him and enjoyed going out with him. Yet, sometimes I worried about being with him. Then, one evening he showed his real card. He wore his black SS uniform! This stunned me! I had had no idea. I became scared and felt like running, but my feet were as heavy as lead. Now I understood why he could take me to all the nice places. The SS had everything at their disposal. He told me of his nice new apartment and mentioned I could live there with him. This seemed dangerous to me and I wanted to go home. I never went out with him again!

When he called or came by, although not easy, my mother found plausible excuses for my not seeing him again. Frau Bartsch asked *Muti* why I wouldn't go out with him, and said he was a nice young man.

Mother answered, "Yes, but he is SS!"

Frau Bartsch said, "That doesn't make any difference. Some of them are very nice."

40

I didn't want anything to do with the SS and Mother agreed. We felt it was too dangerous. Pretty soon after that, he transferred out of the area. Fortunately, I hadn't allowed anything serious to happen between us because the SS seldom took no for an answer. The Lord must have looked out for me.

In the year after Hitler's invasion of Poland, German soldiers occupied Denmark and Norway, and then moved on to Belgium and the Netherlands. On June 5, 1940, German troops marched into France. Five days later, Italy's Benito Mussolini declared war on France and by June 14, 1940, the Germans occupied Paris. Everything went very fast.

All of this frightened me. My worst fears had come true. I still feared things falling from the sky as my teacher had told us years ago in the fourth grade. Now, I was fifteen years old, and all these things seemed to be happening. Violence and war surrounded us. My mother talked about the horrors of World War I and my grandparents grumbled that they'd already lived through one war and they didn't want to go through another. Many friends and neighbors felt the same way.

I feared the Army would draft my father. Many men in his age group, forty-three, had already gone to war, but the bank where my father worked needed him for special services. They saw to it that he could stay in Berlin. This made Mother and me very happy. Yet, people talked ill of Father, the only man in the neighborhood.

A few months later, he felt he had to wear the uniform, and in 1940 he volunteered his services to the army. The Nazis sent him to France and Belgium to serve with the occupation troops.

Shortly after that, Mother received news that *Vati* was quite ill and had to be hospitalized in Koblenz at the Rhine River. We learned later that he'd had a nervous breakdown because of the horrible things they had to do to the French people. Mother left Berlin right away and went to see about him, leaving me, at fifteen, alone in our big house behind the big old fence. Of course, my grandparents lived right next door, but they felt I could stay all by myself in the big house. My mother stayed several weeks with my father. Whether I liked it or not I had to sleep in the big house all by myself for what seemed like a long time.

Finally, my mother came home with my father. Because of his nervous breakdown, the army released *Vati* from the service. Under a doctor's care, he needed patient, quiet, and loving care. We had to tiptoe around him. When we asked what was going on with him, he didn't want to talk about it and said nothing. After about six months, he recovered and went back to work at the bank on February 23, 1943. *Vati* worked a short while and then decided to go into the service again. He felt he needed to fight for his beloved Fatherland like everyone else. He was sent to Poland and later to Russia. The German government reported him missing in 1944.

Quite a few years after the war, my mother had to declare *Vati* dead to get a pension from my father's bank and the military. This was very difficult for her, but she had to have money to live on. With him reported missing, the government and the private sector refused financial aid to his widow.

Finally, in 1960 the International Red Cross informed my mother, who had moved to the States in 1958, of my father's death along the Russian-Polish border. He had been patrolling the border when Polish partisans shot him in the back. The Red Cross also told Mother that he is buried in a Catholic cemetery in Warsaw. It took 16 years to get this sad news to our family.

I can still see my father standing in the yard in 1941 reading the only newspaper we had in Germany which was the *Voelkische Beobachter*. My father read a big headline, "America Declares War on Germany"—a Goebbels propaganda trick. The Japanese were conveniently not mentioned. At the time, we didn't know about the sneaky attack of the Japanese on Pearl Harbor which resulted in America's declaring war on Japan and Germany. Since Hitler had declared war on England and sent bombs and rockets over there, we understood why America felt it had to come and help. After all, England was America's mother country, however, we didn't understand why America declared war on Japan. I've never forgotten what my father said when he read that America had declared war on Germany and Japan, "We will lose the war now when this big giant comes in." Unfortunately, for us, events showed my father right.

By 1940, however, explosives fell from the sky just as my teacher had said when she had upset the whole class. The British bombing had started. My mother and I sat in our cellar by ourselves. I was very scared. I did not know what was happening, and I felt fenced in. We could hear the explosions in the distance over Berlin. I could hear the airplanes. Since I didn't know whether they were German or enemy airplanes, I asked my mother, "What is going on? What is this noise?" My mother always answered, "I don't know. I don't know."

These bombing attacks meant running several times during the night into that cellar because, at first, the British bombed us only during the night. Often we sat four to five hours in the cellar, but they never hit near us. I remember my father, before he went to war, getting after me because whenever the sirens went off they scared me so badly I always had to run to the bathroom.

At first my grandparents and the neighbors didn't come into the cellar. The English bombing us Germans? That couldn't happen. After all, my grandparents said, the English and the Germans had a common ancestor in Queen Victoria. They didn't believe the seriousness of the situation.

Our cellar lay partially underground and partially under the house and was very uncomfortable. At first it had no places to sit. It had no windows, and a single electric bulb hanging down from the ceiling gave little light. It had air vents even with the ground. Before the air raids, we used the cellar only for storing potatoes, carrots, cabbages, apples and pears. Mounted on the walls were many shelves used to store our canned vegetables and fruit. In the summer we used it as a refrigerator to keep our little bit of meat and sausage and butter. The cellar always felt very cold and damp to me. Perhaps it seemed so cold because of my fear. Later, my grandfather made benches for us to sit on during the air raids. The benches didn't make it much more comfortable. We took pillows and blankets along with us to keep warm as the cellar had no heat. It always smelled damp and musty. I remember its musty smell now, as I write. I hated to go there, but I surely didn't want to stay in the house with the bombs falling.

People living in the center of the city had bunkers, but most Berliners, those living in the suburbs, used the cellars of their apartment houses or homes.

The cellars protected people from flying debris, but a direct hit would destroy the house and kill the people in the cellar. We all knew this, but from 1940 to 1945 our cellar bomb shelter belonged to our way of life and kept us fenced in.

In the cellar, we talked; some people told jokes or some kind of tall tale. I enjoyed knitting, a fad at that time. Everyone knitted sweaters in Swedish patterns. I did too. It kept us occupied and our hands busy. The stories and jokes helped, too. People laughed and forgot for a moment the seriousness of the situation. Of course, when we heard the flak or explosions near us, knitting, reading, and conversations stopped, leaving a deathly silence. We all huddled together. When I heard the whistling of a bomb, I felt relief. We heard if you heard the whistling of the bomb, you didn't get hit. Only when you didn't hear the whistling did it hit you.

These bombing attacks were England's answer to Germany's missile attacks on London. Hitler had also planned a landing of the 6th and 9th armies in Dover. This landing never took place because the German air attacks could not succeed in weakening the English sufficiently.

Since the early bombings happened at night with the streets completely dark, we could hardly see other people walking and easily ran into one another. Someone, I don't know who—probably the government—came out with some phosphorus pins.

We put them on our overcoats or jackets so we could see each other coming and going. The pins came in shapes and forms like butterflies and bugs. We had to buy them; the government didn't give them to us. Before we went out at night, we had to hold them under a lamp to redo the phosphorous. When we wore hats, we put them on our hats. As teenagers, we young people enjoyed them.

At night even the headlamps of the cars were dark. People placed caps of oilcloth over them allowing only little slits of light through. Of course people covered every window in the houses and apartments with shades or blankets so that no light could shine through. After all we did not want to show the bombers our town.

In 1941 the war with Russia began. Constantly we heard: Special News: Ivan, Stukas, air raids, and bombs. Reports told us Ivan's location, what our German Stukas destroyed, where air raids had hit, and what the bombs had knocked out. We had total war, west and east. We were fighting with France, England, and Russia.

At first, the German propaganda machine, with Goebbels as the head, proved quite successful. They constantly told us about war victories. Hitler said he had a terrible weapon to win the war for us. Before Stalingrad, we actually believed it. After that horrible experience, there in Russia, we didn't believe the propaganda any more.

The propagandists also lied to our soldiers about winning the war and told them New York lay in rubble and ashes. What a rude awakening for German soldiers transported as prisoners of war to New York to see the city intact! They found out first hand the whole Nazi Regime consisted of lies.

At the end of the war, I remember talking to a cousin taken prisoner. He told of his shock when he saw New York in one piece. He also told of his experiences in Texas where the Americans treated him well. He had a large sack of things, canned foods and other provisions the Americans allowed him to bring home. His family couldn't believe the Americans permitted him to bring so much. At that time, after the war, we had very little to eat.

45

In addition, this cousin brought from Texas a large turtle he kept for a long time. Of course, later on, I heard how everything in Texas is bigger. My cousin said he'd like to have stayed in Texas if he could have. What a different view of the Americans we got after the war! Yet, during the bombing, we hated them.

Later on, we took a radio into the shelter so we heard the locations of the bombing. I always hoped the antiaircraft guns didn't shoot too much since when enemy planes came under cross fire from the guns, the pilots dropped the bombs aimlessly. Then the bombs hit houses rather than factories, a much more dangerous situation for the private citizens.

One evening, while visiting Andreas, one of my good friends who lived in an apartment house, we got caught in an air attack. Everybody went as fast as possible into the shelter. We all sat as close as we could. Some people covered up with blankets; others covered themselves with heavy coats. One man calmly read his book, a woman slept, two children fought and a third one cried. The woman responsible for the shelter opened a big package of sandwiches with sausage and ham. She ate in front of everybody and enjoyed the sandwiches to the last one. Being too scared to be hungry, I wondered how she could eat at such a time.

Only Nazis held shelter warden positions since part of their job involved identifying the Jews. This one treated Andreas and most everybody in the cellar in a very unfriendly manner.

I wondered, too, how the Nazi shelter warden had so many sandwiches. Our ration card allowed us only 30 grams of bread, "too little to live on and too much to die on." I assumed she was a Nazi because party members could get everything. We didn't have bread, but we had plenty of brandy and cigarettes. After big bombings, the newspaper announced we could get extra brandy and cigarettes. We resented these because they seemed intended only to calm us. They didn't help the growling of our stomachs. The wardens intimidated us because we knew they could always report us to the SS and make trouble for us. This shelter warden could afford to eat her sandwiches nonchalantly without fear of anyone complaining.

Suddenly, somebody in the shelter yelled: "Fire, fire!" A bomb had exploded close by and had blown off the roof of the apartment house. Everyone ran upstairs where a Jewish man had had his apartment. He lost all his prized possessions, his books and writings. "My life's work is all gone," he mumbled calmly. I felt very sad that this man had lost everything. Everywhere around the apartment house, one saw destruction and sadness.

The fact we shared the cellar with a Jewish man didn't bother me. Apparently, the shelter warden didn't object to him either. Some shelter wardens threw Jews out if they tried to enter as happened to Sara and Martin. I couldn't imagine the fear of being caught without a shelter.

Once, while in our cellar during an air raid, we heard a crash and a big explosion very near by. An air mine flying by us hit and destroyed the cellar across the street from us. We called the air mine a *Luftmine*. The *Luftminen* flew low and did not go into the ground. This one killed all the people in the cellar across the street. They all sat up in their chairs and looked alive. When the *Luftmine* exploded it sucked the air from their lungs which burst and killed them all. Although upset because we knew most of those people, we also breathed a sigh of relief it had missed us.

Always after a bombing, a low cloud lay over the city. A fine rain of soot and ashes came down and covered the ruins. The soft daylight was indistinguishable from the reflection of the fire that raged in bomb-torn Berlin. The beautiful capital of Germany became a macabre scene, black from soot and disfigured from thousands of craters. In the center of the city the once wide streets and boulevards had disappeared. Complete businesses and living quarters didn't exist any more. The bombs left a picture of bleakness and hopelessness.

Throughout the war, and in spite of the Nazi regime, films of American comedians like Laurel and Hardy and tap dancers like

Shirley Temple rolled through our land. Despite the Nazis insistence on all things German, in the area of entertainment the people's opinion asserted itself. Even the Nazis had to give in. Amazingly they allowed Shirley Temple films. I always enjoyed them and saw as many as I could. Even Adolf Hitler himself sat in the King's Box to enjoy the musical *Happy Traveling* by the Austrian Jew Eduard Kunnekein who had moved to America.

Later, the Nazis didn't allow fun events like dancing, especially swing dancing, viewed as an English thing. At this time the Gestapo made anybody who coughed at the wrong time and place to disappear. Artists, criminals, political opponents and, of course, Jews vanished.

One day our flak hit a B-17, one of the flying fortresses. This one had a Canadian crew and a very tall Canadian lay dead in the middle of the street. I remember my grandfather saying, "Come on, Giesse, and look at this big dead Canadian lying in the street. He is tall! Come on, Giesse." I didn't want to look at a dead man so I didn't go. Many from the neighborhood gathered to look at him. People were astounded at how tall he was. Since only one plane ever came down in our neighborhood, we thought the flak didn't hit very much.

Later in the war, when the Russians began bombing Berlin, we learned we need not go to the shelters. When the Russian planes attacked, we slept right through. We knew they couldn't hit anything and they had such small bombs. We laughed at them.

In the morning after a bombing attack, we still had to go to school by 8:00 a.m. Many nights I had only 3 or 4 hours sleep. Nobody thought of it as a strain on us. We only had school until 1:30 or 2:00 p.m. At home, I had a lot of schoolwork to do, but I also could sleep a little.

When I look back to those war years, I don't know how we survived, but I know one can get through most anything in life if one has the will and perseverance. In spite of the war, in spite of hard times, in spite of rationing and the terror bombing, we teenagers stayed positive and tried to have a good time as often as possible. I enjoyed living, and I still do.

In 1940 Hitler had the bright idea to send all fifteen-year old students to the country so we could find out how we got our food. He thought people from the city didn't know that. Our schools closed for six months. One teacher went along for each class. Every morning we had lessons from 9:00 a.m. till noon. At 12:30 p.m. we ate lunch together and then we went into the fields. We girls went to individual farms. I had to work as a farm hand in the sugar beet fields, hard unpleasant work. We had to move around on our knees, but we had a sack to kneel on to soften the hard ground. We had to let the strongest plants stand and cut the others out.

I worked with foreign workers, including Frenchmen with whom I had interesting conversations. I took the opportunity to practice the French I studied in school. I also worked with Russian girls the Nazis took from their homes in Russia and brought to Germany to do work in the fields. We weren't allowed to speak to the foreign workers but I did anyway. After all, they were human beings too.

For six months we had to work in the fields. I didn't like physical labor, and I didn't like getting dirty. My hands got dirty and crusty because we didn't have any gloves. Hitler wanted us to help because the men served on the front lines. We still had three hours of school each day, but we only had one teacher, so some subjects weren't taught.

Fortunately, I didn't have to stay the six months because I grew ill. The farmer's wife feared I had tuberculoses because I was so skinny. She started feeding me to fatten me up. My body could not consume these heavy and fatty foods and I developed boils all over. I itched and then scratched the boils. I almost developed blood poisoning from the boils. The doctor called my father and asked him to pick me up and take me home. I was not unhappy at all to go home. Later, some of these boils turned into carbuncles and had to be lanced. Our doctor had to watch over me quite a while.

With the schools closed, I had to get a private tutor. As a result, I had advanced much further along in my studies than the students who worked in the country for the full six months. I was glad I would not have to make up all of the studies. I was even happier that I did not have to get dirty in those fields!

Since I went to a high school for girls, I needed, somehow, to get together with the opposite sex. Soon my mother enrolled me in an upper middle class dancing school. Because we lived in a very class-conscious society, my mother wanted me to meet young men from the same social structure. The dancing class met twice a week, and I enjoyed learning ballroom dancing and meeting young men socially.

By the time I turned sixteen, I'd become an outgoing and fun loving person. I had a lot of friends, both boys and girls. We danced, went on picnics, rode bicycles, went ice-skating on the frozen lakes, and had wonderful times. But when we kissed our friends good night we did not know if we'd see each other the next day. A bomb could come during the night and end it all. In other words, we lived on the edge, with fun and good times and with death and sadness. As we know, man does not live by bread alone, and often we even did not have enough bread. We could party, however.

Because I was a good dancer, another dancing school in Wilmersdorf, an area closer to the city, asked me to attend. They needed more girls to dance with the boys there. At the Zehlendorf dance school I had a good and close friend named Rudi Bindhardt. At the Wilmersdorf dance school I formed a close friendship with Gunnar Fossum. I enjoyed the company of both young men, nice, tall, and pretty good looking. We met not only during the time of our dancing lessons, but on other days in other places. We went to the movies, concerts, operas, and out on the town. I was sixteen years old and it was war, a very serious time. I had fun, however, in spite of the horrors of war.

Soon there came the time of the Rose Ball, a very popular and elegant event. As fate wanted it, both my dancing schools came to this festivity in Zelendorf. Both Rudi and Gunnar asked me to the ball. Before I could make a decision, both somehow found out I'd been asked by the other. How embarrassing! Both young men became quite angry with me, and both withdrew their invitations.

I had a pretty new dress made by Bartsch Modell Haus and no one to take me to the ball! I suppose it served me right. I cried my eyes out. The Rose Ball meant so much to me, and I wanted to go badly.

At the last minute, Dieter Dehrmann, another friend from the dancing school, came to my rescue. He called and said, "Do you have a date?"

I don't remember whether I told him about Rudi and Gunnar, but I happily accepted his invitation.

During the Rose Ball the custom was for the men to give bouquets of roses to girls they liked. I had twelve bouquets of roses. I had the most and felt very happy. Gunnar's and Rudi's plan to keep me from the ball didn't work out. Dieter took me home after the ball and kissed me passionately.

Dieter and I became close friends. We had many rendezvous and enjoyed our time with each other. On most of our outings we went to concerts or to Lake Wannsee. Dieter had a wonderful paddleboat and we spent many pleasant afternoons on the lake. Often he paddled us into the reeds where no one could see us; so quiet, so sweet, and so private. Of course, we only kissed passionately, but how wonderful it was!

I remember these times with warmth and great happiness in my heart. Besides Dieter Dehrmann I had another good friend by the name of Clemens Lessing. While Dieter lived in Wilmersdorf several stations by train away, Clemens lived in Zehlendorf not too far away from where I lived. We could walk to each other's homes. I met him through our book club. Six girls and boys who enjoyed reading interesting books and discussing them started the club. We picked a book, read it during the month, and then got together in a friend's home and discussed it. A different member of the club acted as leader each month. We learned from each other and made the club interesting and educational. Of course, we only allowed intelligent young people involved with the studies for the *Abitur* to belong to this club. We were absolutely snobbish about it.

One month Clemens Lessing, a friend of one of the boys, appeared on the scene. A serious, intelligent young man with a great interest in good books, Clemens fit right in with the rest of us in the club.

Clemens continued to participate, and one evening after we had finished our discussions, he asked me if he could walk me home. I accepted, and our walk gave us a chance to get a little better acquainted. From then on, he waited for me at my school, whenever possible, to walk me home. Very often, he invited me for ice cream at the *Anneliese,* the local ice cream parlor and teen hangout. He also had a paddleboat like Dieter's, and quite often we paddled on the Spree or Havel rivers.

Before long, Clemens took me to meet his parents. I found them very nice, and often Clemens' mother invited me for dinner at their home. She seemed to like me.

Quite frequently, Clemens' mother invited all the members of the book club to a dance at their home. Often, we decorated the cellar and had our dance there. When the air raid siren sounded, already in the right place, we kept on dancing and celebrating. We called these Dancing Teas but had punch and snacks rather than tea. With the punch often spiked with wine or champagne, we felt very grown up and sophisticated. My father always wanted me to be home by my twelve o'clock curfew. When the dance lasted longer than that, Mrs. Lessing called my father and talked him into letting me stay longer. I always liked that very much, but my father didn't. He gave in, but he wasn't pleased. I could not walk home by myself. Since Clemens always walked me home after the parties, my leaving would've broken them up early. In spite of the bombing, we found as much joy as we could.

Every so often, Clemens visited me at my home. He brought his flute and we played duets, I on the piano and he on the flute. We both liked Mozart's "A Little Night Music" and played it often. My mother always sat there with embroidery or some kind of handwork. She only left the room when she offered us cakes and something to drink. Then we smooched a little bit and made up for lost time. Clemens and I frequently went to concerts where he insisted we read along in the score. We enjoyed music so much and liked doing these things together.

My grandfather also played his game whenever Clemens came to visit. He'd meet him at the gate in the big old black fence in his work clothes, wrinkled and covered with paint spots. This always embarrassed me very much. Clemens soon caught on to Grandfather and didn't seem to mind, so Clemens and I enjoyed our little tête-à-têtes very much.

Between Clemens and Dieter and my other friends, I tried to have a lovely time in spite of the war. As long as the bombs missed the theatres and concert halls and the Nazis left them open, the performances took place. We often had to stand in lines for tickets. It did not matter how long we waited, just that we got them. Of course, sometimes we stood in line and the bombing started so we had to run to some kind of cellar. With all the government buildings, factories, and businesses concentrated there, the center of Berlin was very dangerous. The center of Berlin was the main target of the bombs. There were only two public bunkers, so often we used the cellars of apartment buildings. Yet, we went to plays, concerts, operettas, and operas.

In all this mess, I had my last year of high school in front of me. This meant preparation for the *Abitur,* the dreaded test that decided all: University or stupidity. If you passed this examination you could go to a University; if not the young men went into a trade school or ended up an apprentice to a master craftsman.

Women went to business schools or *Handelsschule*.

When I was 10 years old the principal of the elementary school had recommended me for high school, an academically oriented public school. It required some tuition and private purchase of textbooks. It was much like a prep school. In order to go to a university one had to graduate from such a prep school. I had passed the test and qualified. When I started high school, we had sixty students, divided into three classes of twenty. Twelve students of the sixty made it into the twelfth grade. What happened to the others? Some of them had to go back to the less challenging public school, and others did not keep up with their studies and dropped out.

On the 23rd of February 1943, I stood in front of the whole faculty of the *Gertrauden Gymnasium* to take the oral *Abitur*. Every teacher had the right to interrupt and ask a question about any school subject. If one had a grudge against a student, he or she could make it very difficult for that student. A group of friends and I wanted to get around the *Abitur* and talked about joining the army instead. We had heard terrible stories about the difficulty and how so many had failed it. When my father got wind of that idea, he set me straight really quickly.

Since we knew of the two part *Abitur's* difficulty, we studied a lot. By the big day in February, I had already passed the written examination. On the oral exam, I had no earthly idea on which subjects they'd test me, so I prepared for everything. In the first subject, biology, they asked me to discuss the areas of natural preservation in Germany. After ten minutes, they stopped the biology exam, a good sign.

The second part tested me in my worst subject, English. I had to read something from Oscar Wilde I'd never seen before. Then, I had to translate the paragraphs into German without a dictionary. Finally, I had to answer questions and discuss the paragraphs intelligently in English. The whole thing took twenty minutes. I passed the *Abitur* with a 2; angry I had not made a 1. Yet, when I heard that of the twelve tested, only nine had passed, I felt happy and relieved. I felt the test opened the door to any University in the world.

That night, my mother gave me a party. She invited my friends and relatives. We had a very good time, but that night all hell broke loose. Several bombs of the smaller kind fell around our house. Phosphorous canisters flew everywhere around the yard. The roof was badly damaged and the explosions knocked big holes in the stone walls of our house and blew out all the windows and doors. We found them in the street and in the neighbor's yard.

Phosphorous lay everywhere, burning our shoes and socks, even our feet as we walked around. The roof and the second story of the neighbor's house burned from the phosphorous. Even as the bombing continued, we ran for the water hose and got the fire under control. That night was one of our worst nights. The next night, we found flyers in our yard that read, "We will not bomb here anymore. We'll come and live here." We laughed and didn't want to believe it, but later it became a sad reality.

After completing the *Abitur*, the time came for me to leave Berlin. I enrolled in a teacher's college in Bad Godesberg. I had dreamed of becoming a biologist in a research laboratory. However, since becoming a biologist involved a long study of five years, *Vati* convinced me to become a teacher. It involved a shorter study, and I had the possibility to earn some money sooner. The change was not so difficult because I had enjoyed playing school as a child with my dolls and teddy bear.

Times grew much harder. With less bread and less food, long lines developed at the markets. Often when you got through the long lines the clerks said, "No more food; go home." Thus, people spent a lot of time hungry and uncomfortable.

After Stalingrad became Hitler's Waterloo, everything went from bad to worse. All my male friends ended up drafted as soldiers. Two of them had already died. I learned the Allies had captured Werner Erdmann and sent him as a prisoner of war to

Ottawa, Canada. For him the War was over, and this pleased me. Maybe we would see each other again. I wrote him letters and sent him pictures of myself and of Zehlendorf. Surprisingly he wrote back. When I told him about studying to become a teacher, he got very upset and told me in the letter he'd never marry a teacher because they think they're smarter than anybody else. I thought it was very ignorant of him to have such a viewpoint, so I never wrote him again.

When the American planes came, we could feel them before we saw them. Their bombs hit and destroyed. One could see street after street with nothing but ruins and rubble. The bombs the Americans dropped seemed bigger and more destructive. The Americans also used phosphorus bombs that set fires. We really hated the American bombers. Additionally, Goebels and the German propaganda painted the Americans as horrible creatures.

We always liked bad weather because the planes didn't come, and we could sleep for a night. No air attacks. No phosphorus from the sky. Later, towards the end of the war, the weather didn't make any difference because the flying fortresses came. B-17s could fly in any weather.

When the Americans began saturation bombing, it became even more terrible. When they shot four flares, which the Berliners called Christmas trees, they bombed mercilessly. They destroyed everything and killed nearly everybody. You cannot imagine the destruction. It made us angry and we wished those Americans in the planes the worst. We wanted revenge. The propaganda told us to hold steadfast with determination, not easy to do in this horrible situation.

Even the soldiers from the front line did not want to come home for furlough. They could not stand sitting in a cellar and waiting until a bomb hit. At least on the front line they could see the enemy and defend themselves, but in the bomb shelter the soldiers felt helpless and fenced in like everyone else.

One might think that you get used to the bombs and the

56

shelters, and the sirens. You don't! Every time the sirens blew, fear struck again as we hid in the dark cellars and bomb shelters. You knew it might come again at any time, but you never knew what awaited you.

Now, I compare the bombing to a tornado. I have lived in Texas for 41 years and have experienced a tornado. You have the same feeling of terrible insecurity and fear. You take shelter from flying debris, and wait until the storm or bombs hit. I feared the bombing, and I now fear tornados. Both give me the same fenced in feeling.

Once the American bombers came, we didn't do much knitting and storytelling any more. We heard bombs whistling and explosion after explosion. Then every one fell quiet and listened. Death surrounded us. We die a little every day, but during the war we died a lot every day. That we kept our heads clear and our nerves under control still amazes me. I never got used to the bombing; I always feared I might lose a leg or both, maybe an arm or even my life.

Toward the end of the war the sirens went off but the planes started bombing before we could get to the shelters. We decided that the sirens might as well not even blow. We found it shocking planes got through without notice. After 60 years, I can still hear the noise of those planes as wave after wave came over Berlin. It became a war of nerves.

Later, the war of nerves really got bad: 30 minutes in the cellar, 2 hours out of the cellar, maybe in bed; the siren blew again, this time, 1 hour in the cellar and 30 minutes out of the cellar. In this fashion it went on through the night. The British came in the evenings; the Americans came during the night and at noon. These noon attacks brought incredible devastation. They flattened everything beneath them. You can't imagine the horror of sitting in a cellar and waiting, expecting something to hit and kill you any second.

My mother grew tired of the bombing, and one time she

exclaimed, "Let a bomb come and kill us all."

I called out, "O Lord, do not listen to her. I'm so young, I still want to live."

I made only this one prayer through the whole war. Kind of selfish I've always thought, but a friend has since told me he thought it quite normal and understandable.

Times got harder, and we had less and less to eat. Germany was filled with empty stores and hungry people. However, alcohol and cigarettes remained plentiful. These did not quiet a growling stomach.

Before the bombing started, Hermann Goering stated that not one bomber would fly over Berlin. If that happened, he said he'd wear bathing trunks and all the Germans could call him Mister Mayer, a very common German name. When wave after wave of American or British planes passed over Berlin, we all shouted: "Wear your bathing trunks Mister Mayer!"

The terror bombing grew increasingly worse. Once, our neighbors and I sat in the cellar for 45 hours under constant bombing. During these days Berlin became a bomb cellar community. In four months, Berlin had 145 air raids. No wonder the city consisted only of rubble and craters. All the time, houses and factories burned and fires smoldered everywhere. Everything looked and smelled like death.

Chapter 5

Becoming a Teacher

From April 1943 until April 1944 I studied pedagogy, the art and science of teaching, at the teachers' college in Bad Godesberg on the Rhine River in western Germany. Berlin had universities but no teachers' colleges. I enjoyed being away from Berlin and from home. Bad Godesberg, a beautiful little town, had little business other than the teachers' college. The school had one old building where we both lived and went to school. Unfortunately, Bad Godesberg lay on the Rhine River with its factories, so Allied planes attacked the area often. They never bombed the school, but the sirens sounded regularly.

In April 1944, I passed my first teacher's examination. They cut the normal two years of study in half. This meant that with only one year of study, I could teach under the supervision of a master teacher! The school administration sent me to a one-room country school. They believed if a teacher could teach eight grades in a one-room school, she could teach anywhere.

So, I went to Steinwehrsruh, a large self-contained farm called a *Gut* in German, located in the eastern part of Germany close to the Oder River. It had a beautiful mansion like a little castle, stables, and other out buildings, all surrounded by a lovely park.

They had cattle, horses, pigs, sheep, chickens, pigeons, and peacocks. I hated those birds when they came close, because I hated feathers.

As a three-year-old child, a rooster flew at me out of the backyard and clawed himself into my little chest. I can still feel him when I remember the incident. Of course, I screamed. My mother tried to pull him away from me and had a difficult time to get the thing lose. The big old rooster clawed and fluttered and the wings flapped in my face. I still see how the wings hit my face like mad. Mother got the rooster away and threw it into the yard. Then, she hugged me and took me into the house. Ever since then, I've hated birds and feathers.

Later, as our family ate on the terrace during warm weather, a sparrow landed on the table. I screamed. My father couldn't stand that so he took me into the house and gave me a spanking. I got so many spankings because of my fear of feathers caused by that rooster, and as a result, I detest all birds, and I feared the birds on that farm. This just proves many events in our formative years go with us through life.

That *Gut* at Steinwehrsruh had many large fields with wheat, barley, rye, flax, and corn for the hogs. It also had a large garden with beans and peas, different kinds of cabbage, spinach, and other vegetables. They had a big orchard, too, with pear, apple, plum, and peach trees. In addition to the main house, the farm had bunkhouses and individual homes for the year-round and seasonal workers.

My mother came to stay with me on the *Gut* because my father felt he might not return from the war and wanted Mother to save herself for Gisela. The farm in the country was much safer than Berlin.

Thick pine woods separated the farm and the nearby little town of Lepene. When Mother and I wanted to go to Lepene, we walked down the paved road through those woods. Wild boars roamed the woods, and, occasionally, we'd hear of them killing someone. We always looked for a tree we could climb in case one of those boars attacked us.

Lepene, a nice little farm town, consisted of quaint old buildings. One could find all sorts of farm equipment, but they also had dress shops there. Naturally, those interested Mother and me. The town also had a movie theatre and one café. We usually took in a movie and had some dinner at the café. Mother and I always enjoyed our little outings.

Under the supervision of the local schoolteacher, I taught the children of the hired families from the *Gut* as well as those of the small farms around the area. The owner of the farm allowed Mother and me to live in one of the small homes on the *Gut*. It had a bedroom, a nice size living room, a kitchen and a bathroom. Not a big place, but comfortable.

Major von Eckersberg, the *Gut's* owner, often drove me to school in the morning with his horse and buggy, and sometimes picked me up in the afternoon. Often, he sent his son instead. Otherwise, I had to walk several kilometers. I saw the Major, a man in his fifties, as a father figure. He often said he wanted me to marry his son. I found his son unintelligent, and I didn't care at all for him.

The major, a womanizer, had married a lovely lady, not very pretty, but wealthy. Quite often she came to mother and me and poured her heart out to us. A sweet old soul, she appeared sickly and sad, not surprising considering the womanizer husband of hers! She had the money; I never understood why she put up with him. Her husband even made little overtures to me, a very young woman. He always tried to embrace me and kiss me, actions I detested, as I disliked his strong cigar breath. Since we lived on his farm in a little house, rent-free, he felt that obligated us somewhat, but I did not care. As a strong young woman he didn't intimidate me.

It was awkward and straining, riding with him back and forth to school every day. I eventually had to tell him off because he tried to overstep his territory. I didn't kick him out of the buggy, but I kicked his feet and gave him some strong words to remember.

"You damned old man, keep away from me."

Hearing such words from my sweet lips struck him speechless. That ended the episode Von Eckersberg.

The country schoolteacher, Herr Lehmann, my supervising teacher was just as bad as Major von Eckersberg. He made me do all of the teaching and gave me very little critique.

He always said, "Oh, you're doing very well."

Often he made me very angry, and I wanted to tell him off, but I needed a recommendation from him, so I played it cool. Off and on I played a little roller coaster game with him. If he acted just friendly, we visited together, but if he tried being affectionate, I ignored him.

Herr Lehmann also had a lovely wife, but she knew him too. She told me to just blow him off, but not hurt myself with the recommendation. She said he flirted with every young female teacher that came along. After six weeks of teaching in that one-room country school, I received my recommendation from him as a teacher trainee. Now, I could teach in a classroom by myself without a supervising teacher present. I only had to have a conference once a month with the supervising teacher.

As a result, the school administration sent me east to the Baltic Sea area. Mother stayed at the *Gut* until I could find sufficient accommodation for both of us in the town of Neuteich located in Danzig, Westpreussen. There, I taught a very spontaneous fifth grade. I had a good time teaching these great kids. I was supposed to move across the border to teach German to the Polish people later after we had won the "glorious war." Hitler always said that he had something up his sleeve to make us victorious. Being young, we hoped for that miracle. Of course, we never learned what miracle Hitler thought he had.

In July of 2003 I saw an interesting television program about Hitler's miracle weapon. A Jewish printer, a survivor of the concentration camps, told how Hitler saved about 150 Jewish craftsmen for his war machine. This Jewish man told the Americans the Nazis had hidden this weapon in Lake Toeplitz in Austria, the deepest lake in Europe. Hitler probably thought nobody would ever find his miracle weapon. If some evil is done in secrecy, my first husband, Louis always said, "The sun will shine it out."

American divers with their latest technical equipment brought the waterproof boxes containing the "weapon" out of the lake. I could hardly wait until they opened the boxes.

When the officials opened the first box the Jewish man cried out, "My goodness, I printed these pound bank notes!"

Hitler had printed the first dollar notes when the Russians neared Berlin, so he had to stop printing and pack up his miracle weapon and throw it into the lake. Hitler wanted to undermine the British, American and Russian economies with false pounds, dollars, and rubles and win the war this way. Of course, by 1945, it was much too late for this miracle weapon to work.

Very near where I taught in Neuteich sat the city of Zoppot, the oasis of the rich. The navy had a submarine station in the area. I found lots of fun things to do. On the weekend, I usually rode the train to Zoppot with my girlfriends, and we walked the boardwalk in our bathing suits. We also went swimming and lay on the beach. The submariners came by and whistled at us. We ignored them at first and then, perhaps, flirted a little.

There, I met Dieter Dehrmann, my dancing school friend, again. It felt strange, as I didn't know he'd be there. Dieter served as a submarine captain. A very nice, decent guy and shorter than I, a good thing for a submariner, Dieter and I often met on the weekends, and we enjoyed each other's company very much. We swam in the Baltic, went sailing, and walked on the Boardwalk. Every so often his mother, whom I knew from Berlin, came to visit Dieter, and I met her again in Zoppot when I visited there. A very pretty woman, and also a very vivacious and lovely person, his mother, Dieter, and I had fun together. I knew that this could not last very long, because the subs had to leave and go into action. This terrible war interrupted all the situations of life.

The sub left after several weekends, and a few weeks later, I received a call from Dieter's mother with disturbing and sad news. She told me his sub experienced problems on the bottom of the Indian Ocean, and officials doubted the sub's ability to surface. I remembered our wonderful weekends in Zoppot where I so enjoyed their company. Unfortunately, because of the unstable times, I later lost contact with Dieter's mother, and I never saw or heard from her again.

During this time, my mother remained in Lepene. I wrote and told her I was trying to find a place for us to live in Neuteich. At the time I lived with another teacher in one small room hardly big enough for two. We each had a single bed, a chest of drawers and a small night table. The room didn't have space for a table and chairs so we had to do without. I tried diligently to find an apartment for my mother and me in Neuteich, but never succeeded.

During the winter of 1944-45, a very scary time in Neuteich, we really didn't do much. Every night we heard the artillery fire from the Russians at Thorn. People from East Prussia trudged through with their carts and few possessions trying to escape the advancing Russian army.

The Russians did not advance like the Americans and the English in a long, extended front, but in "kettles" as we called them, or in circles, creating a crazy situation. We did not know where the Russians were at any certain time. For example, Mother, in Lepene, lived farther from the Russian border than I, in Neuteich. Yet, Russians had already occupied the area around Lepene before they came to Neuteich, farther east and closer to Poland. Because the Russians advanced like this, we never knew where to expect Russian troops.

With the Russians advancing on Neuteich, everybody who could, left their homes to escape another bad situation. Neuteich, a lovely town with about 5,000 inhabitants, had nice shops in the inner city. Fashionable, good quality dress shops lined the streets along with shops for men's clothes and very cute toyshops for children. Neuteich also had excellent restaurants and good *Konditoreien* or pastry shops with cakes and delicious tarts. I had a favorite *Konditorei.* The small and cozy store served heavenly cakes and tarts and I visited it whenever I could. I enjoyed living in Neuteich.

Now, unfortunately, everyone wanted to get away, creating a *Voelkerwanderung* or mass migration. We heard the Russians killed and raped, and they did.

Two girlfriends of mine and I wanted to get out too. I taught fifth grade and they taught fourth and sixth grade in a German public grammar school. We talked of leaving, but didn't know how to do it.

A few days later I heard by the grapevine, a munitions train en route to Berlin planned to stop in Neuteich. The next day the train arrived, and I went down to the station to ask for the commander of the train. Fortunately, I found him and pleaded with him to take three German schoolteachers with him. At first he hesitated, but after a while, he gave us permission to come aboard. I believe he just acted hesitant. After all, what normal young man didn't want to have three good-looking young women come along? Three intelligent and talkative girls with positive attitudes in spite of the serious situation certainly made for good company for the German officers.

I asked if he'd scheduled any stops before arriving in Berlin. He told me of a planned stop in Lepene for a few hours. That gave me hope of getting in contact with my mother. Maybe she knew about the train and waited for it at the station. Before I left to talk to my girlfriends, the commander said, "Bring a few clothes, but please, no books."

I saw my friends, and we talked the situation over. We hated to leave the school and our students. We couldn't say anything to anybody. We also knew the school couldn't stay open much longer. People were coming from all directions fleeing from the Russians. We had to leave to save our own skins. Worried, afraid, and concerned about the future after we lost the war, and also worried about leaving our jobs and letting the students sit there without a teacher, my friends agreed, hesitantly, to leave the school and the students and go on the train. We all packed a few things and boarded the munitions train. We felt a bit like cowards for running away, but we simply had to do what we had to do in this situation.

The Russian artillery sounded as if it sat in front of our door. Droves of people fled on bicycles, in wagons, with pushcarts, or even on foot. Everyone ran for their lives. Much later, I learned that all the teachers who stayed at the school in Neuteich died. I heard they hid in the cellar of the school, and when the Russians came they shot the men and raped and starved the women to death. The Russians, it seems, killed all of the intellectuals they captured: teachers, ministers, professors, and doctors.

The train consisted of an old and uncomfortable combination of passenger and freight cars. The cars rode roughly and constantly swayed. We three girls rode in the same car with the officers. The commander of the train wanted to make it comfortable for us, but the seats in this compartment, though upholstered, were very worn and shabby and not very comfortable. I feared that we might pick up fleas and lice from them. At least the soft seats made sitting for long distances a little easier to endure. Despite the discomfort, we felt fortunate to have those accommodations. The kitchen on the train supplied us with soup or sandwiches. The soup gave not only nourishment, but a comforting, warm feeling. The other passenger cars had wooden benches but not enough to go around. Many people had to sit on the floor of these cars. I do not know how the mothers and babies survived.

The Russians tried constantly to bomb us, but fortunately, they didn't hit the train. Often the train had to stop or detour because of broken rails. When they could, the crew tried to fix the rails. If they could not fix the rails, we had to find another route. A trip that normally took about eight hours took us from the beginning of January to late February. We had many air raids and attacks. The Russians tried very hard to hit us. It was a miracle we made it through.

The train also had to stop for potty calls. We had to run to the fields or woods to take care of our toilet business. This went on for the whole six weeks.

When we came to the middle of the Dirschauer Bridge over the Weichsel River the train stopped. We found ourselves in the middle of artillery fire. The Russians shot at the Germans, and the Germans shot at the Russians. A lovely battle boomed right over our heads. We sat on a munitions train in the middle of the bridge in the middle of a battle! How wonderful! Any minute I expected the train to take a hit and fall as little atoms into the Weichsel River. Finally, I resigned myself to death. Suddenly, the firing stopped. The bridge stood intact and the train could go on. The Lord and His angels must have held their hands over us.

Finally, we reached Lepene. The station, the town, everything burned and smoldered. The Russians had arrived in Lepene a long time before us. They raped, they killed, and then they set everything on fire. The train didn't stay, and I hoped against hope my mother had gotten out of this hellhole.

One of the worst parts of traveling on this train involved the morning cleaning process. We had hot water from the train and had to clean ourselves in freezing weather in front of everyone. Ever so often we needed to strip down and clean the whole body more thoroughly. Embarrassed, I avoided looking at anybody. I didn't know if anybody looked at us three girls. It did not matter anyway. We really had other things on our minds. Most of us thought of food and saving our lives.

The Lord must have held his hand over us again and again, although I didn't realize it at the time. Travel grew harder and harder on the train. It seemed half of the population of Neuteich rode on it. The temperature dropped below freezing outside and inside the train. The longer the train ride lasted, the less food we had. The train had elderly people, mothers with small children, and even pregnant women who gave birth on board. How they survived I don't know. Today, I know they only survived by the saving grace of God.

On February 21,1945, my twentieth birthday, we finally reached Berlin. My friends and I had to say good-bye. I went on home and they went to their aunt's home in the eastern part of Berlin that later became part of the Russian Sector. I never saw or heard anything from them again. Friends, relatives, and, often, whole families lost contact through this terrible war.

The condition of Berlin shocked me. The whole city lay in rubble and ashes. What a waste and what a horrible destruction! Anyone who hadn't seen it could hardly believe it. Getting to the district of Zehlendorf, some 14 kilometers away from the station where I arrived, presented a challenge. With no taxis, no busses, no streetcars, and no subways, I had nothing to transport me home. I still had two feet, and so, I started walking. I stumbled over rubble and walked across ashes and death until I reached home, a terrible, long walk.

Joyfully, I found our house still standing in one piece. There I stood in front of the big old black fence ringing the old garden bell that hung on the fence. It felt so good being home again.

I had to ring the bell several times until someone answered. Grandmother Loebel called out from her home, "Who in the world is ringing at three o'clock in the morning?"

I could hear the disgust in her voice. I answered, "It is Gisela."

She slowly came to the gate and could not believe her eyes when she saw me standing in front of her. She unlocked the gate and hugged and kissed me. Grandfather Loebel survived too. But, what about my mother? I hadn't found her, and she hadn't arrived at home. That only meant one thing. She didn't get out of the hell's kitchen in Lepene. We really worried about her.

I stayed during the day with my grandparents next door, but at night I slept in the big house in my own room. The house lacked heat because we had no fuel to heat it. Normally one undresses before going to bed, but with it so cold in the house, I put on sweaters, a jacket, long pants and even gloves. Then I got under the feather comforter and kept warm.

At the beginning of March 1945, Grandfather Loebel fell ill with strep throat. He had very high fever, and one could see death in his face. The doctor refused to come to see him anymore. He had the attitude that people of grandfather's age had lived long enough to die.

I told him, "Not yet!" I needed my grandfather badly. I shouted at the doctor and took him by the arm and dragged him to the house. I'd never done something like that before, but I felt I needed to do everything possible. Whatever the doctor did, it worked. My grandfather got well and lived twenty more years.

Since, I'd stayed with Grandmother and Grandfather Loebel, I decided I should stay with Grandmother Koch for a while. I didn't know she had rented one of the three bedrooms in her apartment to a young soldier. When I arrived there, I met the roomer. He was a young soldier with a large bandage around his head. We spent time together and decided after the war we should get married. He gave me a gold band for our engagement. A tall, nice-looking young man, I don't even remember his name now. Then, however, we both felt we needed someone to hold on to. We were able to help each other in a time of need.

All this time we never heard anything from my mother. They told us in June of 1944, of my father's disappearance. Now it seemed I'd lost both of my parents. Thankfully, I still had my grandparents.

At this point, we all knew we'd lost the war, and we had made white flags of surrender, hoping for the Americans to take Berlin. Instead the Russians came closer and closer from the east, and we feared they might take the city. I enjoyed living again at home but didn't like the air attacks with carpet bombing which seemed worse every day. The allies really wanted to force us to our knees. Just living seemed simply nerve racking.

Chapter 6

The End of the War

Around April 18, 1945, my grandmother and the young soldier, my fiancé, advised me to leave Berlin. They feared the Russians would take Berlin and possibly rape and kill me. Because they couldn't hide me on the property, my fiancé told me to go to Homberg via Kassel in southwest Germany, to the home of his elderly grandmother. He planned to meet me there after the war. I agreed and hoped to get there safely.

I took a few belongings and left all by myself. The first train went no further than city of Brandenburg where I arrived on April 20th, Hitler's birthday. The Americans must have wanted us to celebrate because they really gave us a party. They gave us one big bombardment that seemed worse than any other. Afterwards, it looked as if a great earthmover had pushed up the soil in some areas and left deep craters in others.

I rented a small apartment for a few days until I could board another train to western Germany. Suddenly, the siren sounded, and I started to the cellar, but then, I decided to run across the street to a bunker built under an old barracks. A bunker seemed safer to me than a cellar. Two bombs of the smaller kind, however, fell on the bunker and exploded. They blew the roof and two upper stories into the street and the air pressure tossed us from one side of the bunker to the other, all in all a very traumatic experience.

When the bombing ended, everyone wandered around in a daze looking at the destruction. Suddenly, the father of one of my Berlin girlfriends appeared and asked how I came to be in Brandenburg. I told him my plan to flee the Russians and go to Homberg.

Then he said, "Why do you have a pillow on your head?"

I suddenly realized I still held a pillow over my head and close to my ears. I had held it in the bunker and didn't realize I still had it. My girlfriend's father told me they had hit us with smaller eight hundred pounders. I told him I lived in the apartment across the street. He pointed out the smoldering ruins where the apartment building had stood!

Along with my apartment, bombs had also destroyed my few belongings. Fortunately, the Lord led me to make the right choice. I had lived because I had gone to the bunker instead of the cellar. As a result of my clothes disappearing in the raid, I had to stay in the same outfit for six weeks. Before long, it smelled to high heaven, but you don't worry about such things while running for your life.

A few days later, a train came, and I continued my trip to western Germany. During the train ride, I met a young girl traveling to the same area. We bonded and made the trip together. During this time of the war, nothing functioned well anymore. The trains could not go long distances, so we changed trains constantly, and pretty soon we'd reached the end of the line. In the area of the Harz Mountains, both train and bus service ceased. Very frightened, we stood on the street and didn't know how to continue our trip. After we overcame our panic and got our senses together, we looked around and found a pile of men's bicycles German soldiers had left behind. We picked out the best bicycles and started through the Harz Mountains.

We walked and pushed the bikes up the mountains, followed by the absolute pleasure of coasting down so fast and furiously. Whenever we got hungry we stopped at some farmhouse and told the farm people about escaping from Berlin and fleeing from the Russians. The people treated us well, usually providing food and bedding. Many times we had to sleep in barns on a pile of straw. It didn't bother us. We relished having something to eat and a place to sleep. In the morning we could always clean up and then have a good breakfast waiting for us. We never had to pay anything.

Off and on, we also heard shooting. We didn't know whether the Germans, Russians, or Americans did the shooting, as we didn't know the location of the different armies in the thick forest of the Harz Mountains. We hoped that we wouldn't cross into a Russian area.

After making the trip through the mountains, our bicycles broke down. The chains often came off and the tires went flat. Since we didn't know how to fix them, we left them and continued on foot.

As we walked in the forest unsure of our location, we suddenly heard more shooting. It was dusk and we couldn't see very well in the dark of the thick trees. Suddenly, we saw something white hanging in the air. It looked rather spooky. We walked towards it, and guess what? We saw a black soldier who smiled at us showing his white teeth. He was so black that in the dusk we couldn't see his face, only his teeth. Heidi and I had never seen a black person before. What an experience! As we got closer we could see that he wore an American soldier's uniform, and we knew that we had walked into the American lines. We trembled, as we had no idea what the soldier might do to us with the huge knife he had in his hand. We feared he might cut our throats.

With butterflies in my stomach, I gathered my courage and my English vocabulary together and asked for the head officer of this outfit. The soldier motioned in back of him. We walked to a clearing and found an officer sitting at a table in front of a barbed wire fence. He looked very important. I walked up to him and told him we'd come from Berlin, running from the Russians. When he heard that, a half grin played around his lips. He motioned for

Heidi and me to go behind the barbed wire fence. Again, I was fenced in.

We had heard from German propaganda the Americans shot Germans, old and young, women and children, so, we feared how they might treat us.

We joined the young people, children, elderly people, and women sitting, standing, or lying behind the fence. The soldiers gave us something to eat and ordered us to sit on the German farm wagons. So Heidi and I sat with three other girls on one of those wagons. Since it had no buildings, the area offered no protection from the weather and April in Germany can be quite cool and sometimes very cold. Everybody, young and old, had to stay in the open air. Many of the people sat on the bare ground; others had blankets and pillows.

Once darkness fell, some of the soldiers came and said to us, *"Fraeulein, kommen Sie mit."*

Then one put something against my chest. In the dark, I suppose he wanted me to think he had a gun. I touched it and found a flashlight. I yelled at the soldier and threatened to scream if he didn't get off the wagon. Boy, they left fast, and we did not see them again the rest of the night.

The next morning, the soldiers told us they had to leave because they had to give this area to the Russians. When I heard this, I wanted to leave too because I feared the Russians more than the Americans. The Americans released us from the wire fence. We moved along with them until we reached a river. Heidi asked what we should do next. I told her, a timid young woman with limited English, we had to get to the other side of the river and stay with the Americans. We heard from other Germans fleeing that this was the Elbe River.

Since we didn't have a map, we really hadn't known our location. Knowing we had reached the Elbe made us happy. I believed if we got across the river we'd make it behind American lines. We knew now the Americans didn't plan to rape or shoot us.

We also knew they'd feed us.

Getting across the Elbe River presented a problem. The Americans had a boat service for their people, and sometimes they took German civilians too. The river narrowed at this crossing and one could swim across, a dangerous idea in this weather.

I asked a soldier to take us across, but he refused, so I said to him, "Well, if you don't take us across, we will jump into the water and swim across."

He then agreed to let us cross on the boat. When we reached the other side, we knew we'd crossed behind the American lines. We knew the Russians couldn't reach us, and we felt much safer. We found some more bicycles the German soldiers had left and continued our trip.

Finally, after almost six weeks, we neared our destinations. Heidi went to Fritzlar and I to Homberg. I never saw or heard from Heidi again. She didn't know her aunt's address, and I didn't know where I'd settle.

When I arrived in Homberg, my fiancé's grandmother had no room for me. All their relatives from Berlin had come, and they had no space to take in another person. Boy, when I heard that, my feelings sank to a new low. What to do?

My fiancé's mother went next door to her neighbor, an elderly lady who lived alone. She had a well-furnished attic and would rent it to me for very little money. The cute little place had a comfortable couch that made into a bed. It also had two armchairs and a table with four straight chairs. As with most German living rooms it had a small china cabinet filled with cups, saucers, a few dinner plates, some glasses, and two crystal vases for flowers.

Fortunately for me, this attic room carried a very reasonable rent, as I no longer had a job. I still had a little money from Neuteich, but Germany had only a few schools still open because of the war and the terror bombing.

The small town of Homberg lay in central Germany. We heard the Allied planes fly over to attack Berlin, and I worried about my grandparents. Hearing about the bombing in Berlin devastated me, as I knew first hand what it was like. How could they stand it? I still find it amazing what a human body and mind can endure.

People in Homberg soon found out I taught, and before long I had a private school going in my room in the attic. It helped my money situation, and it helped the students to advance their studies. The children liked coming to the cozy little attic and having school, and so the kids and I had an enjoyable time.

Bombs, shells, and the constant rumbling of the artillery fire ended May 8, 1945. Germany surrendered unconditionally. The American troops in Homberg celebrated and most drank far too much as they had gotten into the wine cellars. I went outside to see what had happened. Everyone had taken to the streets. The war had ended!

Suddenly a car stopped! "Get in," said the soldiers in German, "We are trying to get through to Denmark."

That sounded good to me so I got in! Anything to get away from Germany! The soldiers wore battle dress, but when I looked around in the car, I saw the soldiers for their real selves: SS! I wanted nothing to do with them! I decided I didn't want to go to Denmark! Not with the SS! I asked them to stop the car, telling them I had to use the bathroom in the open air. I ran as fast as I could into the bushes and stayed there until they left. Fortunately, they soon sped away. If the American soldiers had caught us, I can't imagine what they might have done to a girl in a car full of SS. I had to walk back to town and back to my upstairs schoolroom.

We heard later from the Americans that people had sat in the cellars for days in Berlin and waited. Without news reports and newspapers, few Berliners knew the war had ended.

I felt sad we lost the war, but the fact it ended made me feel good. I got into trouble about that. Most folks were upset by the German surrender, but sleeping through the night was more important to me.

Chaos ruled in the big cities. Most people had little money and few jobs and hardly any place to live as so many houses had been destroyed. Busses and trains no longer ran. Water, gas, electricity, and food were extremely scarce in this catastrophe. The stores lay empty and very few could afford the black market prices for the few things available, so in Berlin and other major cites, most people didn't have enough to eat. It might seem odd, but during this time when people had little to eat, many actually stayed healthier. The loss of weight and minimal diets led to fewer gall bladder illnesses, heart attacks, stomach problems, and kidney problems.

No longer at war, we felt free and peaceful despite the hunger and lack of proper clothing. In Homberg, a small town, the situation didn't get quite as bad. Everybody had a place to live as the bombers had by-passed the town. Although we had a limited food supply, we at least had something to eat.

By May 12, 1945, four days after the war, a strange silence fell over the town. No planes flew overhead, no bombs exploded, no shots echoed, nothing. The only unusual sounds we heard for days came from the Americans as they yelled and screamed as they celebrated their victory over us Germans. The Americans had defeated the Fatherland, but I just felt glad the fighting and bombing had stopped.

Chapter 7

After the War

One day, an American appeared on the doorstep of my landlady's home with a big machine gun. She called me down to the door. The soldier said, in broken German, "Would you wash my clothes?" I said to him, "If you put your machine gun down, I'll talk to you." I also told him we had come through the war without a scratch and, "we do not want to get shot now." He understood and smiled and put the gun on the ground. My landlady washed, already, for another American soldier. She had asked if I'd do laundry for the Americans, also. I didn't want to wash clothes, but my landlady told me I could get cigarettes, chocolate, coffee, and soap that way. I didn't need most of those things, but I could trade them on the black market. I agreed to wash for Bernie.

He brought his clothes once a week, pants, shirts, and underclothes. I had to press two pleats in the front and three pleats in the back of his shirts. Washing the heavy jackets on a scrub board took a lot of effort. My fingers bled from rubbing the clothes. Life had taken a confusing and hard turn. I found myself washing clothes for an American soldier, formerly the enemy. I had to scrub his clothes and then hang them out, and I had no experience with such work. Mother or a washerwoman had always done the wash at home, and we had never had heavy jackets such as this. I did ironing too. I absolutely could not stand it. Yet, I had to "bite into the sour apple" and do the work. I found it difficult to converse with the soldier with my limited English. I had to strain to get all the words together. I still taught in the attic, but in my situation with a very limited wardrobe I needed to have something to trade.

Soon after the war, the U.S. Army camp very close to the house where I lived in Homberg closed, and the soldiers went home to the United States. Happily, I lost Bernie, my enemy client for whom I had washed clothes for several months.

Since the schools had opened again, I tried to get a teaching job. Of course, because I had no certificate showing my qualification as a full-fledged teacher trainee, I had trouble finding a job. I told the reluctant officials they could observe me in my job and find out if I could teach. After several discussions, the personnel director hired me. I had to swear I had earned my certificate as a teacher trainee, but that I had destroyed my certificate in fear before the Russians invaded Neuteich. They hired me to teach in a village school outside of Homburg.

Again, I had to teach eight grades in one classroom. I found myself the only educated person in the village. Whenever someone in the village had to fill out forms or something, they came to me for help. I lived in a very nice apartment above the classroom, comfortable and well furnished. I had everything I needed. The living room had a nice couch, several armchairs and a full china cabinet. The bedroom had a double bed and a big armoire. The kitchen contained a gas stove, a tiny fridge, and lots of cupboards with cookware and flatware. A small dining area with a table and four chairs took up one end of the kitchen. Of course, I also had a bathroom. The bathroom had a bathtub so big and tall I almost needed a ladder to climb in and out.

In bad weather, I could get to school very easily without getting into snow and ice. Everything really worked well for me. I enjoyed the students and the people in that area. The people, always kind and helpful, often invited me for dinner or brought meat and sausages to me.

I might have had a perfect life if I had heard from my grandparents and mother. Every day I wrote a letter. When someone came through the village, I asked him where he was going. When I heard Berlin or Leipzig, I sent a letter along. It went on like that for months. I feared losing my mother and grandparents, my only immediate family. I didn't want to lose them. I didn't want to be left alone in the world as had happened to so many, but I didn't hear from Berlin or Leipzig.

Every day I wondered about my grandparents and my mother. Were they alive? Were they well? Did the house still stand? Was Grandmother Koch's apartment still intact, or had the bombs found it as well? These questions repeated themselves several times a day, but I had no answers. I also wondered if my mother ever made it home. Was she well? Did the Russians still have her? Worrying really didn't help and didn't get me anywhere, but I couldn't stop. It almost made me sick.

At this point with everything unsettled, I had other concerns as well. Would we all have to work for the Americans from now on? Would we have to speak English from now on? Our beautiful Germany lay in shambles, and rubble and ashes now made up Berlin. I didn't know what to do. Would the Americans take everything away from us: our homes, our money? Our spirit was pretty much broken, and this is what I thought the Allies wanted. All these questions added to my worries.

Thousands of people, separated from each other because of this terrible war, now moved about the country looking for family members. All over the country, communication had broken down, making it very difficult to get in touch with someone. I don't know how many letters I wrote, but one letter got through to my grandmother's sister in Leipzig.

I learned later, my mother remained on the *Gut* at Steinwehrsruh. She lived at the farm headquarters with a number of young Russian women taken from Russia to work on the farm.

When the Russian soldiers arrived and occupied the farm, the women identified Mother as a good woman not to be harmed. However, the Russians shot the owner old Herr von Eckersberg. He had mistreated the Russian women. The soldiers also raped his wife and dragged her off.

Near the big farm sat a cluster of five small farms and farmer's houses. As the men had left, the Russians made the women and children work the fields on the small farms. Mother told me later she had moved into one of the houses with one of the women and her children to keep from starving to death on the big farm. The women, all in their thirties, and Mother, the oldest in her forties, did what they could to survive. The beastly Russian soldiers came through almost daily to harass, beat, and brutally rape mother and the farmers' wives. Over a period of two months, Mother later told me they raped her twenty-seven times.

The Russians soldiers moving through the countryside dragged women out of their houses, threw them on the ground, tore off their clothes, and raped them in the open. Often, the children, my former students now in their teens, witnessed the Russians' brutality and rape of their mothers. Then the Russians moved on and others came.

Rumors circulated that the Russian soldiers had the worst venereal diseases that didn't make them sick or bother them, so the women feared they might contact a venereal disease or possibly get pregnant. Mother later said that if she had gotten pregnant with a Russian child, she'd have hung it on the next tree. My mother prepared douches of Lysol for herself and the other women to use after each physical contact with the Russians. The doctor whom they visited much later told them that the douches protected them from pregnancy and disease.

Mother told us, that on one occasion, after a Russian soldier had raped her, he stayed to visit. He showed her several fish and indicated he wanted to wash them. Mother didn't want to have anything to do with the fish. When the soldier started towards the toilet, she motioned for him to go to the kitchen. He did not understand and kept going. He threw the fish into the toilet bowl. Then he pulled the chain to flush the toilet, thinking to wash the fish. Imagine his surprise when he saw the fish disappear. He looked at Mother with big eyes and didn't know what to do. Much to his shock the fish didn't come back. Mother just laughed and felt that it served him right.

On another occasion, Mother said, the Russian soldiers told her the bombed-out homes in Germany looked better than their houses in Russia. The soldiers told of sleeping on the stoves to keep warm at night. They also told her of their outhouses behind their homes. Many of the Russian soldiers clearly lived in very primitive circumstances.

Mother also told of a very cold night when the Russians ripped off the women's clothes and pushed them naked into a barn and locked it. The women feared that the Russians might set fire to the barn and kill them by burning them to death. Fortunately, that did not happen, and the next morning they let the women out.

Mother said she prayed every night for the Lord's mercy and to die during the night. She hated the situation. She wished to die rather than suffer the rapes and other abuses. Of course, she fought the soldiers off, but when they pointed a gun at her chest, she gave in, not wanting to die a violent death. When I mentioned this many years later in a talk to a group of American women, several said they would've taken their own lives rather than suffer the brutal attacks. Easy to say, but who is to say what one might do when threatened with a gun?

The Russians entered an area, and then left, replaced by another group with a repeat of the brutality. Later, Stalin ordered the rape and brutalities to stop.

About that time, my grandmother told me later, Russian officers moved into our house. My grandparents, astonished, asked what the Russians wanted? The officers smiled and said in broken German, "*Wohnen hier.* Live here."

"*Du Deutsche kaputt. Wir Sieger.* You Germans are losers. We are victors."

The six Russian officers moved into our big house.

Every night around ten o'clock they came down to grandmother's kitchen and ordered supper. Apparently, accustomed to eating very late at night, they brought their own food because grandmother had nothing to feed them. As she cooked their supper, the Russian officers stood around grandmother and the stove with cocked rifles. The officers watched her very closely. That made grandmother nervous and also afraid. When grandmother finished cooking they made her eat some of the food first. They waited several minutes and when she did not get sick or fall over dead, the Russian officers ate. I suppose they feared grandmother might poison them. This happened every evening for six months. Oh, she hated that, she said.

All in all, the Russians didn't, steal or ruin anything in the house. In fact they brought a very nice Persian rug from somewhere and left it in the living room. After the Russians left, grandmother took the rug out and aired it for several days because she feared they'd left it full of fleas and lice. I really don't know what she finally did with the rug. I think Grandmother probably put it in the apartment of Frau Dahlke, the lady who rented from her.

Grandmother, worried about my mother, considered talking to the Russian officers about mother's situation, but realizing they couldn't speak enough German, she felt it a useless undertaking. Instead, grandmother kept hoping for Mother's release and return home. Her wish finally came true.

One day, a Russian officer called my mother into his office and asked her if she wanted to go home to Berlin. When she nodded, the officer told her to get on the truck waiting outside. She climbed on the truck not really believing they intended to take her home. Yet, they did, and delivered her right to the front door of her house. Unbelievable! But the Russians were always very unpredictable. What great joy! I was surprised that my mother, although only 46, didn't come home as a little old lady, but she survived the suffering well.

My grandmother also worried a great deal about her sister Anna and her husband in Leipzig, not knowing if Anna and her husband still lived. Since Grandmother's health prevented her going to see about her sister, my mother went into the Russian Zone to find out about her, a brave act considering what Mother had experienced at the hands of the Russians. When she arrived at her aunt's house, she found both her aunt and uncle well. As my mother began talking about my disappearance and lamenting about it, my Great Aunt Anna gave her my letter. They all had feared the worst, but now Mother knew I had survived.

Then, mother started writing letters to me and giving them to people going to look for their families in the Kassel area near Homberg. She hoped her letters might reach me even though authorities hadn't restored public communication. Can you imagine a country without phone, mail, newspapers, or radio service? People cannot feel it and understand it unless they have gone through it. It made life absolutely awful.

Chapter 8

Back to Berlin

After several weeks, one of mother's letters finally reached me, but I didn't find it uplifting at all. She told of starvation and illness. I quickly went to the school administration in Homberg and resigned my position as a teacher in the little one-room schoolhouse. I had to get back to Berlin! The parents of my students understood. Although saddened I had to leave, they all thought I needed to go. They loaded me with meat, sausages, potatoes, and bread for my grandparents and mother. I appreciated their kindness very much. I never saw that little town again.

Homberg lay in central Germany in the American Zone, but very near the Russian Zone. The Allies divided Germany into four occupation zones, one each for the Russians, the English, the Americans, and the French. The Russian Zone completely surrounded Berlin, in northeastern Germany. To reach Berlin, I had to take a very long journey through the Russian occupied area.

When I arrived at the Russian Zone, I saw barbed wire fences everywhere. People had to slide underneath them, something very hard for the elderly. All these people wanted to get to the other side. The Russians used German soldiers as guards, under the supervision of Russian officers. The German guards helped a lot because they knew when the Russians had their vodka time and did not pay attention. With their help, we crawled under the fence and

I continued on my journey.

Ahead of me, I had a long, hard trip. Getting home to Berlin would still be difficult because only a few busses, trains, or subways worked. Sometimes, I could ride a train for a short while. When the line came to an end, a bus might pick up the passengers and transport them to the next one-horse town. Mostly we walked. Sometimes a horse drawn farm wagon came by and took some of us along. Then we walked again. Then another horse and farm wagon took us a short ways, and so on. Once I slept on the steps of a railroad station. Usually, we slept on the ground. We couldn't bathe at all.

I finally reached home after a month, a trip that before the war took less than twelve hours by train. Happily, I found our house standing in one piece but a little war-torn. The walls had some holes, but most of the roof remained so at least we had something over our heads.

Elated, I found my mother and Grandparents Loebel alive, but weak from the months of hunger. Elderly and not working, they had the number six graveyard ration cards. This card allowed them very little food. I could see that they were starving. Fortunately, I had brought some food along. The smoked meat and sausage survived the long journey, but Mother and grandparents had to make sure they didn't eat too much at first. Too much food at once might have made them deathly ill. I would later find that Grandmother Koch was alive and well. She still lived in her home and my aunt and uncle took care of her.

I found conditions in Berlin far worse than I had thought. Four girlfriends from before the war who lived in the neighborhood came to see me when they found out I'd made it home. They said, "You should have stayed in the American Zone where you had something to eat. Here we starve." They didn't have jobs. They wanted jobs in German businesses, but there weren't any. I said, "I can't understand how you all sit around and live on ration card number six. Why didn't you go to the US Army and ask for work?" Self conscious of their English, they feared they couldn't make themselves understood. I said, "Fiddle dee dee, I'm going to the US Army and look for a job. I'll make myself understood." After all, I had already washed for a US soldier. I think they had too much pride to work for our former enemies. I told them, "We came through the war without a scratch. Now, we don't want to die of starvation."

I knew I had to get a job somehow. Since we had ration card number six, I didn't need a job for the money, I needed it for the food! At this time people had only two thoughts, food and staying alive. I went to an official of the US Army and asked for a job. In a few minutes, I had one for me and for my four girlfriends too. Very menial work cleaning up the soldiers' quarters, the jobs kept us alive because now my friends and I had number two ration cards. We could eat in the mess hall of the American soldiers, and I could give my mother and my grandparents my number two ration card. This way they had more to eat as well.

Every morning at 6:00 a.m., my friends and I went to work at the little town of Wanusee traveling by S-Bahn, now that it ran again. After a fifteen-minute walk, we reached the soldiers' quarters. The soldiers lived in two-story German apartment houses. Each one of us had one house to clean, not exactly fun, but not so bad either. The war left wounds and scars with rubble everywhere, houses in ruins, and, of course, scarce food sources. Women whose husbands served in the Nazi party had to clean the bricks and stones for reuse. Mother had to do that work, too. Slowly Berlin began to rebuild. Not very much had changed from the war days, but we could sleep through the night.

One thing, however, had changed. The American leaflets from the planes had said, "We are not bombing this area. We'll come and live here."

We used to laugh about that message. Then reality set in. They meant what they said, and we had to cope with this difficulty. One day, the U.S. Army occupied our large home. They did not want anyone else on the premises and Grandmother and Grandfather, and *Mutti* and I had to move out. They also moved the lady who rented the room in the back. They kept our home for one year. Six officers lived in our big house.

I must say they tried their best to destroy the house. They poured beer into my mother's piano and ruined it. They ruined our steam heating system by using it without putting water into it. They pulled down the chandelier in the living room and pulled all the other hanging lamps in the house out of their sockets. We wondered if they had swung on them like monkeys. They also stole my father's desk. They may have put it in another house, I don't know, but it left our house.

While they used our house, we had to share another house with four families. Each family occupied one room, and we slept on the floor because our room did not have enough beds. My elderly grandparents had great difficulty sleeping like this. Five women had to use one kitchen. Four families made that one house very crowded and very uncomfortable. No one had children which would've made life even more complicated.

One day my grandmother got the idea to go home to see about the fruit on the trees. She had not handed over all the keys to the Americans. She needed the key for the gate in the big black fence.

While she picked fruit from the trees, suddenly a loud voice yelled at her in broken German, "*Wenn nicht weggehen Du ich schiesse.* If you don't leave, I'll shoot."

Grandmother answered, "*Schiesse, ich bin alt genug zu sterben.* Shoot, I am old enough to die."

Then the officer smiled and motioned for her to come upstairs. He had just fried a chicken and had made mashed potatoes and gravy, and he invited grandmother to eat. Then the officer told her she could come and pick the fruit off the trees as often as she wanted.

One morning, either the alarm did not go off, or I did not hear it and I overslept. It made me so angry I took the little clock and threw it against the wall. That didn't help a bit. I broke the clock and hadn't gained a thing. I just knew I'd lose my job when I arrived late. As I said before, I did not need the job for money; I needed it for food, so that my mother, grandparents, and I could survive. I did not understand how Americans dealt with people who came late to their jobs. I arrived late, and they seemed glad that I had arrived. My girlfriends arrived late too because they had waited for me. Had I worked in a German firm and arrived late, I'd have been fired. The Americans, however, didn't do anything. They were just happy they didn't have to clean their own apartments.

Sometimes, I enjoyed my job because the soldiers treated me well. They knew I had to do this work to survive. Every Friday the MP came with white gloves and inspected the apartment, and I always passed. The soldiers then showered me with soap, coffee, cigarettes and candy that I exchanged for food for the family.

One day an MP came to me and asked if I knew a German man who could take care of the heating system of the apartments. It wouldn't be hard work, as he only had to put coke in the furnace when it grew low. He could sit warm and comfortable by the furnace and read as he kept the system going. I thought maybe Grandfather could do that. He could ride with us to Wannsee, do his job, eat with us in the American mess hall, and receive ration card number two. When I came home, I made this proposition to Grandfather, and he accepted.

The next morning my four girlfriends, Grandfather, and I entered the train for Wannsee. Grandfather enjoyed eating in the mess hall, the warmth of the cellar, and reading without Grandmother there to tell him what to do. He liked the Americans better than the Nazis.

Later, I decided to go back to teaching. This upset my grandfather because he didn't want to ride to Wannsee alone. The girls still went to Wannsee, but Grandfather soon stopped. The girls thought me silly to begin teaching and lose the advantage of eating in the American mess hall. I felt it better to go back to my profession as a teacher. Besides, I still received ration card number two.

In 1946, the schools, closed during the worst part of the war, reopened. I still had not taken my second examination to become a full-fledged teacher, but because of my job in Homberg, I had my teacher trainee certificate.

The school office in Berlin hired me for the *Nordschule*, a public school for boys in Zehlendorf. Mister Dienerowitz, a very nice man and an excellent school official, served as principal. With many school buildings bombed and destroyed, we had to double up in the remaining ones. This meant we had terribly overcrowded classrooms. I ended up with sixty fourteen-year-old young men in my class.

At twenty-two years of age, I worried about motivating these boys and maintaining discipline. Somewhat scared, I told Mister Dienerowitz I didn't know if I could handle it.

He said, "Oh, yes, you can handle it. You are strong and have a good personality."

In spite of the strain of the job, I managed to stay above the situation.

I wanted to be a teacher, but I did not want to look like one. Those old German teachers, my goodness, you could recognize them a mile a way. They never had many dresses. They didn't take care of themselves. At this time, of course, we had to have ration cards and enough points to buy clothes. Ration cards had coupons (points) and numbers on them. Different items required different numbers of points. Often we had to collect these coupons over a long period of time to buy items like clothes, shoes, or such. Fortunately, my grandmother didn't use all her coupons and she saved them for me.

One of my teacher friends had a brother who owned a fantastic dress shop, *Model Haus, Bartsch.* Here I bought very chic dresses at cost. My mother also took the curtains down in the sunroom and dyed them bright yellow. I took them to *Model Haus, Bartsch* and had them made into a most elegant dress with pleated skirt and a bodice laced with brown shoelaces. The yellow with my dark hair looked very good. I always wore American nylons and brown, very pointed high-heeled shoes with it. Mother gave me the cover of a sun umbrella, red with big white polka dots, and I had it made into a beautiful red skirt with big white polka dots. It looked very nice. We saw American women wearing very bright colors, and we all wanted to dress like the Americans.

When the parents of my students came to a parents' meeting or open house they told me, "Oh Miss Koch, we know all about everything you wear and the way you dress. Our boys tell us all about it."

Most of the teachers in this school, advanced in age and careless about their appearance, conducted classes in the same boring way. Only the teacher spoke, and the students listened or dozed. These teachers tended to ignore questions from the students. Because I had youth, good looks, and energy on my side, I conducted my classes in groups with questions and answers. This made it very lively. Students learned to give interesting reports in front of the class, and sometimes we just had sessions where the pupils told about personal experiences.

Mister Dienerowitz, my principal, liked me and arranged for me to meet his eldest son, Hans-Juergen, a very good-looking young man. Six foot tall and slender, he had brown hair and beautiful blue eyes, always warm and smiling, especially when he saw me. He was also intelligent, loving, and kind.

Hans-Juergen had just come back from the war in Italy. Of course, he had no job and took it easy. He could have gone to the university, but worn out from the war and uncertain what he wanted to do, he just rested. Our friendship grew and we had fun together. He'd been engaged an Italian girl, but broke the relationship off after he fell in love with me. I liked him very much, but I don't think I loved him.

91

At that time I didn't know what love was. I enjoyed having young men look at me and try to date me, but I couldn't endure long relationships. I decided I shouldn't have lasting friendships and I should never get married. Engaged several times, I had broken those engagements off. This disgusted my mother and girlfriends. I suppose I was too young to be serious with my boyfriends. The Lord apparently had something else in mind for me.

My sex appeal performance worked, and the students practically ate out of my hand. They worked and learned well. I enjoyed them very much. Every month we had a field day. One time we took a steamboat ride on the Havel River to the castle of Queen Louise of Prussia. Other times, we went to the museums of Berlin and the castles in Potsdam and Sans Sousci.

One day we took a swimming excursion to Lake Wannasee. From Zehlendorf to Wannsee we rode the train that had only just come fully back into service. Riding a train with sixty fourteen-year-old boys wasn't easy. One does these things when young. Naturally, they pushed, ran, and made lots of noise getting on the train. When we arrived at the station in Wannsee we had to change to a bus. Again, the boys pushed, ran, and yelled as they climbed on the double-decker bus. I'd made safety arrangements ahead of time with Hans-Juergen and instructed the students not to swim beyond Hans-Juergen's paddleboat. Sure enough, when we arrived Hans-Juergen met us with his boat.

The boys quickly stripped to their bathing trunks and jumped into the water while I went into the bathhouse. A little later I appeared in my bathing suit, very self-conscious with all those males, though at that time I had a good figure. I must've looked great in my tight swimsuit since the boys and Hans-Juergen stared at me. He smiled very lovingly, and the boys did too. They obeyed well, and we had a wonderful day swimming, playing in the water, splashing, and sun bathing.

At noon, we ate our picnic lunches. The kids loved it. In the early afternoon, we all arrived happily back at our school from where the boys walked home. Hans-Juergen and I met later in the evening for a nice tête-à-tête in a restaurant. When I look back to those different field days, I shake my head and think only youth can undertake such bold things. The students and I got along well. Being young, fashionably dressed, and vivacious, with a modern outlook on life helped motivate the students and keep them in line.

Later Hans-Juergen told me I looked very good in a bathing suit. He and I had a good relationship. We both liked art, music, and the theatre. We went on bicycle trips and had good times on the river steamer and on his paddleboat.

In spite of everything, I needed space from Hans-Juergen. I could not see him every day as he wanted. Every so often, we had quarrels about this. He wanted to make a commitment and talked about engagement and marriage. I dragged my feet. I didn't want to marry so young and have children. In fact, I never wanted to get married. I wanted to travel and see the world. In the summer of 1948, he wanted me to go on vacation with him. He still didn't work and really had vacation every day. I agreed to it because I wanted to see if we could get along almost twenty-four hours a day.

We went to Heidelberg to see his brother, a dentist. Then, we traveled together farther south in Germany. We traveled for three weeks staying in hotels, he paying his way and I paying mine. I enjoyed sharing the beautiful views, sights, and experiences. We hugged, kissed and held each other tightly, but never had sex. I did not want a commitment.

Perhaps, I treated him unfairly. I didn't want commitment, but he seemed ready to settle down after the war. On what? He had to go to a university first and then get a job. He probably thought I had a good job and my family had our own home, all around, a good deal for him. By the time we returned, we had been together every day, and I didn't enjoy his company anymore. Something irritated me, and I stopped speaking to him. After a year of a close relationship, I told him good-bye. Later, he left for Freyburg to study medicine at the university there. I heard he later married a girl who could've been my twin sister.

After that, I met Darby, an American who cooked in the mess hall. He had also worked as a cook in good restaurants at home in Georgia. I met him because Mother had a bottle of Schnapps she wanted me to exchange for food. At the soldiers' quarters, Darby exchanged the bottle for me and then drove me home in a jeep. Thus, he knew where I lived.

Darby visited often and became a good friend of the family. He always brought something, a small present from the PX, perfume, or food. He never came empty handed. He often brought food he had cooked in the mess hall for the family. He sometimes invited me to the PX where I learned to love milkshakes and hamburgers, new treats to me.

Once when Darby visited, he brought a handful of German Marks. He handed them to me and said, "Here, this is for you." Afraid he might have stolen the money, I told him I couldn't take it, but he said he had gambled all night and the money came from his winnings. He said he didn't need to take it back to America and told me we should fix up the house or something. Thus, from Darby's gambling winnings, we repaired our home.

Although we had spent little time alone, Darby and I decided to marry, and he gave me a gold band. Whenever Darby came over, my mother watched everything we did. Sometimes, Darby came to the house drunk, and I didn't like that. Then, one time he didn't show up as planned. I knew where he lived and went to the American quarters to look for him. His friends told me he was in the hospital drying out. I asked what they meant, and they told me he was an alcoholic. They explained drying out meant overcoming his alcoholic addiction. I decided I didn't want to marry this man who gambled and drank. After that, Darby came several times to the gate, but we refused to open it to him, and he finally got the message. I didn't have a diamond ring, just a small gold band. He didn't ask for it back, and I didn't give it back. Once again, the Lord protected me from making a big mistake.

Shortly after I started teaching again, I had to think about working on my second teacher's exam. Still a teacher trainee, I felt it high time I begin studies to earn a full-fledged teacher certificate. I couldn't go to the famous Humboldt University in the center of Berlin now located in the Russian Sector. Workers had laid the groundwork for the Free University in the American Sector of Berlin, but no buildings existed yet. Consequently, classes took place in different schools throughout the American Sector. During the day, I taught my students, and in the evenings, I studied on my second exam. It took three years to complete my work. In 1949, I passed my state board exam and became a full-fledged teacher. Now I could teach from the first to the eighth grade in the public schools.

To teach high school, I needed three more years at the University for my doctorate. All high school teachers in Germany had to have a doctor's degree. I never began work on my doctorate since the only advanced degrees were offered at Humbolt University in the Russian zone.

After the war, the Americans, British, French, and Russians met at Yalta and divided Germany into four parts. The four nations met again at the Cecilienhof not too far away from Berlin to make the decision a reality. A beautiful hundred year old building, Cecilienhof is now a museum and a very expensive restaurant. The Allies turned Berlin into an island completely surrounded by the Russian Zone. We Berliners called our city an island in the Red Sea.

Not only did the Allies divide Germany into Zones, but they split Berlin into small sectors. The Americans had the southwest or best part of Berlin with beautiful houses, wonderful lakes, nice landscapes and little bomb damage. The rich people and the big shot Nazis had lived in that area. The Russians occupied the industrial areas in northeastern and central Berlin, the most bombed part of Berlin. The French occupied the southern part of the city, and the British the northwestern part. These Sectors also had suffered greatly under the bombing. The Americans knew where to live in comfort.

In 1948, we had a scare in Berlin when the unpredictable Russians closed the highways and railroads across their Zone. This cut off all travel from the Western Zones of Germany to the Western Sectors of Berlin except for air travel. The Russians had fenced us in since Germans weren't allowed to fly. Trucks and trains carrying food or other products to Berlin couldn't cross the Russian Zone. The Russians planned to starve two and a half million Berliners to death in order to control all of Berlin. The Americans reacted quickly, however, starting the Berlin airlift. At the airlift's peak, American planes landed at Tempelhof airport loaded with food and other supplies every three minutes.

Berliners facetiously called these planes the raisin bombers. Of course they brought not only raisins, but lots of coal, raw materials for the industry, parts for machines, and commodities for our livelihood. Two days after the blockade, the airlift started. There were 500 flights in 1948 and 2,800 flights until May 1949 when the blockade ended. The planes carried over 2,000,000 tons of supplies into West Berlin.

I shall never forget when we received the first cans of sweet potatoes. We had never heard of them. We opened the cans and tasted the horrible stuff, but hunger drove it into our stomachs. We didn't know how to fix sweet potatoes, and ate them straight out of the cans. The instructions for preparing them were in English but we couldn't read them. Had we known how to prepare them, we couldn't have anyway because we had no butter, no sugar, or spices. They gave us marshmallows too, but again we didn't know how to eat them, especially with sweet potatoes. Many years later my American husband, Louis, fixed sweet potatoes for me with marshmallows, brown sugar and lots of butter, and I liked them very much.

We got meat, vegetables, and fruit in cans. We got Spam too and liked it, but the American soldiers threw it away. They couldn't stand it. Often the soldiers gave us their rations, and we couldn't believe they could give away such good food. Rations had Spam and chocolate. I especially enjoyed the chocolate. I had not had sweets for six years. We saw American soldiers as spoiled. They, surely, were not hungry. We were hungry!

Some planes unfortunately crashed, killing the crews. Now, it made us very sad that men died doing such good deeds. In May 1949, the Americans, British, and French negotiated with the Russians and finally the Russians let trains, trucks, and busses drive through to West Berlin.

Then came the years of the 50s with the economic wonder, the Marshal Plan! America gave Germany the money to rebuild. We got food, too. Every German got forty marks under the new government since Nazi money carried no value. With this we started over, everyone equal. American troops occupied Germany and protected it. American soldiers liked the Frauleins and enticed them with chocolate, perfumes, petticoats and nylon hose from the PX. Germans began to prosper and share the wealth and rebuild the nation.

By that time I had finished my second teacher's examination, earned full teaching status, and still taught eighth grade in Zehlendorf. I taught one English class. I spoke English to the Americans and could get by, but I didn't feel my English good enough to teach others. I prepared for my English class each evening and taught the material the next day. I believe, sometimes, I even made up some words. I had fun, we got along well, and my teaching went well. The world had improved for me extensively by the beginning of the 1950's. Things, however, soon changed a lot more for me.

Chapter 9

Off to America

Since the war, I had met so many nice and interesting American families among the occupation troops in the American Sector of Berlin. I felt closer to the country for knowing these Americans, and I wanted to see their country.

I especially liked the American women because they fixed themselves up so nicely and wore makeup and beautiful clothes. As teachers, we had rules against makeup. I wore polished fingernails and lipstick, anyway, and the principal once told me I couldn't wear lipstick or fingernail polish because it made me look like a fast woman. I told him he shouldn't look at the outward things but should look at how I taught my students. Nobody said anything more. I wore lipstick, painted my fingernails, and dyed my hair reddish brown. I loved that chestnut hair, but one day I ran my fingers through my hair at the top of the back of my neck, and I found a big bald spot as big as the palm of my hand. I was horrified! I went to a doctor, and he fortunately gave me something to treat the area. My hair finally grew back again, but I didn't color it again until many years later, after I had moved to America.

Some time during 1949, I saw an article in our newspaper about scholarships given by the United States government through the Institute of International Education. It encouraged teachers and students to apply, and I did. At the time I was engaged to a fellow teacher, Hans Sauer. We had taught three years together at the same school, but he didn't like the idea of my going off to America for a whole year of study. Seeing the possibility as exciting and advantageous, I applied in spite of his objections. I had to think of myself and my future as a teacher.

To get the scholarship, we took many examinations both written and oral about general education, math, English, geography, and literature. I suppose the American educators wanted to know if we had the mental capabilities to handle the study. They also wanted to know if we could communicate in English so we had to answer questions in English and write why we wanted to study in America.

We also had to fill out questionnaires about our Nazi memberships. They wanted to know when we entered the Nazi youth organization, how long we belonged, and if we belonged to the Nazi Party. Of course I told them I spent eight years in the youth organization, but hadn't joined the Nazi Party.

One afternoon when I had to take one of the examinations for the scholarship, an FBI man told me I had belonged to the Nazi Party. I nearly fell over! I really wanted to go to America. I learned from the FBI man that at 18 years of age, without saying anything to me or asking my opinion, the Nazi party took me in. I'd never attended a meeting or anything. I simply got out of the Hitler Youth and thought I was free. Normally parents signed up their children to join the Nazi party. However, the FBI told me that for those born in 1925 the Nazi party just took them without asking or informing them. I went home and told my mother I'd lost the scholarship and the FBI probably thought I'd lied. I might even have to go to prison I thought. I was very upset.

Fortunately, my Nazi party membership didn't affect my scholarship. The Americans gave amnesty to the entire group of those born in 1925, and I received a letter from the Institute of International Education telling me that I had gotten a one-year scholarship for study in the United States. Sixty-five teachers and students applied in Berlin and only nine of us received scholarships. This made me very happy! My selection for this wonderful chance also pleased my students, my mother, and my grandparents.

Of course, I faced a significant difficulty. With my father still missing in action, Mother didn't receive a pension from the bank. I provided her only financial support. The school administration agreed, however, to allot me half of my salary. This, mother could have. I didn't need it because the scholarship paid everything for me. Mother also applied for and obtained a good job with the US Army. She decorated and prepared houses for officers and their families moving to Germany from America. Then she stayed in the houses until the families moved in. Sometimes it took a month for a family to move into a house, and she had very little to do, except live there and wait. This took care of Mother financially for the year the scholarship took me to America.

The scholarship letter told me to be at the airport in Tempelhof at 9:00 a.m. on August 13, 1950. American planes flew us from Berlin to Frankfurt and then a train took us to Cannes where a ship took us to America. How exciting, flying on an American military plane. What terrible fear we had had of the Americans during the war. What excitement! During the war I saw America as the big giant on the other side of the ocean, the feared enemy! Now I had a scholarship to study there! How fast things changed!

My mother took me by taxi to the airport. Like most Germans at that time, we didn't have a car. When we arrived at the airport, there stood my sixty boys all with flower bouquets in their hands. When I saw them, tears came to my eyes. It made me feel so good that they came with their parents to see me off. Unfortunately, I couldn't take all the flowers with me into the plane. Mother had her arms full of them. Before I entered the plane I said to the boys, "In one year, I'll see you again." Little did I know America would become my new home.

When we landed in Frankfurt, we boarded a train that took us to Cannes on the French Riviera. But, boarding the ship at Cannes proved an ordeal. Shallow water prevented the ship from reaching the shore so we had to get on small boats that took us to the ship. Then, we had to climb a steel ladder on the side of the ship. I hated that. By nature a little clumsy, now I had to climb a narrow ladder to board.

The sailors shouted at us, "Don't look down! Don't look down!"

Of course, I looked down, a very scary, long way down, and I almost froze up, but I wanted to go to America, so I climbed.

Finally, all six hundred fifty German educators and students with scholarships from the Institute of International Education safely boarded the ship. I had never been on such a ship before and neither had the others.

Excitement filled the air! When we left Cannes, the music played, and we waved to the people who stayed behind. What a great experience! I almost forgot about the terrible war five years earlier.

We sailed first-class on an Italian cruise ship with excellent service. I shared a very nice stateroom with another girl. After we unpacked our clothes, we went on deck with our life jackets for safety training. The ship had a swimming pool where we could swim in the afternoons, and the crew offered us something to eat all of the time. We had excellent food and lots of red wine. It all contrasted to war-torn Berlin so much. I'd never experienced anything like it.

The first night after dinner, we had a dance. Of course I went. I loved to dance and always had a good time. I didn't have a partner, but that didn't matter. I knew I'd find someone in the course of the evening. Sure enough, a young man whom I had known from Berlin came and asked me to dance. Some others came too, but the young Berliner came again and again. I had a wonderful evening with a beautiful dance. The ship sailed on the Mediterranean Sea under a clear sky and the shining moon. We stood by the railing, and then he walked me back to my stateroom and said, "Goodnight."

The next day we passed the Rock of Gibraltar and stopped for a day in Lisbon, Portugal. There the ship could dock in the port and we disembarked via the gangplank. If they had made us climb a ladder again, I'd have stayed on board. Since we had a six-hour stay in Lisbon, we took a tour the city.

Lisbon had beautiful old buildings typical of a Mediterranean city with areas built on terraces up the hillsides. One thing surprised me in Lisbon. In the residential areas, we saw beautiful homes built right next to shacks. Apparently, they didn't have building codes. The interesting and exciting tour of Lisbon, strolling through the beautiful city, lasted until evening when we boarded the ship again.

Leaving Lisbon, we sailed into the open sea of the Atlantic. That evening, we had a lovely dinner consisting of several courses. After dinner, the band invited us for dancing. Some people went back to their staterooms, but of course, I stayed. I had already made friends with the young teacher from Berlin. He stayed for the dance too. We had a good time dancing together. Some other young men came and asked me to dance also. Then a little later, a very good-looking young man came towards me and asked me to dance. Very tall, something over six feet at least, Hermann Bader had a slender build, with broad shoulders and narrow but tight buttocks. He had black, wavy hair, blue eyes, and very white teeth. His mouth looked absolutely inviting. I expected arrogance, but quite the contrary, I found Hermann very nice with a good sense of humor. We had fun together, and he danced with me the rest of the evening.

The next morning, he knocked on my door and asked me to breakfast. I went with him, and then we spent the whole day together. At the dance that night he danced with me every dance and didn't let anyone near me. Hermann, a good dancer, intelligent, exciting, and the best looking guy on the ship, made for a wonderful shipboard romance.

We took the Southern route to New York with our next stop in the Azores. When we arrived there, the natives came to the side of the ship in their lantern-lighted boats to sell their goods. In boats decorated with flowers, the women wore their colorful native outfits, making a very beautiful scene. For the first time in my life, I saw a pineapple. I bought it, but didn't know what to do with it.

One of the stewards watched me, took the fruit from me and said, "I'll fix it for you and give it to you tomorrow."

The next evening, Hermann and I stood by the railing holding hands when the Steward brought us the ice-cold pineapple covered with Champagne. It tasted heavenly, and Hermann and I feasted

After we left the Azores, we caught the tail of a hurricane. The ship rocked from side to side and back and forth and I grew terribly seasick. Everyone had to lie in their beds with the sides up to keep them from falling out. Later, after things calmed down, Hermann sat by my bed and fed me green apples. It helped settle my stomach a little. We were en route to New York, to the big giant called the United States, and I was so sick. In spite of the seasickness, the trip kept me very excited. Off and on, I had to pinch myself to make sure it wasn't a dream.

Early one morning they called us on deck. There before us lay New York. We passed the Statue of Liberty, and the huge skyscrapers towering behind it. With the sun just rising behind the city, the sky looked almost like gold. I will never forget that wonderful sight as long as I live! I had never seen a building over seven stories high. I had never seen a skyscraper. The city overwhelmed me, so gigantic, so fantastic. I couldn't hold back my tears.

I had wanted to come so badly to America! Arriving, I finally felt safe and secure. With my native Germany in such shambles and my hard life behind me, here I felt free and not behind a big old fence. After fifty years, as I think about it, I still cry. I know then, I felt blessed, but didn't know just how blessed.

After waiting a while on the ship, the Institute transported us all to Columbia University by bus. From there, most of us went in all directions, but, fortunately, I stayed at Columbia, an excellent university. Already a teacher, I took only classes that advanced me in my profession.

At Columbia, I met a very nice and intelligent young American student named Thomas Koch. How strange to find someone in America with my last name. We had several classes together and spent much time with one another. He showed me New York: Radio City Music Hall, the Met, different theatres, Broadway, and Times Square. The fact that all the Times Square stores remained open at 2:00 o'clock in the morning impressed me. The lights shone so brightly I could read a newspaper. In Germany we had had so little light for so long. Yet, here in the bright lights of Time Square I bought a pair of shoes at 2:00 o'clock in the morning. Unbelievable!

After one semester at Columbia we scholarship students again went in different directions. The scholarships introduced us to America and American ideas for us to take back to Germany. I hated to leave Columbia University, which I liked very much, but I needed to see another part of the country. As a result, I left New York for a Teacher's College in Spearfish, South Dakota. What a change! From the lights and excitement of New York to the plains of the Midwest certainly let me see different parts of the United States.

I found South Dakota a very nice state with friendly people. I easily made friends who invited me to go somewhere almost every weekend. Many of the girls took me to their homes, and I met their families. They often took me to the memorable sights in South Dakota. I saw Devil's Tower, Mount Rushmore, and Custer Park as well as many other places. Parts of South Dakota reminded me of Germany. When I visited the Black Hills I thought of the Black Forest in Germany.

South Dakota did not, however, meet my expectations. In

Germany we thought South Dakota full of Indians, so I expected to find Indians everywhere. Indians did come to school there, but they did not look like the Indians I had expected, for they did not wear native clothes. They wore blue jeans and sweaters and looked very nice. When they went to their reservations, they dressed in their native dress. I learned to like them very much. Invited to the Sioux reservation in the Bad Lands, I spent a day and a night there where I had the chance to dress like a squaw. I found this visit interesting and enjoyable. I discovered a civilized South Dakota and not the wild country and people I had heard about.

In Spearfish, I lived in a dormitory where I had a roommate. In Columbia, I had had a private room. My roommate in Spearfish studied nursing. I wasn't too thrilled having to share a room. She, along with some other girls, immediately told me I had to get rid of the hair under my arms and on my legs. I didn't know how to get rid of the hair, because in Germany we didn't worry about the hair. They told me I should shave my legs and under my arms. I told them I might cut myself, so they did it for me. They "Americanized" me in this manner.

Later, my roommate asked me what I thought of a dress she had on. I told her I thought she looked better in some of her other dresses. This offended her and made her angry. In Germany, I answered peoples' questions honestly, but I learned to exercise care when telling Americans the truth!

They told me how cold South Dakota could get. I said, "It's cold in Germany too."

Later, a couple of girl friends took me out on the street. I had never experienced such cold! They told me to keep my mouth closed and covered to keep the cold from damaging my lungs. I couldn't believe how cold the winters got and how much it snowed.

On the first Sunday in South Dakota, my roommate invited me to church. Going to church? Why? All these many years I hadn't gone, and no one had said a word or invited me. Why should I change my routine now? My roommate kept on asking and bugging me. Finally, several Sundays later, I gave in. We went to a Lutheran Church, and my goodness, I felt so uncomfortable. My heart pounded, I could hardly breathe, and I grew very anxious. In fact, the service made me nervous. I didn't enjoy it at all. I found it strange, but at the same time interesting how many different denominations existed. Just one God and, yet, so many different ways to worship Him. I couldn't understand it.

Off and on, I went with my roommate to the Lutheran Church, but I still didn't feel comfortable. My heart pounded, and I often felt like running. Sometimes, I could hardly stay in my seat. From what or whom did I want to run? Did I want to run from the devil or from the Lord? I didn't know.

One Sunday evening, several of my friends invited me to a different church. They told me the congregation prayed loudly. Of course, I thought of the Lord's Prayer. In every Lutheran Church, they prayed it loudly, although I didn't know the Lord's Prayer in English or German. That evening, I went with my friends to their church. Everything went fine until the altar call. Men and women went to the altar and started shaking their bodies, raising their arms, moving them back and forth, and making noises. I looked around me, and I saw people kneeling and hitting their heads on the pews. Some people rolled on the floor while others shouted. I thought all of them had lost their minds. Suddenly afraid, I ran out of the church. I ran until I could not hear them any more. I wondered what kind of church I'd visited, as I'd never seen anything like it. I suppose it takes all kinds of ways to worship the Lord, but I knew this wasn't the church for me.

The pastor and my friends came looking for me afterwards. Embarrassed, I explained I'd visited churches where people prayed out loud, but I'd never seen a church where people made so much noise and rolled on the floor. I never went there again. This one-time experience was enough for me.

One Sunday much later, I went to a Methodist Church. For the first time in my life I felt comfortable in a church. I felt peaceful, loved, embraced, and secure. My heart did not race, and I found I could sit quietly in my seat. The sermon made me feel good and gave me strength. I felt the Lord put his arms around me, a lost sheep. Could He care maybe about me, such an insignificant person? What did He want with me? For the first time in my life I heard that God was love and not a punishing God. Sunday after Sunday, I went back to the Methodist Church, and I felt like I had come home.

Chapter 10

Louis

As Christmas approached and we prepared for two weeks of Christmas vacation, I wondered where I'd spend it. An earlier experience in Germany provided the answer. After the war, American organizations and civilians had sent CARE packages to Germany. At first they bombed us to pieces and then they helped us! One day, we received a CARE package with all sorts of goodies like cans with meat, cans with vegetables and fruit, dried beans, rice and even some candy. We had not had sugar and sweets for years. The Round Rock, Texas family sending the CARE package had written their name and address in it. I wrote them a letter in my very limited English and thanked them for their kindness. They wrote back and sent us some clothes: sweaters, blouses and skirts, all new. Fortunately, everything fit, and I proudly wore clothes from America. I wrote back, and we kept corresponding.

From Spearfish, I wrote them again, and they invited me for Christmas. They even sent me a bus ticket to Round Rock for the Christmas vacation of 1950. I appreciated their kindness very much. They had written that they lived in the country a little outside of Round Rock.

What a different life I had during those holidays. When I

received the invitation and the bus ticket, I grew excited because I had read a book about Texas and the Wild West. The book almost scared me from wanting to come to Texas, but I looked forward to seeing the saloons and the cowboys on horseback and the shootouts. When I actually got to Texas, I found nothing like that, only prairie country. I had never seen so much space in my life. Imagine my surprise to find cars in Texas since I thought everyone rode horseback with a six-shooter on his hip. To my shock, they even had universities!

One day my Texas friends mentioned German students studying at Southwestern University, a small liberal arts university in Georgetown, Texas, only a short distance away. They drove me over there to meet the German students. Not only were they part of the same group with which I had come to America, but guess who I met there again!

I found my shipboard romance, Hermann Bader. While at Southwestern, he had received money from his rich uncle in Munich and had bought a second-hand car. We went all over creation with it. We drove around Georgetown, and to San Gabriel Park, and we drove the thirty miles to Austin, the Texas capital, and saw the sights, including Mount Bonnell, the Texas capitol building, and Zilker Park. The traffic lights started blinking at 9:30 in the evening. In 1950, Austin was a lovely little town and we had a very good time.

Hermann told me he and his very good American friend, Louis, liked to go to a local restaurant. They went there together in the evening to drink hot chocolate and eat onion rings. Louis, studying German, enjoyed practicing his German with Herman. They also enjoyed going to a German bakery.

Herman took me to the bakery and I met the Raths, the German family who owned the bakery, the only bakery in Georgetown. We visited in German, and as we talked, the Raths asked me where I stayed. I told them about the family who lived in the country near Round Rock, but also told them I didn't want to wear out their hospitality. The Rath family invited me to stay in Georgetown with them, so I spent the rest of my vacation with the Rath family.

While the Raths worked and their children went to school, I spent the days with Hermann. One day down the street from the university, the siren blew at noon. I hit the ground!

Hermann asked, "What's the matter with you?"

I said, "Get down. It's an air raid. Didn't you hear the siren?"

He laughed and said, "You've lived too long in Berlin. It's twelve o'clock noon. This is America. That is the noon siren."

I didn't know many American towns blew a siren at noon to indicate the beginning of the noon hour. I learned pretty fast.

One day, Hermann took me to the cafeteria at Southwestern University for lunch. I found it strange the boys had to stay in one line and the girls in another when later on, they sat together and ate! This made very little sense to me. After we sat down to eat, Hermann yelled, "Snowdy, come here; here is a German girl who wants to meet a ministerial student." Embarrassed and blushing, I didn't look up from my plate and didn't see the student he called Snowdy. I think I only glanced up once. In Germany a girl did not want to meet a man, she only wanted a man to want to meet her.

Later, I learned he thought I was engaged since I wore a diamond ring on the fourth finger of my left hand. In Germany we didn't have the custom of diamond engagement rings. We wore a simple gold band on the fourth finger of the right hand to indicate marriage. Conversely, a gold band worn on the forth finger of the left hand indicated engagement. I had simply brought a pretty ring to America. I didn't know it had any special significance worn on the left hand, and no one had told me what it meant here. Snowdy later asked Hermann why he wanted him to meet an engaged woman. Hermann knew I wasn't engaged, but only wearing a family ring and explained.

The next day, January 8, 1951, as the Raths and I ate dinner, the doorbell rang. Frau Rath went to the door and opened it. A young man with a very pleasant voice asked for the German girl. He didn't know my name. I could see him at the door and thought him very good looking. Frau Rath told him I couldn't visit with him then, being at the dinner table. He let her know he'd already eaten and offered to wait in another room and read the newspaper. A real persistent young fellow it seemed. I finished my dinner quickly, excused myself, and went to him. I didn't want him to get bored and leave. A handsome young man about twenty-three years old, he had dark brown, wavy hair, blue eyes, and long eyelashes. He stood about six feet tall, neither too thin nor too fat. It was Hermann's American friend, Louis Snoddy.

We talked a little, and I explained I planned to leave for Oklahoma City to visit another friend that very evening. Ruth, my teacher friend from the school in Berlin, had married an American GI and now lived in Oklahoma. Before leaving, however, I wanted to say good-bye to some friends in the country, whom I had met during my stay. They had a big ranch outside of Round Rock. The Raths had planned to take me, but Louis talked them out of it. He offered to drive me.

Before I knew it, I sat next to him in his friend's car. All of a sudden the car jerked, and I had a feeling it didn't want to go anymore. Quite embarrassed, Louis found out the car had run out of gas. No wonder the car stalled! Louis walked to a gas station and brought a can of gasoline back. Then we drove to the station and filled the gas tank. Quickly we went to the ranch of my friends.

I enjoyed my time with Louis, a nice young man with a good sense of humor. I learned he'd moved from his birthplace of Lake Charles, Louisiana, to Beaumont, Texas when just two years old. He had lived there with his parents, his older sister Marie, and his two older brothers, Leon and John. Louis had gone to school at French High School in Beaumont and had lived practically all his life there. The first time he left Beaumont was when he went into the army.

His father had a wholesale grocery business and a gas station. Louis clearly loved his father and talked fondly of him often. When Louis was eight years old, Mr. Snoddy fell sick with lead poisoning. Years later, Louis told me of his sadness and fright during his father's illness. During the night his father actually passed away, Louis woke up and saw an angel sitting on his bed. Then Louis said he felt very peaceful and knew he didn't have to fear anymore as he felt God's presence. After his father died, Louis' mother lost her sight. She developed glaucoma and had one eye removed. Almost immediately, she lost the sight in the other eye. Sometimes illnesses and misfortunes build character and make people better; sometimes, when people don't have a strong faith in God, illnesses and misfortunes make them bitter. Mrs. Snoddy grew very bitter and very obstinate. If lunch came at one o'clock, she had wanted it at twelve. When one brought her coffee, she might throw it on the floor, saying she wanted tea. She made the whole family miserable. When she died, some years later, the family felt relieved.

Towards the end of World War II, the U.S. Army drafted Louis. When Louis was twelve years old he had felt the call for the pastoral ministry, and in the Army he heard the call again. He went to Ft. Leavenworth, a Federal Prison, as a chaplain's assistant. There he ministered to those hardened criminals. Maybe that's why he later wanted to work as a chaplain in the Texas Prison System.

Since Louis' mother was blind, the Army allowed her to stay with Louis in the house they assigned to him off base. This pleased the mother and the whole family. Because of her negative attitude, no one of the family wanted to live with her. Only Louis, with his patience and good humor, seemed able to get along with her.

Later, after we married and Mrs. Snoddy moved from one relative to another, she'd come and stay with us for six weeks. Louis tried to get her to live in assisted living near us; he tried to get her to go to the school for the blind; he tried everything. She stayed obstinate and against any suggestion. Still, Louis remained

112

kind and understanding with her. Of course, at the time this man happily drove me to my friend's ranch to say good-bye, I had no idea about all this.

Before we returned to the Rath family, Louis stopped the car, looked me deep in the eyes and said, "If you do not want to go back to Germany, you do not have to." This shocked me a little. I didn't know what to make of it, and I didn't know what to answer. In those situations I had learned not to say anything.

I said good-bye to the Raths, and this stranger, Louis, drove me to Belton, about thirty miles up the highway, to catch the bus. I could have caught the bus in Georgetown, but he wanted to spend more time with me. He told me he had exams or he'd have driven me back to South Dakota. When I said good-bye to Louis in Belton, he gave me a small picture of himself; I suppose to remember him by. Then, he shook my hand. It disappointed me he didn't even give me an address or something so we could write to each other.

When I reached Oklahoma City and showed my friend Ruth Louis' picture, she said, "Forget him. He is much too good looking. He has a girl on every finger." I stayed with her a few days before I left for South Dakota. She lived in a lovely well-furnished three-bedroom house and anxiously awaited the birth of her first child. I enjoyed the few days with her and her husband, and we had a good time together.

When I arrived back at the dorm in Spearfish, two girls ran towards me with letters in their hands.

They called out, "Gisela, you have two letters from a man in Texas. Did you meet a rich oilman?"

"No, just a student," I answered. One letter maybe, but I had two letters already! It overwhelmed me.

Louis wrote every day. He wrote in longhand and I couldn't read his letters, so had to have a girlfriend read the English to me. Finally, I got the courage to tell him to type his letters because I couldn't read his handwriting. He said "Okay," and from then on he always typed his letters. Later, I asked him not to use $.50 cent words because my English wasn't good enough to understand his big words. He wrote every day, sent a small present every week, and called once a month. It was wonderful to hear his voice.

He wrote nice, newsy, and enjoyable letters. I looked forward to his letters and tried to answer in the same way, both of us truthful and open with one another. Only this way could we get to know each other well. After a month or two, we both knew we were meant for each other. I longed for him and could hardly wait until the mailman came.

On Valentine's day, I received a huge heart. The girls said, "Oh, you received a big Valentine. We've never seen such a big heart."

I had never heard of Valentine's Day. I didn't know what it meant. The girls had to explain it to me.

Another day, I received his class ring. I didn't know what to do with it. He hadn't explained what it meant or why he sent it. The girls told me I had to wear it around my neck because it meant we were going steady. I really didn't know what that meant, but I wore it proudly around my neck.

Because I had so many speaking engagements around Spearfish, I found it difficult to write Louis every day. Every club wanted to know something about World War II and the time during the Hitler regime. At that time, it seemed all Americans thought of all Germans as Nazis. Maybe only ten percent had belonged to the party, but most Germans didn't. I talked about the war and about where I had lived in Berlin. Americans wondered about life before the war and about what happened during the war. For the Rotarians once, I said, "In Berlin, I was a fast girl, but in America I am even faster." They all smiled. I meant life had moved very fast in Berlin, but in America, life moved even faster. Later an elderly gentleman explained why they had smiled, and that the term "fast girl" had a different meaning. I blushed and felt like going through the floor.

The long distance courtship went on from January 8th until the middle of May 1951. One day, Dr. Jonas, the President of the College, called me into his office. It scared me. In Germany one gets called into the President's office if one has done something terribly wrong. I didn't think I had done anything out of order. Dr. Jonas mentioned to me that Louis had written him a letter asking for my early release from the College. Louis wanted to get married on June 2nd. The Central Texas Conference of the Methodist Church met in Ft. Worth and he had to go there.

In the Methodist Church each local church belongs to a local District. A group of Districts make up a local Conference. Each Conference, headed by a Bishop, met annually where the Bishop appoints the preachers of that Conference to the churches.

As a student pastor, Louis had to attend this yearly conference, which took place the first week in June, and he wanted to take me with him not as his girlfriend but as his wife. After Conference, on the 5th of June, he had to attend Perkin's School of Theology at Southern Methodist University in Fort Worth to study Theology for the next three years. While he studied at SMU he wanted to live in the parsonage of his student appointment, and unless we married, we couldn't live together there. In other words, June 2nd was really the only free day for him to get married, and for this reason, Louis wanted me released early from the Teacher's College so I could join him. He explained this to Dr. Jonas in his letter. He did not, however, tell me about this situation.

I hadn't the faintest idea about Louis' writing Dr. Jonas. Somehow, I felt a little uncomfortable about it. We had corresponded for four months. At least Louis could have mentioned it in his letters. We'd agreed to marry some time in the future, but I didn't realize the future came so soon or that the church might determine when I got married.

I absolutely wanted to marry Louis, but this date was very sudden. I felt we really hadn't known each other long enough. In Germany, people usually knew each other a long time before they married. After I thought about it, I changed my idea about this German custom. It didn't really matter how long two people knew each other. After marriage a couple really only then begins to know each other. Without a foundation of love and a commitment to Christ, things often go wrong.

I also worried about my immigration status. I had the scholarship for one year and needed to return to Germany in August 1951. Before I came to the United States, officials of the Institute of International Education had warned us not to extend our stay because we could get into trouble with the U.S. government. Staying could mean deportation. They told us when the U.S. deported a person, he or she could never return to the United States. I wrote Louis about this concern after Dr. Jonas had told me Louis wanted to get married on June 2nd.

He wrote back, "Don't worry about it. The Lord is ruler yet. He will work it out."

Louis was right. Later, the Lord did work it out so that I could stay in the United States with Louis.

I never had a doubt about Louis in my mind. I knew I loved him, and I didn't worry about marrying him. I wrote my mother I had found the man of my life, and if I had to live in a tent with him, I would do it. I had never loved anyone the way I loved Louis. Later, I had forgotten about writing this, but my mother asked me if I'd still live in a tent with him. I told her, "Yes!"

Dr. Jonas told me he'd written to Southwestern University, to the Methodist Church in Georgetown, and to Louis' professors. Dr. Jonas did not disapprove of my marrying Louis, but for my sake and security, he wanted to investigate him. It bothered me a little that Dr. Jonas had checked up on Louis. I told him as a grown woman I knew what I was doing. He told me about trying to protect me. He feared that since I had come from a war-torn country, I might've been blinded by this country and by this man. Then Dr Jonas told me Louis came very highly recommended. In fact, Dr. Jonas said he wondered if anyone would be good enough to marry Louis based on such great praise. Then he agreed to release me early from the college so I could get married. Later on, I appreciated his interest in me because I could have gotten hurt. Some German girls did. Louis and I later had friends who married German girls, and the marriages did not last. Louis' and mine did.

I left Spearfish Teachers' College the middle of May, fourteen days before the end of the semester. I rode the bus by myself to Dallas, Texas. We had a rough ride and arrived late because we had to go through storms. We had to dodge bad weather and tornadoes. I didn't know about tornados and wondered why we couldn't go through one. Later, after I experienced one, I understood. I worried Louis didn't know that we were late and might not be there to meet me. I didn't realize the bus company called ahead.

What a relief when I got off the bus and Louis stood there! Then, he kissed me! Our first kiss, since he hadn't kissed me when I had left Belton after Christmas vacation. We hugged and kissed, just happy to be together. He took me out for dinner and then we went to the rooms he had reserved for two nights. Tired from the long bus ride, I went straight to my room and right to sleep.

The next day Louis showed me SMU where we'd spend part of our time while he studied in Perkins School of Theology. I liked SMU and the surrounding area of Dallas. The main thing for me, of course, was being with Louis. With him I felt secure and protected.

When we left Dallas and SMU, we drove to Holland, Texas, a nice little town near Georgetown. Louis worked as a student pastor there while completing his undergraduate work at Southwestern University. In Holland, everybody knew everybody. Louis had lived there on weekends with his mother in the parsonage. During the week he had lived in Mood Hall at Southwestern University in Georgetown while a female church member of his had taken care of his mother at the parsonage in Holland. At the end of January 1951, Louis had received his Bachelor of Arts Degree from

Southwestern University. After graduating, he had lived full time at the parsonage in Holland with his mother.

Because we wanted to get married and Louis needed money for a car, Louis worked at the American Desk Company in Temple about 30 miles north of Georgetown. He didn't have a car at Southwestern but in Dallas he needed one badly. At Southwestern, other student friends and his German teacher took him to Holland for his student appointment. It seems strange for a professor of German at a university to take such an interest in a student outside of class.

Louis' German teacher, however, loved Louis and wanted to marry him. After I arrived in Holland, he told me that she had said to him, "I love you. Let's get married." He said she had told him if he wanted to get his Doctor's degree, she could take care of him and help him get it. He had told her brutally frankly he wouldn't marry a divorced woman with a child. An Austrian, determined to get Louis, she didn't want to give him up.

One evening, before we married, Louis said to me, "I want to introduce you to a very nice lady. She is one of your German sisters. You will enjoy her."

I had no idea she was Louis' German teacher and in love with him. When we arrived, I could see that her face fell a few inches because I'd come along. She wore a very low cut Dirndle dress, a native Austrian dress. It looked to me as if her breasts might fall out of the dress any moment. I couldn't believe Louis had contact with a woman who dressed like that. She barely spoke to me and seemed unfriendly. Louis introduced me as his fiancée and told her all about me. I'm sure she didn't want to hear all that. I was glad when we left. Only then, did Louis tell me all about her and all about her bothering him constantly with suggestions and proposals of marriage. I realized he did this to make sure she understood he wasn't going to marry her. I grew angry with Louis for putting me in such an uncomfortable situation.

From the time we began writing to each other, Louis and I

took it for granted we'd marry, but he had never asked me. After I moved to Holland, Texas, finally, in the driveway to the parsonage, he proposed to me as we entered the car.

Louis said, "We've set the date and the time to get married, but I haven't asked you to marry me. Do you want to marry me?"

I answered, "Well, now you ask the question. We've made all of the preparations. I can hardly back out!" Then I hugged him and kissed him and said, "Yes, I want to marry you!"

We had met on January 8th and on June 2nd, we would marry.

In Holland, I met Louis' mother for the first time. From the beginning we got off to a bad start. When I first met her, she had a glass of milk in her hand which she dropped and splashed everywhere. I had to jump to the side so my dress didn't get dirty. She told me right then she intended to continue living with her son whether I was there or not. From then on, any time I went to visit, she ignored me. I said "Hello," and she didn't answer. Fortunately, I didn't have to stay at the parsonage until after our wedding.

During the short time before our marriage, I stayed with an elderly lady named Mrs. Kelly Dugger, a member of the church. She had stayed with Mrs. Snoddy during the week while Louis studied in Georgetown at Southwestern. Right away, I felt at home with Mrs. Dugger, a sweet and kind woman. She felt sorry for Mrs. Snoddy and she understood her in a way, but she did not understand Mrs. Snoddy's bitterness. Mrs. Dugger thought Louis a wonderful man and a good preacher, and said I couldn't marry a better man, but she also said she didn't envy me for my future mother-in-law.

Mrs. Dugger's husband had died a few years before, and she lived alone in a very cute house. It had two bedrooms, one bathroom, a small kitchen and a big living room. The house had a very friendly and bright appearance with walls painted in light colors. Mrs. Dugger had flowers everywhere. She had them outside in the yard and inside in every room of the house. I enjoyed staying there.

In contrast to Mrs. Dugger's house the parsonage seemed dark and unfriendly. The dark furniture, ugly and old, blended right in with the gray walls, dark green carpet, and deep brown woodwork. The living room had heavy, dark green drapes. The parsonage had three bedrooms, one bathroom, a big kitchen, a large dining room, and a good-sized living room. The big, dark house fit Louis' mother's attitude, her bitterness toward me and toward everyone else.

Of course, I found the idea of becoming a preacher's wife quite exciting, but yet frightening. I felt very inadequate. I told Louis that I didn't know God, the Bible, or prayer. He smiled at me and told me he loved me and he had accepted me for myself. He assured me we'd experience God together and I'd soon know the Lord.

He also told me he wanted me to teach Vacation Bible School! I asked him, "What is Vacation Bible School?" I had no idea; I had never heard of it.

He told me, "Don't worry about it. You tell this fifth grade group Bible stories." Then, Louis explained it more thoroughly. Louis always had a way of calming me down and taking away my fear. Louis never wanted me to be afraid. He knew I had gone through lots of hardships and frights during the war. He wanted me never to experience horrible things again.

After our little talk, I felt much better, and I decided to prepare for Vacation Bible School. Louis gave me some books from which I should tell the children stories. I didn't understand what I read in those books. I needed something simple, so I looked into the children's Bible in the Sunday School room and used it for my preparations. Those stories I could understand. I still had my limitations speaking and understanding the language. The children, a lively group of fifth graders, made discussing the stories a difficult matter.

I worried about my heavy accent, afraid I might butcher the grammar and the pronunciation badly. While this can make life in a foreign country quite difficult, Louis had a wonderful way of simplifying everything. He got me into Vacation Bible School and I learned more about God and Jesus Christ. I learned God is Love. Mother had always told me if I misbehaved, God would punish me. The Lutheran preachers in Germany said the same thing. Yet, teaching Vacation Bible School from the Children's Bible helped me learn of the love and steadfastness of God.

At first the children sat quietly, but as I continued to try to teach, they soon began talking and asking questions. Often their questions didn't have anything to do with our study. The children wanted to know about my home and why I talked so funny. Some of the kids said they liked to hear me talk. I had to stop and explain I'd come from Berlin, Germany. I asked them if they knew about Germany and explained it as being on the other side of the Atlantic Ocean. That satisfied them. After the first few days of Vacation Bible School, I grew more confident. The children began responding to me. Their enthusiasm made it an interesting experience for me.

Chapter 11

My Marriage

Once Vacation Bible School ended, my excitement about our wedding in Beaumont, Texas, grew. Beaumont, a very unpleasant, humid city close to the Gulf of Mexico, lies east of Houston. First, we had to pack our luggage. Then Louis had to see that his mother's brother picked her up and took her to his home. She had to stay with her brother and his wife for a while.

Louis' blind mother had lived with him most of his life. A very bitter and obstinate person, Mrs. Snoddy felt God had punished her with blindness because she had had an affair with Mr. Snoddy. After her first husband died very suddenly in the 1918 flu epidemic, she had nursed the first Mrs. Snoddy until her death from cancer. Then, at age thirty-six and with three children from her first marriage, she married Mr. Snoddy, twenty-one years her senior and with three children of his own.

After nine years of marriage, Mr. Snoddy died of lead poisoning. Then, Louis' mother developed glaucoma and the doctors removed one of her eyes. Soon she went completely blind. She never seemed satisfied or pleased about anything in life. No one, not Mr. Snoddy's three children or her own, wanted anything to do with her and wouldn't take care of her. Only Louis got along with his mother. I always thought her unpleasantness stemmed from her blindness, but one of her sisters told me later she had been always difficult.

The whole family believed Louis would never marry and would always be available to take care of his mother. He mentioned many times to everybody, however, he planned to marry whenever he found the right woman. Louis' family seemed to hope he'd never find the right woman. Yet, when his brother and his sister-in-law visited Louis, they suspected he had met someone whom he might marry when they saw my picture on the nightstand in his room. Louis hadn't told anyone in his family about me or his intention to marry me. He seemed very secretive about it.

Louis knew his mother, and he probably didn't want to face the music. After he told the family about our upcoming marriage, every one acted shocked and standoffish to me. His mother felt she'd lost her home and her security.

Some years later, family members openly complained about keeping Mrs. Snoddy. Then, Louis again suggested his mother live in assisted living. Aunt Zelma, one of her sisters, agreed and encouraged the family to accept Louis' idea. His brothers and the rest of the family so hated the suggestion they didn't talk to us for three years! In a way, I was glad they didn't associate with us, and we didn't have to put up with all the commotion.

When we went to Beaumont for the wedding, we stayed in Louis' brother John's house. This felt very uncomfortable with everybody upset with me. When his mother visited, she cried all the time and made a scene. The rest of the family didn't try to visit with me. I still had trouble with my English, and I often couldn't understand the conversations. How terrible for me, here in a foreign country without my mother or any relatives of mine and not accepted by the family of my future husband. Although it frightened me and sometimes I felt like running away, I loved Louis so very much that I faced all these obstacles.

Louis' friends, however, made me feel welcome. They entertained us with lunches and dinners and wedding showers. When Louis said, "We are having a wedding shower," I thought he meant rain. I had never heard of a wedding shower. I asked Louis, "Does one get wet?" Louis told me we had to wear raincoats, otherwise we might get wet. I believed him! We wore raincoats to the first one, and people looked surprised. I saw gifts on tables and wondered why we wore the raincoats. Then, Louis explained to everyone and everybody laughed, but now I understood. Of course, I felt like a fool. The shower turned out to be a lot of fun. Louis enjoyed pulling my leg all the time. Sometimes, I think he married me just to have entertainment. At these showers and parties, we found a real difference in our personalities. He rather liked the quiet with a few friends and family. Big parties and goings on didn't fit his style. I, by contrast, enjoyed partying very much.

Finally, the second of June 1951 arrived. We held the wedding ceremony in the North End Methodist Church in Beaumont, Louis' home church. It was a beautiful new church with some parts still under construction, but they had completed the sanctuary, a beautiful place to worship. On this most important day of my life the dark clouds from the family overshadowed a warm and sunny day.

In contrast to me, Louis grew up in a large family. He had two older brothers and one older sister, all of them already married. Most of his family drove in from Lake Charles, Louisiana. His aunts, uncles, and many cousins came, naturally curious about me, and wanting to see Louis's "Nazi bride." I met many strangers whom later I didn't remember. From the beginning, I felt very close to Aunt Zelma, one of Mrs. Snoddy's sisters. A wonderful woman, she made me feel welcome with hugs and kisses, and she, unsuccessfully, encouraged Mrs. Snoddy to accept me.

I asked for, and we had, a lovely candlelight service. A friend in South Dakota loaned me her beautiful wedding dress and veil. The dress fit as if made for me. It surprised me for a girl I had known only a few months to loan me her wedding dress. This wouldn't have happened in Germany, but I found most Americans very trusting and giving individuals.

Louis practiced the vows with me a few days before the wedding because I had difficulty understanding the words I had to know and say. Louis' eldest brother, Leon, gave me away; his youngest brother, John, stood as the best man; and his sister, Marie, served as my maid of honor, three people I had met only two days before the wedding.

The only person I knew before the wedding was Louis. I had known him only a few months by letter, and then, personally for two weeks. I saw the others as strangers. I couldn't even speak and understand the English language well. As a result, all the guests probably thought Louis had married a nitwit. You most likely will think me out of my mind, but not at all! Love, very strong love, bonded me to Louis. Of course, today, I know the Lord led us to each other.

We had an okay wedding reception at John's house, nice, but nothing special. Louis' mother didn't attend the wedding or the reception. I can still hear her scream as I left the house to go to church to marry her son. She stayed home alone because she didn't want Louis to marry anyone, especially not me. She resented me from the beginning. Many times, she told me I came from the devil's country and that I had the devil in me. This made me very sad, and I often cried about it. This very bitter and unhappy woman made her surroundings very unhappy as well.

Before I met her, I had told Louis she could live with us, because I grew up with older people around. Louis smiled and said it wouldn't work out. He knew his mother.

After we left John's house, we drove to Galveston on a one-day honeymoon. We stayed in a lovely hotel on the beach. We were married! Fantastic! Here for the first time we made love, an exciting, almost spiritual experience. The next day, I floated on cloud nine! That Sunday morning, we lay in the sun, went swimming, and relaxed on the beach. I left behind the unhappiness of family and a wedding amongst strangers in a foreign country.

Marriage to a wonderful guy made life good. We had very

little money, but we had each other and lots of fun together. I wished I had listened to my mother and learned how to cook, but before I married, I had absolutely no interest in any kind of homemaking. My job, my friends, and my pleasure interested me, not cooking, baking, and cleaning house. At that time I selfishly had only fun and pleasure in my head and never thought of anyone outside my family. I never helped anyone. For example, I hurt the teacher Hans Sauer very much. Engaged to him when I left for America, I married here and wrote him a "Dear John" letter.

When Louis met me in Georgetown, I must have changed, because I couldn't see him falling in love with such a selfish, flighty, and fun loving girl. He might not have objected to the fun loving girl, but surely the flighty and selfish one.

I loved Louis so very much and wanted to make him happy. I wanted to do anything and everything for him. Yet, I had no idea about housekeeping, cooking, or baking. I felt terrible. I remember the first steaks I cooked for him. Hard and dry, they didn't stay flat in the pan. If I had thrown the steaks at him I'd have put a dent in his forehead. He ate everything I put before him. I got thinner and he got fatter!

I watched him eat and thought, "Louis, you can't possibly eat this stuff."

After three months, he asked me, "Sweetheart would you like to learn how to cook American dishes?"

"Of course," I answered, and he put a *Better Homes and Garden Cookbook* on the table.

When I opened it and looked at the dishes, I couldn't understand a thing. I had studied Shakespeare, Oscar Wilde, and Charles Dickens in school, but not recipes. I didn't know the vocabulary. I stood in the kitchen with the cookbook in one hand and a dictionary in the other. I bought all the ingredients necessary and followed each recipe very diligently. At the end of the month, Louis and I had a $200 bill at the grocery store, and we got only $87 a month! Surprisingly, Louis only said to me, "Sweetheart, you don't need to buy everything in the book! You can leave some things out."

Louis often invited friends for dinner. When they asked me if I had cooked a German dish, I answered: "*Better Homes and Gardens* Chapter 3 page 15." I had no idea what I'd made. We always had a good laugh, but the dinner always turned out well. *Better Homes and Gardens* was foolproof. I developed a very good cuisine and became a good cook. In fact, I learned to enjoy cooking very much. When my mother came for a visit, I shocked her with my cooking and housekeeping. In Germany she used to say: "I feel sorry for the man who will get you as a wife." When she came here to America, she said: "It is uncomfortably clean in your house." She loved my cooking and everything I did.

Chapter 12

Divinity School and Student Preaching

On the afternoon of June 3rd we drove back to Holland, Texas, in time for Louis' Sunday evening service. He preached a wonderful, spiritual sermon. The Holy Spirit must have moved me, and during the last hymn, I got up from my seat and walked slowly to the altar and joined the Methodist Church. This pleased Louis very much, and it made me very happy that he took me into the church.

After the service, the congregation held a lovely surprise get together with cake and punch and very nice gifts. They gave us wonderful, big towels! We got forty towels of every kind, hand towels, bath towels, kitchen towels, and guest towels! Now, we had towels forever! We certainly had towels for many years, and the party surprised both of us.

Late that night, we said good-bye to the congregation, climbed into the car with a big trailer behind it, and left for Dallas. The trailer contained all our belongings including Louis' big, upright piano, which he played very well. Suddenly, we drove into a terrible storm with thunder and lighting. The lightning frightened me. Louis assured me nothing could happen as long as we stayed in the car with its rubber tires. During such a storm in Germany, my grandmother had always gathered everyone in the living room where she read the Bible and asked the Lord for protection. Of course, German storms were never as bad as those in Texas! I soon learned the phrase, "Everything is bigger in Texas" meant even the storms. Louis might have gone on, but the storm and pulling that heavy trailer made me so afraid, Louis decided to stop in Eddy, a small town near Holland. We spent the night there with one of Louis' friends, Charles Fromer.

The next morning, we drove on to Fort Worth where Louis had to attend the Central Texas Annual Conference on June 5, 1951. At the Annual Conference, they appointed Louis to do a student pastorate in Haslet, twenty-nine miles north of Fort Worth and the bottom of the line. No pastor stayed there longer than a year and everyone considered Haslet a bad appointment for a pastor and his family. The District Superintendent had selected an especially good appointment for Louis, but Louis said he did not want any special treatment. He wanted to go wherever the Lord sent him. He did not like to argue or discuss the appointments with the Bishop, so we went to Haslet with the trailer and piano.

A tiny little town, if we had driven through Haslet very fast, we could've missed it. It had one filling station, a grocery store, a café, the telephone office, and the Methodist Church on a little hill outside of town.

We soon learned that life in Haslet centered on the telephone office. Everyone knew everyone in town, and the gossip spread through that office. Haslet still had the old telephone system where the operator had to connect the callers, and everyone could listen in. I never expected to find such an old-fashioned system in America. When we'd go visiting, we never told anyone where we planned to go, but we received phone calls from people in the parish wherever we went. We wondered how they reached us, but we soon found out they'd tracked us through the switchboard.

While at Haslet, Louis preached on weekends and during the week, attended the Perkins School of Theology at Southern

Methodist University in Dallas to work towards a Masters of Divinity. That first week, he left me in the parsonage alone while he went to enroll. The parsonage sat by itself on a little hill. Our neighbors were the cows of an eighteen-hundred-acre ranch. When I said, "Moo" through the kitchen window, they answered me with "Moo."

When we arrived and Louis opened the door of the parsonage, he didn't know if he should carry me over the threshold or not. The bad condition of the house shocked him. Though a big house, we could easily see why no pastor's wives had wanted to live in it. They all went home to their mothers. My mother lived 7,000 miles away, and I could not go home. I did not want to go anyway. I wanted to live with Louis. When I entered the house, I cried about ten minutes and then started cleaning on hands and knees.

Very disappointed, I felt we'd reached rock bottom. From the war-torn Berlin I had jumped into the beautiful and great America, which now offered me very little. I couldn't stand such a dirty place. I knew it'd take several weeks to get the place in shape. Louis couldn't help much because he had to go to school, study, and prepare sermons. The dirty house was my domain. I worked like I had never worked before.

The congregation should have been ashamed to let a pastor and his wife move into such a substandard and dirty place. We scrubbed and painted the walls, doors, and windowsills and cleaned the windows. It took several weeks to get it somewhat livable. Finally, the place looked much better with the painted walls and doors, clean windows and scrubbed floors.

I loved Louis and wanted to help him, so I handled the hard work and felt we served in the ministry together. I still didn't know the Lord very well, and I certainly couldn't understand why He gave us this awful place. The Methodist church I had attended in South Dakota and its minister spoke of love. This congregation certainly hadn't shown us any love. Of course, I didn't understand about tests the Lord gives us to test our earnestness for Him and the Ministry. I thought then, however, I had angered Him, and for this reason, He gave us such a miserable place. I wondered if it might be my fault because I wasn't close to the Lord yet. But, as I've come closer to the Lord, I've come to understand He tested us and we passed when we stayed in the ministry.

A few touches of spring flowers and some pieces of crystal and china which Mother sent me from Germany made the house much nicer looking. It surprised the congregation when they saw the parsonage. It didn't look like the same house. Louis said only a German woman could have transformed it like that. This German woman had also worked like a slave, but she found it very satisfying to see the result of the hard work.

Very early after Louis received his appointment to Haslet, Louis' Aunt Zelma and his sister, Marie, came to visit. Marie turned on the faucet in the bathroom and said, "My goodness, it takes an hour to wet a toothbrush!"

We had very little water pressure in the parsonage because it had a well with a pump.

His aunt looked out the window and said, "Oh, my goodness, you don't have any neighbors."

I said, "There is nothing but land and cows."

I loved this aunt, for she was kind to me. She knew his mother had told me I came from the Devil's country and had the Devil in me. I enjoyed their visit very much, but they agreed the parsonage needed still more improvement. It still had rats!

One evening as Louis studied and I slept, he suddenly called me. "Gisela, come quickly; I have to show you something!"

Just then, three rats ran through the living room! I was appalled at the rats and at Louis! Why did he wake me up for such an ugly sight? Sometimes he had strange humor. Anyhow, I went back to bed, and Louis bought some big rattraps the next day. Little by little, we got rid of the rats and made the house more livable.

The condition of the parsonage should have shamed the

congregation, but the salary they gave us should've shamed them even more. Just $87 a month was too little to live on and too much to die on. Because of the meager salary, Louis worked in Fort Worth in a shoe store after classes on Fridays and on Saturdays to bring in some extra money. I felt very bad because I didn't have my citizenship and couldn't help out by teaching. In 1951, a preacher and his wife in Haslet, Texas found things pretty difficult.

The parsonage had three large bedrooms, a large living room, a separate dining room, a big kitchen, and one bathroom. It had a large porch surrounding most of the house. I liked the porch and sometimes we sat there and ate watermelon. Because Louis worked Fridays and Saturdays and often studied in the library at school, I spent a great deal of time by myself. Every once in a while the so-called "oil king" of Haslett came to keep me company on the front porch. I never let him into the house, and he never got fresh with me, but the gossip went around that he was a womanizer.

By the middle of August it grew very hot and I had a hard time adjusting to the heat. I had trouble sleeping at night, and one time as I rolled and tossed in the hot bed, I got an idea. I got up, gathered the bed sheets, and put them in the bathtub. Quickly, I let water run over them, wrung them out, and put them back on the bed. Then, I let the big, ten-inch fan blow on us. The cool wet sheet felt wonderful, almost like air conditioning. I did this many nights that summer.

For this reason, I spent quite a bit of time in the bathtub, despite the somewhat warm water. I often dropped a bunch of ice cubes into it to make it more comfortable. I usually had a book that I read as I lay there. The parsonage didn't have locks on the doors. I suppose people trusted each other more in 1951. The house only had latches on the screens. One day, I had latched all the doors and jumped into my favorite place. Suddenly, I heard some steps coming down the hall towards the bathroom. I shouted, "Please go into the living room. I'll be there in a minute." The steps kept coming. Here I lay in the bathtub naked and unable cover myself with anything. How embarrassing! A woman member of the church came into the bathroom, sat on the lid of the commode, and started talking to me! I asked her to please go into the living room, so I could get out of the bathtub and join her.

She said to me, "Don't worry, I'm very comfortable here," and she kept on talking.

I had to swallow my considerable anger. After all, as the preacher's wife I had to take it. Rude people exist all over the world including Haslet, Texas. Finally she left, but we had carried on our entire conversation in the bathroom! I imagined her telling her friends she saw me naked in the bathtub in the morning at 11:00 a.m. Just horrible! I don't know that she gossiped about our conversation, but I felt she might! She also undid the latch. How impertinent! What people do!

The situation really upset Louis. He didn't like it at all. The next Sunday, in his sermon he mentioned we had come to Haslet to serve the Lord and the congregation didn't own us.

During this first, hot Texas summer, I didn't feel well. Often sick to my stomach, I thought the heat made me ill so I went to Dr. Funk. There I learned it wasn't the heat. I was expecting a sweet little baby!

One morning, Louis and I stayed in bed, both of us sick. He had fever and trouble with his tonsils, and I had morning sickness. I had to deal with it for the full nine months. Anyway, we awakened to some voices and suddenly, two elderly women stood in front of our bed. They had easily unlatched the doors, too.

Louis sat straight up in bed and shouted, "Get out of here! I'll talk to you in the living room!"

The two old women ran as fast as their legs could carry them. What Louis told them, I do not know, but from then on people didn't just walk into the parsonage.

Later, this happened to us in other parsonages too. People walked in the door and simply said, "Coming in! Coming in!" For this reason, I learned very quickly to push Louis out of the bed before 8:00 a.m. and to get him dressed so I could make up the bed. I knew any time after 8:00 a.m. people might come to the parsonage, and I didn't want them to think the preacher's wife didn't make the bed. People seemed to think they owned the preacher and his family.

Louis continued having difficulty with his tonsils. One Sunday, he had a high fever and could not speak. In order to have a service, I had to go and preach. I just wondered what the Lord had in mind with me, putting me in the pulpit, with my poor English and very heavy accent. Now I know. He often uses people inferior in some things. I lived through it, and the congregation did too. In fact I enjoyed it very much, and I felt one step closer to finding the Lord.

A friend, a minister, took Louis to Methodist Hospital in Ft. Worth. There, Louis had his tonsils removed. Pregnant and unable drive, I had to have somebody from the congregation take me to Ft. Worth. Louis couldn't preach for several weeks, and we had to have a visiting preacher come in. I had, however, experienced the pulpit and did on several other occasions substitute for a sick husband.

Things improved a little in the parsonage when Louis finally received permission from the board of the church to buy an electric pump. Unfortunately, the new pump put extra pressure on the pipes under the house, and they burst. It looked like a sprinkling system under there. Louis went under the house and repaired the pipes. Not long afterwards the pipes broke again, and Louis repaired them again. From then on, it seemed he spent more time under the house than in the house.

The Parsonage needed a major overhaul inside and out. We had old hand-me-down furniture. I had to hit the chest of drawers on the side to open the drawers. When we made love, sometimes the bed slats fell out and we landed on the floor. I wanted to stay on the floor and sleep there, but Louis always set up the bed again. It happened again and again. We always landed on the floor. It got so when we wanted to make love we said to each other, "Shall we sleep on the floor tonight?"

Not only did we have trouble with the parsonage, but also with Louis' second-hand car. It didn't like commuting to Dallas for school very well. One day the car could not take it anymore and just stopped. It needed some work, but on $87 a month, we couldn't afford it.

To save on money for gas and repairs, Louis car-pooled to Dallas with two ministerial students and a female SMU student. One day, fed up with our situation, Louis mentioned to the carpool he wanted to quit the ministry.

A few days later a big black Packard stopped in front of the parsonage. Quite a little congregation of children gathered around the big black automobile. A very well dressed lady came out of the car and walked up the steps to the parsonage. Everyone burned with curiosity. It was Mrs. Wiedeman, a dentist's wife from the First Methodist Church of Fort Worth, the mother of the girl with whom Louis carpooled.

I met her at the door, pregnant, wearing a clean, but unfashionable $3.00 red corduroy jumper with a white blouse. She said her daughter had told her about our situation and about Louis' considering leaving the ministry. This shocked me because he had never said anything to me about it.

She looked around the parsonage, shook her head and said, "It is a shame that a congregation offers such a sub-standard house to their pastor."

She assured me Louis did not have to leave the ministry and that I shouldn't worry about the finances. She said she and two other people from First Church in Fort Worth wanted to help us. Then she put a check for $300 on the table. From then on, Mrs. Wiedeman came once a month to bring us $300 from the Christians of First Methodist in Fort Worth. The people who gave us the money didn't want us to know their names. We couldn't even thank them. We prayed for them and thanked God. He

135

blessed us and held His hand over us. The additional $300 made life much easier in Haslet.

One day Mrs. Wiedemann picked me up and drove me to her beautiful home in Fort Worth. We'd never had a car in Germany and I'd never learned to drive. Mrs. Wiedemann bought materials for maternity dresses, and she made me four beautiful dresses. What a wonderful, giving person. She had the Lord Jesus Christ and the Holy Spirit in her heart. I felt good in those dresses, and comfortable and happy going to the Methodist Conference in Fort Worth at the end of our first year in Haslet.

In November 1951, two sour-faced men from the Immigration and Naturalization Service (INS) came to visit us. According to my visa, I should've returned to Berlin in August, three months after my wedding. Of course, I had married and was now five months pregnant. These men came to arrest me and put me in jail because I'd ignored my time to return to Germany. I didn't want to be fenced in again.

When Louis and I had decided to get married, we had discussed my need to return to Germany. I had only a one-year visa. Just six years after the war, things still seemed shaky and very difficult. Louis feared if I returned to Germany, I wouldn't get back to America for a long time. We feared I wouldn't get another visa or get this one extended, so we decided to go ahead and get married and hope the INS wouldn't notice us. We thought we could get by with it. We found out we couldn't.

Louis told those men that if they put me in jail, they should prepare a place for him too. After we talked with them a little while, they decided against jail and left me with my husband in Haslet.

For one whole year they watched me and visited me again and again. They probably wanted to find out if I had infested the place with Nazi ideas and propaganda. At that time Americans thought that all Germans were Nazis. They asked me the same questions over and over again. They wanted to know why I came to the

States, why I married an American, if I wanted to go back sometimes to Germany, and so on. I thought it pretty stupid, and I told them they had asked me these questions many times before.

I'd had it with them. I didn't care if I earned American citizenship or not. I felt I could live in the States forever without becoming a citizen.

The INS also told us I had to go back to Germany once I had the baby. They threatened to deport me when the baby turned three months old. What a smart idea, tearing a perfectly happy family apart, typical bureaucracy!

Louis and I talked to Mr. Alsebrook who owned the ranch to which Louis had driven me when we first met. Mr. Alsebrook knew Homer Thornberry, the U.S. Representative from Austin and Windgate Lucas, the Representative from Dallas. These men introduced a bill in the U.S. House of Representatives to allow me to stay in the United States. They also contacted Lyndon Johnson, at that time the Senator from Texas. I received a telegram from Senator Johnson stating, "Deportation stopped. I am on the case. Lyndon." I don't remember how long it took, but they passed a private bill for me in the U. S. Congress granting me permanent residence. This thrilled me, but now personally, I wanted to get my citizenship.

One day the INS ordered me to San Antonio to take a test to verify whether I was qualified for citizenship. Becoming an American was a long, involved, but good procedure. Of course, I had to study the political issues of the United States for several months. I passed the test and finally, in November 1956, the ceremony making me a citizen took place in San Antonio, and I felt like I had married a country! Everyone pledged complete loyalty! I have never regretted my decision to become an American.

Christmas Eve 1951, we had Church and Holy Communion, and then we had our first Christmas alone in the Parsonage. I baked some goodies and roasted a chicken since we couldn't afford a turkey. For the Christmas rush, I had worked in a clothing store in Ft. Worth. They needed help and didn't ask for proof of my citizenship. I made a little extra money and bought Louis a nice dress shirt, and he gave me a watch. We couldn't afford a turkey, but Louis felt I had to have a gold watch!

Christmas Day we went to the Wiedemans. We had an absolutely wonderful day, but when she saw my gold watch, Mrs. Wiedeman wasn't pleased. She felt it too extravagant. But that was Louis. A little later their friends the Skinks came over, wonderful people with whom we also felt very much at home.

I had a very bad toothache, and being six months pregnant, Dr. Wiedeman, the dentist, looked at the tooth and said, "That is an infected wisdom tooth and it has to come out." He had an office in his home, and he just pulled the tooth. I went to see Dr. Funk the next day and he hit the ceiling. He said, "You could have had a miscarriage!" I, however, felt much better with the tooth gone. Again, the Lord held his hand over us.

On February 18, 1952 our first son, Andrew, came along. Louis and I had driven to see one of the church members who hadn't come to church. As we drove back on a bumpy, narrow, unpaved country road, Louis hit a big bump, and I could feel it in my stomach.

I said to Louis, jokingly, "If the child doesn't come now, then it will never come."

A few minutes later, my water broke, and Louis knew I needed to get to the hospital twenty-nine miles away in Fort Worth. We went back to the parsonage, and Louis called Dr. Funk, who agreed to meet us there.

Dr. Funk, a jovial man of German decent, worried about me. He knew my mother still lived in Germany and while I had Louis, I had no women family members near by.

When I went back to see Dr. Funk later, with Andrew, he said, "Now, Gisela, don't come back next year. Drink orange juice instead."

And, I didn't come back the next year; I didn't drink orange juice either.

Andrew was a breach birth. Dr. Funk knew this and could've turned the baby, but he didn't. Knowing my anxiety about this birth, he didn't want to scare me. He had to put me under anesthesia. After eight hours, my sweet baby finally arrived. Dr. Funk had to use instruments, and pull Andrew out feet first. Since then, the family has made a joke that Andrew does everything backwards.

Healthy, but relatively small at six pounds and six ounces, Andrew fortunately came two weeks early. Louis couldn't go in the delivery room with me, since at that time husbands weren't allowed.

Before I went into delivery, Louis kissed me and said, "I will pray for you and put you in the hands of the Lord." Then he went into the waiting room and slept. While other husbands worried, Louis slept!

After Andrew's birth, a nurse went in and told him he had a baby boy twenty-minutes old, he asked, "Why didn't you wake me?"

She answered, "Because you were sleeping so peacefully."

I always admired Louis because he had so much faith. He left Andrew and me in the hands of the Lord and didn't worry about us.

As usual, the gossip line in Haslet worked very well, and pretty soon everyone knew about the baby, and many visited me. At that time one stayed five days in the hospital after giving birth. Mrs. Pennington, the wife of the owner of the grocery store and something of a mother to me, visited quite often.

Constantly nauseated before I had the baby, I hadn't eaten much. And while pregnant, I took walks every day from the parsonage to downtown. When I walked by the grocery store, Mrs. Pennington always visited with me, and she or her husband always gave me grapes, about the only thing I could keep in my stomach.

After Andrew's birth, we planned to return to Haslet, but Mrs. Wiedeman made arrangements for us to stay for three weeks with Dr. and Mrs. Skink in Ft. Worth. Mrs. Skink showed me how to bathe Andrew and how to take care of a child. I felt so secure and comfortable in their Christian home, feeling the Lord's presence. After three weeks, when we needed to move back to Haslet, Mrs. Skink cried and I did too. She loved Andrew and she loved me, and I loved her in return. Andrew was like a grandchild to her.

When we asked what we could do for the Skinks in return, she answered, "Pass it on."

I broke down and cried. You can really see how the Lord blessed us. I even cry now, remembering their goodness. We may have been at rock bottom at the church in Haslet, but the Lord showed us He hadn't left us.

When we finally returned to Haslet and entered the parsonage, we had the surprise of our lives. Before I had left for the hospital, I had prepared a drawer in the dresser for the baby's bed after we got home. Someone at the church had suggested that solution. When we got into the parsonage and opened the bedroom door, there stood a complete layette: a bassinet, a crib, a bathtub, diapers, gowns, everything. Apparently, Mrs. Wiedeman and the beautiful people of the First Methodist Church in Fort Worth had been at work once again. I couldn't hold back my tears. Louis hadn't known anything about it. It completely surprised both of us.

Andrew grew and stayed well. Fortunately, I could nurse him for four months. One Sunday morning I woke up about four o'clock to nurse and change the baby. I flushed the toilet and, suddenly, a lot of steam came out of the toilet bowl. It scared me. I had never seen something like that.

I called, "Louis wake up! The toilet bowl is on fire!"

Louis did not wake.

I called louder, "Louis the toilet bowl is on fire. Louis, Louis wake up!"

Finally, he took one look and ran to the hot water heater in the closet and found it short of blowing up. Louis turned off the hot water heater. What a house! We could have lost our lives if this thing had blown up. Again, the Lord shielded and protected us.

One day Louis received an offer from the Navy to give psychological tests to sailors coming back from Korea. Accepting possibly meant leaving the ministry, maybe for a while, maybe for good. Because of our situation, he wanted to accept the job with a better salary. He felt bad about our living in such substandard surroundings.

Actually, I could manage this, having lived through the war in really tough conditions. At least here I had Louis, and we loved each other. It bothered me that he wanted to say "No" to the Lord. Even though I had not truly found the Lord, I knew one does not refuse Him. One has to follow Him no matter what. I pleaded with Louis not to leave the ministry because of financial difficulties. I assured him we'd somehow get through this situation. After I talked to him and assured him we'd be okay, he decided to stay.

The Bishop sent Louis to Haslet to build a church. What a job for a student pastor, to go to school and build a church at the same time. They had had a small wooden church with small houses scattered around which they used for educational buildings. They wanted to build a new sanctuary. The congregation already had the plans, but needed someone to build it. Louis did that. During that year while we served there, they built a very nice little brick church. Then, he wanted to leave.

The congregation seemed surprised when they found out Louis wanted to leave. They asked, "Why are you leaving? Don't you like Haslet?"

Louis explained that since we had a child, we could not make it on the salary offered. The congregation did not offer more. Most of the congregation obviously didn't care about the substandard parsonage or us. They only cared about building the church. We'd lived in that parsonage for one year. We'd had enough!

In June when we went to Annual Conference, other preachers'

wives knew that we came from Haslet, and they shunned me.

I said to one, "Well, we are down now, but we can only go up. You are up now, but you can go down."

Louis received another student appointment, this time to Red River County. He had to preach in four small churches. Since we had to drive so far and due to the horrible shape of our Ford, we decided to buy a brand new car. Louis decided on a Studebaker as our first new car. I don't believe we ever got so excited about a car as we did about that Studebaker. One of the members of the church in Red River had a dealership, and he let us have the car for a reasonable price.

Since Louis still attended SMU, Mrs. Wiedemann pulled some strings so we could move into Hawk Hall on the SMU campus. There we had a very modern apartment with one bedroom, a living room, a kitchen, and a bathroom, far different from the parsonage at Haslet. It had easy to clean, porcelain appliances, all new furniture, and tiled floors. I liked the apartment very much and always kept it nice and neat.

Louis had to preach every weekend, and Andrew and I always went with him. It resembled moving each weekend as we packed the playpen, the diaper pail, the bottle sterilizer, and lots of diapers; a long hard drive for Louis, but somehow, we managed.

During this time, Louis had another job besides preaching and studying. He graded sixteen-millimeter films by content and rated them as films for family, children, or young adults. Because he had these films available, he took them to the church socials in Red River County and also showed the films to ministerial students in Hawk Hall. All of us had a child or two and very little money. That meant we seldom went out. These films provided a handy entertainment for all of us in the three-story Hawk Hall. On movie night, when Louis had to change a movie reel, one person from each floor went to their floor and checked on the sleeping children.

Louis also sold sixteen-millimeter projectors, mostly to Baptist and Catholic churches. Louis enjoyed when the convents wanted to buy a projector. The nuns were very nice and always had something good for him to eat. My husband was a very good-looking young man, and I am sure the nuns enjoyed his company.

For the church socials there in Red River County, we met outside the church. Louis brought a projector and films like *Ma and Pa Kettle*, *Francis the Talking Mule*, and Disney films. We had a lot of fun.

Often, the Baptists joined us and then said, "Tomorrow, we'll catch Hell from our preacher, but tonight we're enjoying it."

I guess the Baptists spending time with Methodists was worth getting chewed out by the preacher. In my opinion, these little films could not have harmed anybody. After the films, we had light suppers and pleasant conversations.

I really disliked the toilet situation. The women all went together to outdoor toilets that had no doors. We could all see each other sitting on the thrones! I thought what strange customs these Americans have. This was "wild-west" to me, no civilization and a far cry from Berlin.

The congregations treated us very nicely. On Sundays, Louis preached four times. We drove up on Friday afternoon and usually stayed with one of the families from one of the churches who had an apartment. During church, various members of the congregations watched Andrew. They, too, treated him like a grandchild. He slept on more different beds! Louis didn't have classes on Monday so we drove home to Dallas on Mondays.

On the long drive to Red River County, Louis looked for some entertainment. He said to me, "Look, there are blacks standing on the side of the road waiting for a bus. Why don't you wave at them? You must take your middle finger and wave. They will be happy to wave back at you." I had no earthly idea what the middle finger meant, and so, I did as Louis had suggested. When I waved at them, they didn't seem as friendly as Louis had predicted. Some of them shook their fists at me. Others made angry faces, and some stuck out their tongues. I couldn't understand their reaction. I innocently kept on waving, and Louis had tears in his eyes from laughing.

Then, I smelled a rat and knew that he'd used me for some silliness as he so often did. He capitalized on my ignorance about American customs for entertainment. When I finally found out what waving this way meant, it made me angry with him.

Every weekend the congregations of Red River County loaded us up with watermelons and vegetables. We took care of all the families of Hawk Hall because we couldn't possibly eat all they gave us, ourselves. Unlike Haslet, these congregations treated us very well.

We really liked our life at SMU. We had a lovely apartment and great neighbors, all ministerial students in the same boat. Everyone had one or two children, little money, lots of studies, and student appointments. In spite of everything, we all had a good time together. I treasure those experiences.

We stayed in Hawk Hall and served those four churches until Louis graduated from SMU in 1954. Studying, preaching in four churches, the long trips, and his part time job took their toll, however. Louis graduated totally exhausted.

Chapter 13

The Preacher's Wife

Of course, at the next Annual Conference, we received a new appointment and moved again. Louis' two cousins and I moved everything from Dallas to Daisetta, 38 miles north of Beaumont. Louis' exhaustion kept him from doing anything. By graduation day, he could barely stand up and receive his degree from the Perkins School of Theology.

Daisetta, a very good appointment, had a new church filled with helpful and very nice people with vision. They were such a lively congregation that wanted to go forward.

With Louis so exhausted, I did everything I could to help him. I took over the responsibilities for Sunday school, kept up with attendance, and taught Sunday school to the teenagers. The congregation wanted a youth choir so I helped establish that. I also sponsored the MYF, the Methodist Youth Fellowship.

When I met with the MYF on Sunday evenings, I asked the parents to bring a little supper for them. The youth led the program, and later, we went to evening services. Louis stayed with Andrew at home and brought him to the evening services where he preached. I had a good time with the youth.

I also helped with the Women's Society of Christian Service, or WSCS, now known as the United Methodist Women or UMW. With the WSCS, I taught some of the missionary studies. Of course, I also took care of my family and the household chores. Obviously I stayed very busy, but I enjoyed working in the church.

While in Daisetta, I got pregnant again, but lost the baby in the third month. I had the miscarriage the same day Louis' mother left after a six-week visit. She left early in the afternoon, and very soon after, I started bleeding. I don't know whether the miscarriage resulted from the stress of her visit, or from some other cause, but Louis always felt the two related. I had a very difficult time getting over the loss of my little boy.

The church community, however, really came through. They visited me in the hospital, since in those days the doctors didn't let you go home for several days. When I did go home, the women of the church didn't want me to clean house or lift anything, and they hired Henrietta to help me every day for several weeks. I felt cared for and supported.

Louis still hadn't recovered from exhaustion. Seven years of University, studying, preaching, and part time jobs had taken their toll. I started making him take a nap every afternoon and saw to it that he got enough rest. A little later, we bought a recliner on which he lay and rested. When someone from the congregation came, he could sit up as if he had been reading or studying. If they had seen him lying down, I feared they'd think him lazy, and I just knew they didn't want a sick preacher. We didn't want to lose such a good appointment, so I did everything I could to make sure the congregation liked us.

Louis' fatigue kept him from working with the young people, like camping or picnics or playing ball with them,so I went with them. When Louis preached, I could see the strain in the muscles of his throat, and I spent the entire sermon praying. Fortunately, little by little his health improved and he did more and more in the church.

Most of all, the people wanted the pastor to visit them. When someone of the congregation entered the hospital, the family wanted to see both of us. I always went along. The same held true for funerals, but for those, I always found something else to do whenever possible.

At that time, I couldn't stand American funerals. American funerals usually had an open casket. Everybody had to look at the dead person. I couldn't stand looking at a dead person. In Germany we always closed the coffin. Can you imagine, I went through World War II and had only seen one dead body? I had seen the big Canadian airman, but then only from a distance. At first, I hid during funerals, but the people of our Daisetta congregation didn't understand and seemed unhappy with me.

Finally, when we went to the funeral of Louis' Aunt Zelma, whom I loved very much, Louis took me by the hand and said, "This has to stop." He led me to the coffin and had me look into it.

Can you imagine? That was the first time I had seen a dead body up close! After that, I handled funerals pretty well, amazed at how good the bodies looked. In Germany, they don't embalm the dead body.

In 1955 while we served Daisetta, I got pregnant again. This time I had a good pregnancy and I could go about my duties, a blessing, because Louis still hadn't completely gotten over his exhaustion. In 1956 close to Easter, Louis drove to Beaumont to buy some chocolate Easter eggs for the elderly shut-ins of the church. This was very important for Louis. I decided to go with Louis, and we took Andrew along too. When we arrived in Beaumont, I felt sharp pains, and I told Louis I had to go to the hospital. I was having the baby.

For nine months, since Daisetta didn't have a doctor or a hospital, I'd gone to a doctor in Liberty. Now, in Beaumont, I had to find a different physician. We went to St. Elisabeth Hospital where I met a Dr. Green. I liked him from the beginning and trusted him even though he informed me I'd have the baby by natural birth. I agreed, though I hadn't really prepared for that.

Since I hadn't counted on this experience, I hadn't brought my suitcase. I had to call back to Daisetta and ask someone to bring it.

Dear Mrs. Denton came with her husband and brought me the suitcase. She scolded me for going with Louis instead of staying in Daisetta. She had warned me not to go. Since I seemed on the go all the time, she had feared something like this day.

She always told me, "You are going so much, you will have that child in the car!"

Since I didn't have my mother with me, Mrs. Denton seemed to take over the role of a mother. I liked her very much, and I appreciated her help.

During this time, Louis took Andrew to a preacher friend of his. He and his wife promised, gladly, to take care of Andrew as long as I remained in the hospital. On March 30, 1956, baby James Earnest entered the world. I had a good delivery with no complications. I praised the Lord for that! We named him James Ernest after both of our fathers.

Louis was still not well. One day while he recuperated at home, Louis kept James while I attended a WSCS meeting.

When I got home, Louis said "James has a high fever. We need to take him to the doctor."

The doctor had told him not to drive while on the medications, so I drove. Louis sat in the passenger seat and we laid James in the back seat of the car. I had learned to drive with the football coach there in Daisetta because Louis had given up trying to teach me.

Suddenly, I heard the bottle drop and looked back. James went stiff and his eyes rolled back. I screamed!

Louis told me, "Stay calm. James is only having a seizure."

I had never seen anyone in a seizure, and this was my child. How could I stay calm? I thought James was dying! I got so excited, I couldn't find the doctor's office.

I drove around and around, and Louis said, "We have to get to the doctor. You need to stop."

I didn't know what I was doing or where I was going. Louis said, "You need to stop. We're at the doctor's office."

Still hysterical after we got into the doctor's office, I yelled,

"My child is dying! My child is dying!"

The doctor said, "No, your child is not dying, but I have to take care of you first."

Pregnant with my third child, the doctor feared I might lose the baby if I didn't calm down! He gave me a shot to calm me. Finally, they got me settled, and I understood the high fever caused the seizure. James often had fevers later, and they often went sky high. After that episode, I learned to put him in cold water to keep him cool and prevent seizures. He has never had another one. Fortunately, the Lord again held his hand over us.

As Louis recovered from the exhaustion, he began to take on more work in the church, and we decided to have a revival. When the churches in Daisetta had revivals, the Methodists went to the Baptist revivals, and the Baptists came to the Methodist revivals.

One evening during one of our services, the Baptist preacher cornered me and asked, "Are you saved?"

He knew I was the Methodist preacher's wife. I answered, "I'm working on it every day."

Then he asked me, "Have you been baptized?" I answered him, "Yes, in my mother's arms."

Then he said, "Since you haven't been immersed, you will go to Hell!"

I retorted, "If I go to Hell, I'll meet you there because you are judging me."

After that, he walked off and never bothered me again. Since then, I have resented that attitude. I imagine when I die the Lord will probably put my soul next to a Baptist soul, just for the fun of it! I know the Lord has a sense of humor! He has proved it to me on too many occasions.

During this time I had difficulty nursing James. A healthy baby, he didn't seem to care for my milk. I tried to nurse him, but he didn't want to drink. Since he didn't empty the breast, the milk caked, and I developed a breast infection and a very high fever.

I felt very bad. I had a breast infection, a high fever, little

James, and I was again pregnant. I also had to pack in order to move! During the annual conference in 1956, the bishop decided to send us to Genoa, located in South Houston.

When the Bishop said, "Move, there's another church waiting," you moved.

Louis told me, "Oh you're tough. You're okay."

I felt I wasn't so tough, but, I packed anyway. During our ministry, the preachers in the Methodist Church moved a lot. We moved to Genoa.

The little town of Genoa grew up near the highway from Houston to Galveston to the southeast of Houston. Yet, everyone there called it South Houston. It is now part of the Houston metroplex and near the Johnston Space Center. We lived just thirty minutes from Galveston and about an hour from downtown Houston.

We found the parsonage a pigsty, the fault of the former preacher's wife. Not much of a housekeeper, she left the house terribly dirty. Louis used an electric drill with a wire brush to get the dirt off the oven. The toilet always ran over. Parsonage toilets always stopped up on us. When Louis cleaned out the drain in the toilet, he found a child's bracelet.

Dirt covered the floors and thick dust coated the few pieces of furniture the parsonage had, all of it old and falling apart. I had to clean all of the windows, and the filthy windowsills. Children's markings and the dirt from little hands coated the walls.

From the time I moved into our first parsonage in Haslet, I vowed to always leave the parsonages in better shape than I found them. I must say I have always kept that promise.

The parsonage also needed a lot of repair. The church members decided to do this while we lived in the house. This proved a very difficult situation especially with a new baby and his sick mother. We had to move the furniture around and the paint fumes filled the house. After a few weeks, they finally finished the work, and we had things under control. Then the renovated parsonage smelled very fresh and clean.

We still had to battle the old furniture. I wanted to get rid of this old junk, but how? Finally I got an idea. One afternoon, I invited the ladies of the church to a tea. I showed them the renovated parsonage and the old junky furniture. Then I asked if they'd feel like living with that dilapidated furniture.

They answered they wouldn't like to live that way, and I said, "I don't either." I told them I had asked Goodwill to come and pick up the furniture. Afterwards, Louis and I went to a good furniture store, and, with our tithe money, we bought new furniture we left when we moved out. We now had a comfortable parsonage, and we did enjoy that.

We found Genoa very difficult. The congregation had two factions, the old guard and newcomers to South Houston. The old guard wanted to keep everything the same. They didn't want new people. The old guard consisted of people who had attended church for years, many of them charter members. The newcomers came from the new people moving into this growing area. As Genoa grew, the congregation expanded and rapidly outgrew the old church building. Instead of celebrating the growth, the old guard wanted to leave everything the same. They dragged their feet about any change. They treated visitors unpleasantly and even mistreated new members who joined the church. They didn't want any growth. This made the assignment especially difficult for Louis since the Bishop sent him to build a new sanctuary.

Louis felt the old guard attitude very unchristian and very hard to work with. He started visiting the old guard at home, one by one. Louis talked to them about his excitement with the church's growth and the importance of new blood, especially the young people. He told them how young people represented the future of the church. He said how unfortunate, even sad, if the church died because young people didn't join.

The unchristian attitude remained, however. The older members said, "We do not care what happens after us." What a selfish bunch of people!

Louis really struggled with them, and I often worried about him. At times, Louis had board meetings until 2:00 o'clock in the morning. The church needed to plan for a new building and no one could agree on anything. They argued about all sorts of things. Some wanted pews and others wanted theater style chairs. Some wanted to spend money on one thing, others on something else. Some wanted stained glass windows and others wanted clear glass. Some members wanted to put names on the pews identifying who paid for the pew. Others opposed having the pews identified. Louis felt that if one gives money, it should be given to the church. If people placed their names on pews or windows, they had their glory here and not in heaven. Louis kept his cool, but I feared his health might suffer.

Then, Louis started painting pictures in his sermons of hardheaded, selfish, unchristian people. Louis stepped very hard on their toes. I feared he'd cause them to leave the church, and I talked to him about it.

He said, "If they leave the church, then the church has not lost anything."

One Sunday morning after church, a lady who always carried a big Bible under her arm cornered my husband. She asked him if he'd let a black person join the church.

"Of course," he answered. "Yes, I'd let black people, Asian people, Mexican people, anybody can join Genoa Methodist Church." His answer really upset her. Then Louis said to her, "Jesus had dark skin. Would you let Him into the church and let Him sit next to you?"

She shouted with her big Bible under her arm, "I wouldn't let any dark skinned person sit next to me." With these words she walked out of the church building, but she did not leave the church. She represented a good example of the old guard.

Another episode that made Genoa a very ugly place for us involved having our dog stolen. We had a very sweet and friendly four-month old German shepherd named Dame (German for Lady), a beautiful, registered animal. One Sunday when we came home from church, she didn't come running to us. We looked all over for her, but we couldn't find her. We drove around the neighborhood, let the congregation know we had lost her, and put flyers with pictures everywhere in Genoa.

Weeks went by, when one evening a couple from the congregation came by the parsonage. They told us they had seen Dame at West Beach in Galveston. They, themselves, had German Shepherds and always went there to let them run and play. The next afternoon, Louis and I drove to West Beach, but we did not see Dame. This discouraged us. Suddenly, Louis decided we should drive to the police station. We told the police officer on duty about Dame and how the folks had sighted her at West Beach.

The officer said, "We just put two young men from Genoa in jail for speeding and cursing the police. They had a little Shepherd in their car."

The officer got the boys from their cell, took them to their car, and picked up the little Shepherd. She came running to us! We had our Dame back. The boys told us their uncle, a member of our church in Genoa, had given the dog to them. He must have picked it up during the church service. They wanted to sell Dame for big money, they said. The boys stayed in jail quite a while.

Officer McManis, the officer on duty said smiling, "We do fast work, don't we?"

The uncle of the boys never showed up in church again.

Another incident occurred one night around midnight. The doorbell rang, and upon opening the door, Louis found the nephew of a church member. He told Louis he wanted to pray in the church. Louis told him they could pray in the parsonage, but the man insisted he wanted to pray in the church. He seemed belligerent, and I felt very uneasy about the situation.

Finally Louis said, "Okay, let's go," and they went to the church.

As soon as they left, I sent Dame, now our big German shepherd, to the church. I told her, "Go! Go to the Church!" She went to the church. When the man saw the Shepherd, he no longer wanted to pray. Louis made him kneel and pray. Then, as both continued to kneel, Louis prayed a long prayer himself. After he and Dame came home, I asked Louis if anything had happened.

Louis said, "No, but he got his money's worth."

Our congregation also had a lady treasurer, one of Genoa's old guard. She seemed very dedicated to the job; so dedicated she called Louis several times during the week to help her with the books and the money. Of course, she wanted him to come to her house because she didn't want to carry the books around. He met with her several times until I told him her interest had little to do with the books and more to do with him. He had told me she fixed coffee and cake for him. When I told him she was after him, he laughed and accused me of jealousy.

This married woman had a family, but it seemed to me she wanted my husband, the pastor. I wasn't jealous so much as concerned about having our marriage destroyed through something silly like that. My husband was very naïve when it came to women. Such men sometimes get into a situation from which they cannot free themselves. Maybe, I thought, she wanted to try to put my husband into an embarrassing situation so the old guard could get rid of him. Time or possibly a sexual advance finally opened his eyes. Louis didn't explain it to me, but he did find a reason to let her go from her position as treasurer.

When Louis replaced her, all hell broke loose. The old guard complained, some members spoke to the District Superintendent, and she and her husband left the church.

Since many of the old guard complained, the District Superintendent wanted Louis to move. However, Louis felt God wanted him to change the unchristian spirit of the Old Guard, and he told the District Superintendent so. As a result, we stayed another year. New people continued to join the church, and Louis completed the building of the first phase of the new church.

Genoa Methodist Church presented difficulty for me as well. Every Monday morning a female member of the church called me. Both the church and the town gossip, she thought she knew everything. I didn't want to hear gossip about people of the church. She also always let me know what the old guard said about the sermon. After Louis started preaching about unchristian attitudes, she told me practically all the time they didn't like the sermon and they wanted him removed. This went on for months. While I should've refused to listen, I didn't want to make her mad. Not a malicious person, she often took care of the children and just liked to gossip. The whole situation made me sick, and I almost had a nervous breakdown. Once again, I felt trapped as if behind that big old black fence.

One day as I stood in the kitchen of the parsonage in Genoa washing dishes, I suddenly heard a voice saying to me, "If you want to see them all, go home."

Go home? I didn't even think of going home. Besides we didn't have the money for me to visit Germany. Still, I ran over to the church and told Louis what had happened. He had no doubt the Lord had spoken to me. When I lamented we couldn't afford for me to go, Louis said, "If the Lord told you to go home, then he also will send the money." Louis was a man of true and strong faith.

A week later, Mr. Schlesinger, Louis' former Sunday school teacher and the man instrumental in Louis' becoming a minister of the Gospel, came to visit. As they visited, Louis mentioned to him the experience I had had. He also told Mr. Schlesinger we couldn't raise the money. Mr. Schlesinger, a very wealthy man and a good Christian, told Louis not to worry; he'd take care of it, and he did.

We had tickets to ride the Eagle to New York and a big stateroom, cabin class, on the SS United States to take us in four days to Bremerhafen. Of course, Andrew and James went with me. Andrew, a very lively five-and-a-half-year old, I kept on a harness with a leash to prevent his falling overboard. I carried James in my arms because he didn't walk yet. An elderly gentleman in the next cabin often held onto Andrew for me and took him to the dining room. A middle-aged lady helped me, too. They thought me quite brave to cross the Atlantic with two little children. I, meanwhile, appreciated all the help I could get. I even woke up at night to check on the boys. We had a porthole in our room. I kept it closed, but feared Andrew might open it or something. Fortunately, the ocean stayed smooth and neither the children nor I became seasick. What a blessing! Even so, we still had a very straining trip.

One day, the captain called all of us on deck and showed us how the Gulf Stream came into the Atlantic. You could clearly see the difference in the motion of the water. It amazed me that this small stream which came into the Atlantic had come from the large body of water in which I swam on the Texas coast. The captain explained how the warm water of the Gulf flows north along the eastern U.S. coast and around to northern Europe. Its flow keeps these areas warm.

After four days, we landed in Bremerhafen. My mother waited there for us. I was so happy to see her. We stayed overnight in a hotel, and I finally got some rest. Carrying James much of the trip and watching Andrew really tired me out. We left next morning on a train to Berlin.

To get from Bremerhafen to Berlin we had to cross the Russian Zone. The people in our compartment of the train soon learned that we were Americans. At that time Andrew didn't speak German so I spoke English to him. These Germans worried about us as the time came for the passport check because the Germans knew the Russians as unpredictable and inconsistent. The Germans had had terrible experiences with the Russians during the war and under the Russian occupation. They feared the Russians. I, however, felt no reason for concern since we had American passports. When the time came for the check, nothing happened. The Russians treated us civilly, and we had no trouble.

We arrived in Berlin in the evening and took a taxi to our

home in Zehlendorf. In mid-March 1957, I could still see bombed-out houses, rubble, and other ugly sights from the war. We greeted my grandparents who seemed in good health and glad to see me, but even happier to see their great-grandchildren. It had been seven years since I had left Germany. I had left as a young girl and now returned as a married woman with children.

The first few days after I got home, I rested. The strain of the trip and the time difference exhausted me. I liked being back in Berlin, but I missed my husband and the American conveniences like a washing machine, a dryer, and a blender. The house in Berlin, comfortable and cozy but old fashioned, was about eighty years old. After I rested up, I called some of my friends, and we went out and had a good time.

One afternoon I went to the flower shop where my mother always bought her flowers.

Suddenly a man's familiar voice shouted, "Gisela, you are here? When did you arrive?" It belonged to Jochen Patschan, at one time a close friend.

We had helped each other to get through the war. Many years had passed since we had seen and spoken to each other. He made an appointment with me to come to our house one afternoon to meet my children. He liked the boys. In fact he was crazy about them. He started coming by daily and bringing goodies and toys to the children, and, of course he enjoyed seeing me too.

One day he asked me to divorce my husband and marry him. He promised me heaven on earth. I mentioned to him he'd had the chance one time and there wouldn't be a second time. He wouldn't take no for an answer and kept on visiting me. Very persistent, he thought gifts, sweet talk, and expensive dinners might change my mind, I guess. Many times he mentioned I would swim in money which might have been true. Jochen had inherited a very profitable and much needed street improvement and repair business from his grandfather. I told him I loved my husband and that money didn't mean anything to me. I told him a person's faithfulness, love, truthfulness, and honesty far-outweighed riches.

He still refused to give up and invited me to his apartment. I went, rang the doorbell, and when he opened the door and wanted to kiss me, a lightning bolt or a bright streak of light came between us. It scared us badly. We both jumped back. It seemed another proof God watched over me. In spite of the light, Jochen asked me to come into his apartment. I told him what had happened was a warning from God. He laughed the event off, but I took it seriously. I turned around and left. I suppose he got the message because he didn't come to visit anymore. In fact, I never saw him again.

Later on, my mother told me that he, however, made a trip to America to see what held me in this country. She said he asked for my address. She did not give it to him. She later said that another friend also visited this country. I did not know either had come. They never contacted me. The country did not hold me, but my husband did.

Six weeks or so after arriving in Berlin, my grandfather developed serious heart problems. At eighty-nine years of age, he had hardly ever fallen ill. The Lord took him home after he spent three weeks in the hospital. My grandfather's death verified for me the Lord had talked to me that morning in the kitchen of the parsonage. Although greatly saddened by my grandfather's death, I treasured the time I had with him for those last few weeks.

One day, one of my former students came to see me. After the war, he had been my neighbor and had carried my briefcase as we walked to school every morning. He was a very good-looking boy when I had him in my class. He was also very intelligent. He knew that I liked the theatre and had offered to take me several times when he was my student. Since he was my student, I had always declined. As we visited, he offered again to take me to the theatre. Since I had turned him down before, I felt it would be nice to visit with him and see a show. This time I could say, "Yes," and go with him. The performance was great, and I enjoyed seeing a play in

German. We stopped for a snack on the way home and had a chance to catch up with the past. He told me of his job, and I told him about my children and my husband and our life as a pastor's family. It was nice to know how this student was succeeding with his life. We had a wonderful time.

The time in Berlin went by fast, and soon I had to leave for America. I hated to leave my mother and grandmother, but I looked forward to seeing my husband. He drove to meet us in New York. We had a great family reunion. For almost two weeks, we took a little vacation through the New England states. Then, we went home to Texas! I enjoyed being home, even in Genoa! After three months, returning to my husband made me very happy.

After I got back, I asked Louis to baptize me a second time. Moved by the experience of going back to Germany, my grandfather's death, and the lack of love for God in Germany, I felt I needed it. Being with my family again and knowing that God had led me to go back had a very deep influence on me. I talked with Louis and told him I felt reborn and felt I needed to make that real. Louis said he could baptize me there in the kitchen, but I said I wanted something more. Louis and I walked across to the church there in Genoa, and he baptized me again. I felt very close to the Lord. I felt I had really come home in a very important way. I also felt freed from the big old black fence again.

Soon after I got home, I became pregnant again. I don't know why, but somehow, I knew this child would be born on Sunday, May 4, 1958.

In June of 1960, the Conference moved us to Port Acres, a small suburb of Port Arthur, near the Gulf of Mexico. We spent time on the beaches there and enjoyed the appointment.

The parsonage was wonderful! For the first time we moved into a brand new home. I was excited! It was a great feeling to move into a house where everything was in tact, where nothing had to be rebuilt or painted. The furniture was lovely too. We rejoiced and thanked the Lord.

The congregation here was not difficult. It was a nice atmosphere, and Louis did not have to work as hard as he had in Genoa. As often as we could, we went to the Gulf and enjoyed the water. By now, Andrew, in the fifth grade, enjoyed his new school and his new classmates. James seemed pleased with the elementary school, and Marcus enjoyed the loving attention of *Omi* and *Mutti* who had moved from Germany and now lived with us. Everything seemed to work out well.

During our time in Port Acres, we started a drama club in the church. The college students from Lamar University in Beaumont, who lived in Port Arthur and Port Acres at home wanted to have dances in the church, but Louis didn't believe in dancing in the church.

He said, "The world is too much with us. We are bringing the world into the church."

He felt, however, that if something was denied, something else had to be put in its place. Louis had done drama at Southwestern University and liked it very much, so, every three months the students performed during the evening services. These were, of course, religious plays about modern Christian ideas. It was a great experience for the students and for Louis and for me.

The congregation liked the plays very much and looked forward to those Sundays when the plays took place. After the plays, I invited the young people to visit us in the parsonage for snacks and cold drinks, coffee, tea, or hot chocolate. Sometimes we were together until 2:00 o'clock in the morning. The fellowship and the experiences with drama were just wonderful. I loved it.

The people of Port Acres were nice, but they had one hang up. They did not want our children in the living room of the parsonage. This room was only to be there for the church members and their meetings. This made my blood boil. I wondered how I could teach these people a lesson. The parsonage was very nice and we had no intention to ruin the place. Our children were well behaved and taught not to hurt or destroy things.

Finally, I had an idea. That is when I began inviting the students for cookies and drinks in the living room of the parsonage. Most of the young people were members of our church or prospective members. I saw to it that the chairman of the board and the church lay leader knew about the young people being in the living room. Pretty soon, our children could be in living room too, and nobody said a word.

Port Acres was a very good church for us. The congregation was peaceful and enthusiastic; the parsonage was pleasant; and we were close to the beaches and the Gulf. Louis enjoyed preaching to this congregation and we were happy with the community. We found life much better in Port Acres and enjoyed our years there.

Chapter 14

Mutti and Omi in America

I came home from Germany in June of 1957. Grandfather had died, and Berlin had ceased being a home for Grandmother. She and Grandfather had lived there together sixty-five years. She wanted to come to America to live with her great-grandchildren, especially with James, for he reminded her of Bruno, the child she had lost when he fell down the steps.

In 1958, Grandmother and Mother moved in with us in Genoa, Texas. At eighty-four, Grandmother spoke no English, but that didn't bother Grandmother at all. She just spoke German and thought people would understand her. She never made an effort to speak English.

Sometimes she'd take Marcus in the stroller and walk through the neighborhood, but she often got lost. When she did, some of the members of the church who lived in the neighborhood usually found her and called Louis saying, "We have Grandmother. She's here having coffee and cake and having a good time."

Louis just went over and packed her, the stroller, and the baby in the car to bring them safely home. This didn't bother Grandmother one bit.

Grandmother had a good time in this country. She loved it here and found it very comfortable. She especially loved all the kitchen gadgets. I had an electric blender and a crock-pot. I also had an electric skillet and an electric knife. My electric stove had a timer on it and a thermostat to keep the heat at a constant level and then it would automatically turn off when done. This was a far cry from the old wood stove Grandmother had cooked on in Germany.

Since we all liked *Omi's* cooking better than *Mutti's*, we tried to get her to cook whenever possible. *Omi* also enjoyed the central heat and air conditioning which made her much more comfortable. Both *Omi* and *Mutti* enjoyed my electric sewing machine that was much easier to use than the old treadle machines they had used in Germany.

Mutti and *Omi* then moved with us to Port Acres. Later, they would move with us to Sugar Land where they would get a home of their own for a short while. It was really good for the kids to have their grandmother and great-grandmother with them. They really helped the kids, and me as well. We still have fond memories of those years with them.

Omi often sewed for the children and patched things or shortened and lengthened. She did a little dusting and straightening. She enjoyed life here. In Germany, *Mutti* had to help Grandmother with everything, but here Grandmother seemed to have more energy. *Mutti* wondered if Grandmother had gotten younger.

Grandmother especially loved the Texas heat. She didn't have to deal with the snow any more. Once we had snow in Houston, and we said, "Oh, look, *Omi*, we have snow!" But she didn't even come out to look at it.

She said, "I've seen snow. I don't need to see it again."

Every Friday, Louis took us driving somewhere in the country. Before Grandmother would get into the car, she would clean it out.

I'd say, "Grandmother you're going to fall over. It's too hot."

She'd answer, "Well, I'll just fall over doing something."

Grandmother had never had a car and naturally couldn't drive. Because, with the children, we would often eat or snack in the car, it was not always in the cleanest condition. She absolutely despised it when we ate in the car. People in Europe didn't eat in their cars.

Later when she lived with my mother on Brook Street in Sugar Land, Grandmother developed a bad habit. After she brushed her hair in the morning, she put her brush into the top of her knee-hi's. My mother told her not to do that because she could fall and have a bad accident. Grandmother did not listen. It was difficult to tell her anything. She had quite a German stubborn streak. Then it happened.

She had the brush in her knee-hi's and she fell. The brush of course didn't give and she broke her hip. She had to go to the hospital and the doctors operated and fixed her hip, but she never really recovered from this unfortunate fall.

Omi lived five years here in Texas until she was ninety. When she died, Louis performed her funeral ceremony, and we cremated her. We sent her back to Germany and friends buried her next to my Grandfather. Grandmother had wanted that, and Mother had very close friends who made the arrangements in Germany.

As grandmother had a bad habit, *Mutti* had a funny one. As a very orderly person, she wanted everything neat and in its place, including the money in her billfold. She hated to see money in the billfold all crunched up. She wanted it nice and straight without any folds, so she ironed it to make it nice and straight. Often, I even had hot money in my billfold.

At the age of sixty, Mother had to come to America because she felt Grandmother, at eighty-four, was too old to come by herself. Mother didn't really want to come to Texas because she had too many friends in Germany. She said she did not believe in living with children. Then she had the language barrier to contend with. Neither Grandmother nor Mother spoke English. This didn't bother Grandmother, but it did bother Mother. Mother, however, came along.

Mother didn't like it at first because she was used to her German culture. She wanted to be able to walk everywhere and be independent. She felt she couldn't walk in this country. Many places didn't even have sidewalks! *Mutti* walked almost everywhere in Germany, and here when she walked to the store or the bus stop, people often stopped and offered her a ride. She had trouble convincing them that she wanted to walk.

She wasn't used to three children either. She loved the children, but found them a strain. Marcus was a baby, and Andrew and James were loud and very active. Andrew always delighted in playing tricks and jokes on her. In the evening they all jumped on their beds instead of settling down and going to sleep. They weren't allowed to do that, but they always did it when she baby-sat for them. As they grew older, she grew much closer to the children, and they developed very close relationships.

Because she did not speak English well, she spoke to the children in German, and they learned German from her and still speak it today. They called her *Mutti*, which means Mother in German, and they called Grandmother *Omi*, the German for Grandmother. My mother didn't want to be called Grandmother because this would make her feel old. She preferred *Mutti*.

Mother improved her English by watching soap operas and did pretty well. She often mispronounced things, but got along. We had fun with her English.. The children especially got a kick out of it. At that time there was a Safeway grocery store in our area where we lived. *Mutti* always said she was going to *Severie* to shop. Because of that, the whole family always went to *Severie* instead of Safeway. *Mutti* loved to go to *Pizza Hoot* and she liked the *Yack in the Bude*. *Bude* means box in German.

When *Mutti* spoke and understood English better, then she liked it better here in America because she felt more at home. She also developed friendships with German people here. Every weekend one of her German friends invited her to visit, or she invited them to our house.

After Grandmother had passed away, *Mutti* flew to Germany every summer for three months to visit her old friends. When I had summer vacation from school, *Mutti* felt that the family could do without her for a short time and that we should spend some time

165

alone as a family, so she boarded a plane and off she went.

These trips gave her a rest from the children. When I went back to school, she returned. Unlike me, Mother loved to fly.

Mutti had her own income. She had a very good pension from Germany, and she felt that gave her a certain measure of independence here. In fact, she often helped us financially. She always paid her own way when we went on vacation.

Whenever possible, we always took *Mutti* along on our vacations. She really saw quite a bit of America. She saw the West Coast up to San Francisco, and she saw Washington State and Oregon. She visited, often, Louisiana because Louis' family lived in Louisiana. She saw New Orleans, and, then, part of the East Coast. Our vacations took us many places, and *Mutti* got to see a lot of the country.

For some reason, *Mutti* never felt completely comfortable with Louis. She felt Louis expected too much of me. She felt the teaching, caring for the children, and being a homemaker as well as working in the church too demanding. The moving around often bothered her, too. Germans don't usually move so often. Grandmother had lived fifty years in the same home, and Mother had lived in our home in Zehlendorf forty years.

Louis had wanted her to come to this country. I think maybe he was a little bit selfish in this case. He wanted her here so I wouldn't go to Germany to visit her. He wanted me at home with him and the children.

Chapter 15

Changing Jobs

We stayed in Port Acres for two years, and then, in 1962, left for Sugar Land and the Texas Prison System Unit, there. We had enjoyed Port Acres, and I had thought everything was great. Yet, Louis, with his restless nature, must not have felt quite fulfilled in this pastorate. One evening, he told me that he felt the call to be a Chaplain in the Texas Prison System. I was not very happy to leave Port Acres, especially the brand new parsonage. Yet, when the Lord called, that meant packing and moving.

Louis had six prison farms under his care with the headquarters in Sugar Land, Texas, a suburb of Houston on the southwest side. We moved onto the prison farm inside the fences that surrounded the headquarters. There, we had again to move into a house that had to be renovated. I was mighty tired of moving into houses that were substandard.

We painted everything, and *Mutti* bought carpet for the living room and dining room to replace the old linoleum that she hated. The only thing I never liked was the color of the walls. The prison system furnished the paint. Every wall in every room had the same color, institutional green. It took about two months, but we made the house livable and more comfortable.

My mother and grandmother moved into the house with us,

and we were four generations living under one roof. It used to be very often this way in Germany, especially when people were living in the country. I understand it was the same way here in America. For our children, it was very good that their great grandmother *Omi* and their grandmother *Mutti* were living with us.

One spring the Blue Bonnets were all over the place. At that time fields surrounded Sugar Land, and there were large open spaces on the prison unit. Everywhere were those beautiful Blue Bonnets. We explained to mother that it was the state flower of Texas. She loved those flowers, but because of her limited English, she never could pronounce the name correctly. When she spoke of them, she always said, "Blue Bons," and since then we have never called them by the correct name. We have always said, "Blue Bons."

The prison farm in Sugar Land was a place where one was not really free. We could not walk all over the place. We were confined to certain areas to walk and ride bicycles. I did not like to be fenced in again. It seems like fences follow me somehow through most of my life. Several times we had a "break" when a prisoner escaped. It was, then, like a little war. It was a little scary. The guards looked all over for the prisoner. They came into the house and looked in the attic and around the house. The children thought this was exciting, but it bothered me. My mother and my grandmother did not like this either. Grandmother was afraid of shooting. She and *Mutti* also feared the prisoners. They decided to rent a nice house on Brook Street in Sugar Land. They enjoyed living by themselves again.

The house on the prison farm was pretty large with a big, screened front porch. Sometimes, when I came home from school, birds were in the front porch. How the kids got them in there, I do not know, but they were there. I couldn't stand anything that had feathers because of the rooster, which had made me very afraid when I was a child. I would not go into the house until the birds were gone. I believe the kids let the birds in on purpose. To this day my kids like to play jokes on me.

While we lived at the prison farm in Sugar Land, Louis felt it would be useful and an advantage to him to get a Masters Degree in psychology. Sugar Land was not very far from the University of Houston, about a twenty-minute drive. He drove back and forth to the University for two years while he took classes in psychology and in law. He studied law just because he wanted to. He received a Master's Degree in psychology and a certificate in counseling. This study was very useful for him counseling the prisoners and later people in the church who were troubled by bad marriages, illnesses, difficulties in their jobs, or other things. He was a very busy man at the time and a very good counselor, I was told. He liked counseling very much. In fact, he enjoyed everything were he could help someone lead a better life.

During this time we lived in Sugar Land, I decided to become a teacher in America. I had been a teacher in Germany and had enjoyed it very much. In order to teach in the United States, I had to go back to school for two years. Since we lived close to the University of Houston, I could go there during the day while Louis went at night. I received credit for most of the subjects I had taken in Germany: math, physics, chemistry, and biology.

My major was foreign language with specialties in French and German. I had to take education, a very poorly taught subject. I also had to take American History, Texas History, English, French, and German. I thought taking German was absurd! As a German native, I thought I should be able to take a test and get credit for the German. I didn't have to take first year German, however, but I did have to take Advanced German.

I had trouble with the professor. At first I wrote all my papers in German and made "C's." I went to the professor.

He said, "Would you please speak in English."

I said to him, "You are a German professor; why can't we speak in German?"

He said, "I would rather speak in English."

I went with him through my papers in English, and he said, "These are very good papers."

Come to find out, he was not really proficient in German and did not understand, completely, my German. I had to write my papers in English and then got "A's" and "B's." He had his Ph.D. degree! He taught English, too.

Later, I received $100 for being the best French student. I was also voted into Delta Kappa Gamma and Phi Kappa Phi, both honorary scholarship fraternities, pretty good for being such a poor German student!

Finally, after the two years, I graduated with a B.A. and could select the school in which I wanted to teach. Foreign languages were in demand because President Nixon had made them very important. As the only French and German combination teacher in Houston, everything opened to me. Because Bellaire High School had a very good scholastic reputation, I selected that school.

I approached the first day of teaching very nervously. What reaction could I expect from the American students? I knew they called Bellaire Little Israel because so many Jewish kids attended the school. That concerned me very much. I also worried about motivation. Could I motivate the students? Bellaire was a very good school and I had excellent students. I really didn't have to worry. Everything went fine, even with the Jewish kids. It amazed me how much easier I could teach American Students. German students often criticized teachers and talked back in very offensive ways.

The school bus took Andrew and James to their school in Sugar Land, and I dropped Marcus at Mother's house on the way to Bellaire where I taught French and German. After school, the school bus took James to my mother's house where she took care of James and Marcus until I picked them up on the way home from school. The children, mother, and grandmother seemed to enjoy each other. They went often to the Dairy Queen and had a little ice cream or something to spoil their supper. Ten-year-old Andrew waited at home until I got there.

While we lived in Sugar Land, I loved to drive fast. I had a very nice little sports car, a Dodge Lancer, which handled very well. I don't know exactly if the car fell under the category of sports car, but to me a car that had bucket seats and drove fast fit in that category. It had a push button gearshift mounted on the dash. Every morning, I pushed the buttons too hard and pushed them through the housing. Each morning, Louis had to push the buttons back out.

One rainy afternoon I drove home from the University of Houston and the streets were somewhat slick. It didn't bother me. I flew down the road. I didn't know that my husband drove just behind me and watched my driving maneuvers. When we arrived home, I received a very firm lecture from my husband. He told me I'd kill myself driving that way in this little sporty car if nothing were done about it. The next morning I had to drive his Pontiac. My beloved little car had to stay home. When I returned from school, my car was gone! My husband had sold it! I shed a few tears.

Louis said, whenever I cried, "Oh, are you reverting back to a three-year-old?"

This always stopped my tears. On the other hand, it made me happy he loved me and cared for me so much he didn't want to lose me through an accident.

Later, he bought me an Austin, an English car that I didn't like at all. It was a little car that looked so conservative and old fashioned, very British.

Not very long after the Austin, Louis had me in a 1952 Rambler station wagon. This car had a stick shift because my husband thought I shouldn't always drive an automatic. Actually, I think he got a good deal, and it just happened to have a stick shift. I couldn't use that stick shift well, so when I drove the car, I had a difficult time.

One Saturday morning, we had some business at Sears. Louis

had to go somewhere else later so we went in two cars. Thirsty, I drove into a drive-in with Louis behind me. After we finished our drinks, we wanted to make our way to Sears. I tried to start the car but I couldn't get my stick shift to work. I fooled around with it and finally forced it so hard, I broke it off. My husband didn't say anything. He just shook his head. I got back into the car with my gearshift in my hand and Louis pushed me over to the Sears garage.

My husband asked the mechanic if he had ever seen someone break off a gearshift. "Not in the sixteen years I have worked here," he answered. Then he smiled at my husband and said, "Be careful that she does not break anything else off."

Louis enjoyed working with the prison system as he always supported the underdog. He had four prison farms to take care of: the main farm in Sugar Land where we lived, and three other farms located around the south of Houston. On Sunday, he preached to the prisoners, and during the week, he counseled them. He had a lot of work to do and had a great responsibility. While Louis preached to the prisoners on Sunday, the children and I went to a Methodist Church in Bellaire.

The prison farm with its breaks and restrictions got on my nerves, and, finally, we decided to live in a private home away from Sugar Land and the prison. In 1963, we moved to Stafford, but the children still went to school in Sugar Land. This time Louis wasn't the driving factor in a move; I was. I couldn't stand living fenced in at the prison farm. Grandmother had died, and *Mutti* moved back in with us. We bought a beautiful new home in a new subdivision and enjoyed it very much. Louis drove to the prison farms each day and I drove to Bellaire.

We bought a large home with three large bedrooms and two full bathrooms upstairs. *Mutti* had one of these and her own bathroom. The three boys had the other large bedroom with a bath, and the third room we used as a den. We had the master bedroom with its own connecting bathroom downstairs. Downstairs we had a family room, a living room, a dining room, and a kitchen. We had ten walk-in closets! Louis fixed one of them as a radio studio. He had a morning devotional program on a local radio station, and he taped his devotionals in his closet studio.

Marcus, our youngest son, never enjoyed school. When the school bus came, sometimes he boarded willingly and other times he absolutely refused to go to school. He cried and held the bus up for several minutes.

When he made such a spectacle my mother said, "*Markilein*, just stay with me, and we'll have some ice cream and fun."

She took *Markilein* to the house and he stayed with her. She spoiled him very much. His brothers still tease him about this.

One day, Marcus didn't want to go to school, and he held up the bus again. This time the bus driver lost his patience. He grabbed Marcus and started to put him on the school bus. When our Shepherd, Dame, saw the driver touch Marcus, she jumped at the driver and caught his pants leg. *Mutti* said he shook all over and almost turned white. Dame didn't bite him, but held his pants leg until he quickly put Marcus down. Then she turned the bus driver loose. Marcus walked home with *Mutti* and again missed school. That evening Louis and I talked firmly to my mother and to Marcus too. This could not go on any longer. From then on, this staying home with *Mutti* stopped.

When Andrew was about thirteen or fourteen years old he wanted to make a little money and decided to deliver newspapers. Since he couldn't drive a car yet, I got the job of driving Andrew through the neighborhood in Stafford after school. He enjoyed throwing the papers. Sometimes they landed in the yards, sometimes not. James and Marcus often came along and had fun listening to the popular song "Chug a lug, Chug a lug." They had a tape and all sang along. Since then, when we hear this song we say, "It's time to start the paper route." After we finished, we sometimes went to the ice cream parlor and had a milk shake or an ice cream sundae. We did this for several months and had lots of

173

fun, but I also taught school and cooked dinner, and after a while, I tired of the extra job, and we stopped Andrew's throwing papers.

Because I didn't care for the principal in Bellaire, I decided to change schools and went to Westbury High, another nearby Houston high school. As the only French and German combination teacher in Houston, I could still select my schools. At Westbury High, I again taught both French and German. I taught three German classes and two advanced French classes. I also sponsored the German Club.

That fall, my German Club wanted to have a Halloween party. Halloween had nothing to do with the German language or the German culture, but, since my students wanted a party and we lived in our big house in Stafford, I invited the students from the German club into my home. They helped me decorate the house after school. They hung colorful garlands from the ceilings of the den, the living room, and the dining room, and upstairs in the children's den. Then we put a colorful light bulb in every lamp in the house, mostly blue and green bulbs that made it a little spooky. Louis used his recording studio in the house and worked out a Halloween program for the students.

We had intercom speakers everywhere in the house, and during the party, he broadcast the program through that system. I had told Louis facts about the students, and they heard funny stories about themselves and each other. After snack time, we had show time. Louis had ordered a very spooky Halloween movie that we showed in the den. With the students and our family, we had sixty-five people in our den with room enough for everyone to sit comfortably on the floor. Some students stayed until after midnight.

In the fall of 1963, Louis finished his Master's Degree in psychology at the University of Houston and decided to move to San Marcos. One day he informed me of this. Then Louis drove to San Marcos. He applied for a job as a counselor at the Gary Job Corps, and they hired him.

Gary Job Corps served as a correctional institution for young people in trouble in their home communities across the state of Texas. They often came from broken families. Some had drunks for fathers or mothers. Others came from poor homes where the children had little opportunity. Louis felt he could really help those young people

Thus, Louis moved to San Marcos. For a short time, he lived in a small apartment just outside of town and commuted back and forth between Houston and San Marcos on the weekends. He lived with a very nice German family. They had a butcher shop, and later, after we moved to San Marcos, I drove out there to buy meat.

Louis wanted his family with him, so he selected a house to rent in San Marcos without consulting anyone in the family. I had stayed in Houston with Mother and the children while we tried to sell the house there. We didn't sell the house in Houston at that time, but after Louis found the house for rent with an option to buy for us in San Marcos, we moved. I suppose Louis thought he did me a favor by finding a place to live, but I could have left the children with *Mutti* and helped him select the house. I felt angry with that, but I went along. He bought a split-level house with the kitchen and den on the lower level and the living and dining rooms on a higher level and the bedrooms on the second floor. We spent a lot of time on the stairs! It was, however, a lovely home. Louis had good taste; he thought he knew what I wanted, I suppose. Life with Louis wasn't dull.

My mother liked San Marcos and went walking all over the place. We lived in a residential area close to downtown and she could walk downtown and go shopping. Marcus, *Mutti*'s favorite, often went downtown with her. Saturday afternoons she took the boys downtown to a movie. Andrew often went with his friends, but James and Marcus went with *Mutti*. James talks, even today, about going to the picture show with *Mutti*.

After we moved to San Marcos, I needed a job so I went to the San Marcos Baptist Academy, a co-educational, military, religious, prep-school and asked if they needed a French and German teacher. They hired me to teach French and German. I expected to hit the place running with only ten students in the class. Was I mistaken!

Those ten students proved more difficult to teach than thirty-five in a public school class. Most of the kids came from very wealthy, but broken homes, the product of selfish and uncaring parents. Many parents sent their children off to school and jetted around the world with their lovers. One of my German students said to me, "She brought me up from Houston, in a jalopy. Now, she goes off somewhere in a fur coat with her lover."

Many of the students told me their troubles. Instead of motivated prep school students, I found students who had many problems and really didn't care whether they went to college or not. The best students came from overseas.

One student said, "Oh, Mrs. Sterling, don't worry. I already have a $500,000 endowment, and I have more to come. I will be a millionaire."

I told him, "Well you will be the dumbest millionaire and may end up in the poor house if you have this attitude."

Most of the students lacked the motivation to study. They wanted to talk about their situations, and they wanted someone to listen. I listened, but after all, we had some material to cover. When I talked about the situation to the administration, they told me not to worry. If the students wanted to talk about their problems, let them do that. I found that hard to do. My Teutonic background told me to teach, and the administration told me let things go if the students wanted to talk.

They told me not to give the students an F. "We need the money," they said.

That made me mad. With a $3000 annual tuition, I felt the students needed to learn something.

These problem children frustrated me. We accomplished very little because the students wanted to talk every day and kill the class. I let them do that a few times, but then I started a Talk Day. Every Friday they could bring up their problems and discuss them. I told the students if they worked hard four days a week, then they could have the privilege of a Talk Day on Friday. This worked better. When they didn't work hard on those four days, I took away the Talk Day. After I did this a few times and stayed firm, the students got the message, and we had less trouble. My motto was "No privileges without responsibility." However, I still experienced great frustration.

If I had begun my teaching career at the Baptist Academy, I would have left the teaching profession. The whole atmosphere made me sick. This administration always took inconsistent approaches with the students and teachers.

I developed such a bad eating disorder I lost 30 pounds in three months. I couldn't swallow food. It took me almost half an hour to eat a mashed avocado. Even the kids noticed my weight loss. Louis, quite concerned, took me from doctor to doctor and they couldn't find anything wrong. They said it was psychological. One doctor in San Marcos who knew about the Baptist Academy told me I needed to quit. Because I wanted to teach the students and wanted them to learn rather than simply listen to them talk about their problems, he felt I could never be happy there. The Baptist Academy made me angry and distressed, and the stress caused my eating disorder according to him. Another doctor said it was like an hysterical reaction. He said I was determined to teach whether they wanted to learn or not. After I left the Baptist Academy, my disorder vanished.

Later, some of the students from the San Marcos Baptist Academy visited me in Austin and told me they had tested out of several hours of French or German at the University of Texas. I guess I did a better job than I had thought.

By 1965, we made a decision to move from San Marcos to Austin. We had moved five times in as many years. We moved to Port Acres in 1960, then to Sugar Land; then to Stafford to escape the prison farm; then to San Marcos to Gary Job Corps; and, finally, to Austin.

Chapter 16

Austin

After living half a year in San Marcos, Louis wanted to move to Austin, his favorite town. While he had gone to Southwestern University in Georgetown about thirty miles north of Austin, he had worked part time at the University of Texas Radio House. He had enjoyed that very much and had fond memories of it. He also had many friends who lived in Austin and Georgetown. I also think Louis wanted to move to Austin to get me away from the Baptist Academy. He worried about my eating disorder and felt if we moved I'd find another job. The doctors had told me I should get out of the academy. I wanted to stick it out because I feared I couldn't get another job if I left in the middle of the year.

We had only lived in San Marcos for six months, and now, Louis wanted to move again. We had just moved from Houston. None of us wanted to leave San Marcos. Even today, the children talk about the friends they had in San Marcos. When Louis made a decision that he thought best for the family, we found it best not to interfere!

We looked all over Austin for a nice home. I saw a beautiful two-story house in northeast Austin with a lovely yard and a cute little brook behind the house. I wanted Louis to buy it, but he refused and explained that cute little brook could become a raging river when it rained. If the yard and house flooded, we might have to evacuate. We could lose all our belongings. Then, I wanted to move to the hills of west Austin.

Louis objected again. "When the roads ice over, we can't get out. We can't drive the car on icy roads."

Of course I didn't like that idea, and I agreed not to move to the hills. I later found out the roads in Austin ice over only every ten years or so. If I had known that then, I might have argued a little more. With Louis, however, one could not argue because Louis always turned it every which way, and I ended up feeling in the wrong. I even ended up apologizing sometimes when I knew I was right. That was Louis.

I finally told Louis he should select the area and the house. Frankly, I had tired of looking for houses since everything I liked proved unsuitable. Louis found a nice home in South Austin so new we had to wait for the builder to finish it before we could move in. We had had a beautiful house in San Marcos, but, no, Louis had to move to Austin. We both had to commute about thirty-five miles back and forth from Austin to San Marcos, but when Louis made a decision, I always thought, "He probably knows best," and so we moved.

No one moved us. We had to pay for the move, and it wasn't cheap. Even when I disagreed with Louis' decision, I gave in, because you couldn't win for losing with him. I loved him deeply and agreed rather than bring conflict into our marriage.

Finally, with the house finished, we moved in December. We decorated the whole house inside and out with Christmas decorations in just five days. Then, we invited our friends and had a dedication of our new home. Celebrating our first Christmas in the brand new house made it very special.

Of course, every Christmas took on special meaning for the children, Louis, my mother, and me. Louis made it so. Each season, he asked my mother and me to leave the house for a few hours. When we returned from our shopping spree, he surprised us with a fresh baked pecan pie, pumpkin pie, and a tasty German stollen. He really made good pies and stollen. Although he did this every year, it still came as a surprise because we didn't know when or if he'd continue it. This year it made me forget all of the moving and difficulties!

In Germany, we celebrated on Christmas Eve. As a small child my grandparents took me to the Evangelical Lutheran church. They always decorated the church with several lovely Christmas trees covered with big, tall, lighted candles. This made it a festive but solemn event. While we attended church, my parents brought our Christmas tree into the house and decorated it. In Germany, the children do not see the tree before Christmas Eve. To see, suddenly, the tree lighted with candles and decorated in all its glory always excited me as a child. Then, I had to say a Christmas poem or play a Christmas piece on the piano. After that, we handed out the gifts.

Christmas Day, we visited grandparents, uncles, aunts, and cousins and had goose, potatoes, and red cabbage, with tarts and cookies for desert. The grownups had coffee and I got hot chocolate. The lighted and beautifully decorated German Christmas tree really made a life-long impression.

I wanted to teach my children a few German customs, and I started with Christmas. Here, in America, we always had two Christmas trees. The big tree, decorated in American fashion, stood in the living room. The *Tannenbaum*, decorated with white lights and silver decorations, like bells, balls, stars, and angels, we put in the den. It looked very simple, but beautiful. We had major and minor Christmas gifts. The smaller gifts went under the German tree, and the bigger gifts under the big American tree.

We celebrated on Christmas Eve the German way. Of course, we all went to church. Then we lit the *Tannenbaum* and exchanged the minor gifts. After that, we read the Christmas story from the Bible. Each of the children and Louis and I had to read a part.

After the prayer, we ate German foods like potato salad and herring salad and sausages and ham. After dinner, my mother played Christmas songs on the piano and we all sang. Always, we had a lovely evening filled with wonderful memories. To this day, James and Marcus often celebrate the German Christmas Eve with me.

The next day, Christmas Day, before the children and I really woke up, Louis came into the bedrooms with his movie camera to take pictures. The children always hated this.

They wanted to run into the living room and open packages and their father said, "No, no, no, we have to do this."

Mutti and *Omi* never got caught in their nightgowns. They got up early and dressed for the occasion. Everyone went to the living room and started unwrapping their gifts while Louis continued taking pictures. Excited and happy as they unwrapped their gifts, everyone had fun and our living room soon looked like a wastepaper basket.

Mutti and *Omi* couldn't get over how many gifts everybody received. In Germany, we had received only one large gift each Christmas. *Mutti* and *Omi* didn't want to open their gifts because they didn't want to tear the nice paper and ruin the bows. In Germany, we didn't wrap gifts, but instead placed them on a table covered with a tablecloth. When it came time to receive the gifts, we just pulled back the cover. During the war, we could not exchange gifts. We were just glad to be together and alive.

With Louis, I got Christmas presents all day long. After I unwrapped a gift in the morning, the intercom came on, and Santa told me to go into my closet to find a surprise. After an hour or two, Santa sent me into the yard or to the children's room or into our bedroom to find other surprises. This went on until the evening. Louis did these surprises in such a beautiful and fun way that it gave me great enjoyment. I think Louis did so much for me because he thought that during the war I didn't have anything, and he wanted to make it up to me. He wanted to make Christmas special for me. When he passed away, Christmas wasn't the same anymore. Louis was Mr. Christmas.

Our new two-story house in Austin had four bedrooms and two baths upstairs, and a big den, a living and dining room, a very small kitchen, and a half bath downstairs. Apparently, the builder didn't think women cooked any more as he made the kitchen the smallest room in the house. The huge den and dining area combined had the big hi-fi from wall to wall and comfortable chairs and an oval dining table and a hutch.

Mother continued living with us, so we let her use the largest upstairs bedroom with a very large walk-in-closet. *Mutti* wanted a sitting room, so she put her bed in the closet and slept there. She used the bedroom as a sitting room with a couch, a small table, and two armchairs there, furniture which she had had shipped from Germany. My mother lived eleven years with us on Tahoe Trail in Austin.

Andrew and Marcus slept in one bedroom large enough for two twin beds with a night table and another table and a desk. They also had a large chest of drawers and a good-sized closet. James, who wanted to live alone, had the smallest bedroom, but still large enough for a double bed, a dresser, a desk, an armchair, and a small round table. All the rooms really seemed a good size.

Louis and I had a huge bedroom. We had a king-sized bed and two octangular night tables on either side of the bed with a triple dresser, a big desk for me, and a big bookcase. We still had room for a table and two chairs. It reminded me of a European bedroom with books and a desk that gave the room a "homey" atmosphere. What a big house! I cleaned it every Saturday. That's why I have a maid now. I'm tired of cleaning.

It was good that we lived in a two-story house. Germans like to look out of windows where they can see what is going on in the neighborhood, and so did *Mutti*. She looked out of her window every morning and waved the children "Good-by" when they left for school.

One day in the fall of 1968, she looked out of her window again and noticed a white Chevrolet pickup stopping in front of our neighbor's house. Our neighbors were a very nice young couple with a little eight-year-old-girl named Sherry, who often played with my youngest son Marcus.

Mutti watched a man get out of the pickup and ring the neighbor's doorbell. The man stayed a long time. *Mutti* knew that the lady's husband had gone to work. She had seen him leave. Mother thought that this did not look good. The next morning *Mutti* made it her business again to look out of her sitting room window. She saw the husband leave for work, and a short while later the white pickup with this man appeared again. He rang the doorbell again, and the sweet lady let him into the house.

During this time James, our middle son, had an hour free between classes. Instead of staying in school and studying, he came home on his motorcycle that he called his "beamer." It was usually close to lunchtime, and he ate with *Mutti*. They both enjoyed it very much.

Mutti told James about the man in the neighbor's house and said in German, "*Ein Kerl ist da bei der Nachbar's Frau.*" (A rascal is there with the neighbor's wife.) "*Schrecklich ist nicht gut.*" (It is terrible and it does not look good.)

James innocently asked, "What do you think he does there?"

Mutti smiled and said, "*Ich weiss nicht.*" (I do not know.) They probably have a *Techtel Mechtel* (an affair).

The next day *Mutti* made it her business to look out of her window again. She saw the husband leaving for work, and after a short while the same pickup arrived. The same man got out, and the neighbor lady let him into the house.

Again James came home for lunch and asked *Mutti*, "*War der Kerl wieder da?*" (Was the rascal there again?)

Mutti answered, "*Ja er war wieder da. So ein schrecklicher Kerl.*" (Yes, he was there again. Such a terrible rascal.)

James got a kick out of *Mutti's* "entertainment." This went on daily for a few months. Then one day, *Mutti* noticed that the husband returned when his wife's friend was there. The husband was of Swedish origin, and he probably let his wife and friend have it. *Mutti* saw the man running out of the house pulling up his pants. *Mutti* said to herself, "*Das ist richtig.*" (That is right.)

Later we heard that the husband divorced his wife and the so-called "friend" left the woman sitting high and dry.

The funny part to me was that mother always accused the man. He came and had a good time because the woman wanted his company and surely the sexual enjoyment. She could have said, "No" and not let him into the house. Both parties made a very unfortunate choice. Too bad that the marriage broke up because then Mother lost her entertainment!

During this time, Mother and Andrew enjoyed Pizza Hut together. *Mutti* called it "hoot," the German pronunciation of "Hut" which means "hat" in German because the top of the building looked like a hat to her. She and Andrew often had a good time drinking beer and eating Pizza. After Andrew began his studies at Southwestern University and when he would come home, *Mutti* would say, "Let's go to Pizza Hoot!" Off they went.

One day however, Andrew had had a little too much to drink. When they both arrived at home, Andrew went to bed and took a nap. Suddenly he woke up because the sheet and his clothes were all wet. He had wet the bed, and everything else. Not only the sheet and his clothes were wet, the mattress and carpet under the bed got their share too. Andrew said to *Mutti,* "Don't say anything to Mom. She'll hit the ceiling." They both got busy washing the clothes and sheets in the washing machine, but they had to clean the mattress and carpet with vinegar water so that the room wouldn't smell. When I came home from school, I didn't notice anything. Very much later I heard the story. Then it was too late to "hit the ceiling."

The music at our house always played so loud I believe one could've gone across the street and listened to it. Louis loved classical music, but he thought he needed to play contemporary music loudly. Both Andrew and James had hi-fi's and played their music quite loud as well. Sometimes, with the doors of the house open, loud music blared from three different rooms, with different music playing in each one. *Mutti* grew very tired of the noise and decided to move into an apartment on Westgate Boulevard almost across the street from where we lived. She still came over almost every day and straightened the house, but only when everybody left and the house was quiet.

One day after about six months, I hadn't heard from her in two days. I called but she didn't answer, so I went over to her apartment. *Mutti* had a terrible cough and a very high fever. We tried all our home remedies, but the cough stayed. We went to the doctor and he took a lot of tests. A few days later when I got the results, it shocked me to learn she had cancer of the esophagus. The doctor told me she had two months to live, but maybe cobalt treatments would help. I was fit to be tied. I wanted to keep her. I did not want her to die.

Mutti didn't understand what the doctor had said, and I didn't want her to know about the cancer. We never spoke of cancer, and I forbade everyone, nurses and family alike, to mention it to her. I really don't know if she ever knew she had cancer or not.

Mother suffered the terrible, inhumane, cobalt treatments. I couldn't stand to take her for them. Louis or Andrew had to take her. The treatments left *Mutti*'s throat raw, sore, and too narrow for her to swallow normal food. Louis and I moved her back to our house. Every morning, I got up at three o'clock and made different soups for her, vegetable, rice, and chicken, and ran them through a food processor to puree them. I fed her and left some for her noon meal. Then I went to my normal morning routine. I never missed a day of school during Mother's illness.

Before she became ill, *Mutti* loved to visit cemeteries. I didn't enjoy it, but I drove her. She had liked Forest Oak Cemetery in south Austin the best and had selected a place under a tree where she wanted to be buried. Whenever we drove by there, she pointed out the cemetery and said, "There's where I am going to be buried."

Unfortunately, the cobalt treatments didn't stop the cancer and it spread into her lungs. Mother passed away in May 1977. Louis held the funeral, and we buried her under her tree at Forest Oak Cemetery.

One evening shortly after mother's death, Louis and I sat in his study watching TV as we had always done while mother lived with us. Suddenly, Louis and I saw the doorknob slowly turning.

I said, "Children do not play a joke. We know you're behind the door."

At that moment the door slowly opened wide. I got up from the couch and looked into the other rooms, upstairs and everywhere, but found no one.

Louis and I were alone in the house. I came back to the study, and Louis said to me, "*Mutti*'s here and paying us a visit."

Another time, *Mutti*'s friend and I sat in the den of our house having tea and cake. Suddenly someone knocked on the outside door. I went to the door and opened it, but found no one there. The friend said, "That was *Mutti* who knocked. She knows we are having tea and cake."

After Andrew and Debbie married, they came to visit. They slept in James' room. In the middle of the night, Debbie needed to go to the bathroom. In the hallway an ice-cold wind and a figure rushed by her. She ran back to Andrew and told him *Mutti* frightened her. I guess *Mutti* wanted to see who Andrew had married. Debbie made Andrew go with her to the bathroom, and from then on, she refused to spend a night in that house.

We heard strange things in our house other times as well. One afternoon, as I ironed and James kept me company, we heard the outside door open and heavy steps come up the stairs. They stopped on the third step. I said, "Louis we know it is you. Just come up." The steps did not come up. I looked out of the room and

187

saw no one. *Mutti* wouldn't have had such a heavy step. We later heard our house sat on an old Indian cemetery.

Since we now lived in Austin, I left the Baptist Academy in San Marcos in the spring of 1965, and looked for a job closer to home. I went to the Austin Independent School District administration office, and Lawrence Buford told me to call the principal of Austin High School who needed a German Teacher.

When I talked to the principal on the phone, he said, "If you look as good as you sound, you got the job."

I went right over to the school. I went to the office and found Mr. Robbins by himself. I said to him, "I'm the German teacher who just called you. Do I look as good as I sound?"

He smiled and said, "Yes, you're hired."

I found Austin High School an excellent school with excellent teachers and felt fortunate to get the job. My students all came from very good homes in Terrytown and well-to-do parents with academic backgrounds. I had mostly boys in my German classes, most of them in the upper two percent of the school. I enjoyed teaching them, and I knew we accomplished things together. I felt very successful.

Later, I took the students on trips, twice to Germany and Austria. It excited the students when they found people understood when they spoke German.

Some told me "Those words are real. We thought you just made them up."

If I hadn't so hated flying, I could have taken students to Europe before.

Previously, I had tried flying with Karl, a friend from Austria who visited this country. I knew we had to fly to Europe and I didn't want to have a hissie fit on the plane in front of my students. I wanted to see if I could stand it calmly, so I flew with him as far as Houston and met Marcus, who lived in Houston at that time. We had lunch with Marcus and I stayed with him until my plane left late in the afternoon. Karl flew on to San Francisco, and I flew back to Austin by myself. Karl gave me a little prayer to carry with me. I prayed it, and I made the trip safely. I really think Karl first interested me in flying and traveling. Once I got started, I found I really enjoyed it and I've wanted to travel ever since. This freed me from another black fence.

I also took students to German contests in San Antonio, San Marcos, New Braunfels, and even New Orleans. My students usually did very well, and we often won. I'm quite proud of those accomplishments.

Sometimes, we put on some German plays for contest. Then Warner Dahlberg helped me a little. He taught English and drama at Austin High School. I understand his students performed excellently in plays and musicals. Unfortunately, due to my busy schedule, I never saw any.

When I came home from school around 4:00 p.m., I went straight into the kitchen and prepared and cooked dinner. My husband wanted dinner ready at 5:30 p.m. We all had to sit around the big table to eat and socialize because this was really the only time of the day all of us got together.

When I taught foreign languages in Austin High School, I enjoyed inviting my students to small parties in my home. It fulfilled two purposes. I got to know my students better, and the parties motivated the students to better learning. I also thought it good for the students to get to know me better outside of the teaching environment. They found out that teachers are human beings too.

One time, we had a Mardi Gras dance and party. Some students came early and helped me with the decorations for our double garage. We hung colorful crepe paper on the walls and ceiling. Everyone dressed in some kind of funny outfit and had a mask over their eyes. I wore my clown suit I used when we went to the Shrine hospitals for burned or handicapped children. My husband hooked up the music with his big amplifiers so it carried two or three blocks away. Since we lived on a very small street with only eleven houses, a few days before the party, I told all the neighbors about our Mardi Gras street dance and asked their permission to make noise and dance in the street to very loud rock and roll music. Everyone said okay, and once the party got in full swing, the neighbors came out and joined in the excitement. At 12:00 o'clock we had the demasking, and the student in the funniest outfit received a big teddy bear. We had the party on Saturday so they could sleep in on Sunday.

I had preparations for five classes. I believe I had the hardest assignment in the school. I taught classes of first, second, and third year German and a combined class of third year German and fifth year French. I also taught second year French. The combination class of French and German proved the most difficult, and I had to prepare to use every last second of the class. I taught the German students fifteen minutes orally. The French students had to write and answer questions about the material they had prepared at home. Then the German students had written tasks, and the French students had to do oral work. Then both groups had grammatical work and reading to do, and I walked around and helped individuals.

For a while, each student had a tape recorder. Each student recorded answers to questions or made statements in the language they studied. In the evening, I took the tapes home and listened to each and responded to their work and corrected their mistakes on the tape. In class and on the tapes, when the students addressed me and asked questions they had to speak in the language they studied. I found myself speaking French and German back and forth, very straining for me, and really not a sound teaching method. Yet, what else could I do?

Because I had such hard and straining assignments, I had to do something fast to free myself from the daily stress. I decided to join a fitness center close to our home. Every morning I went there when it opened at 6 o'clock. I swam for thirty minutes, went into the sauna, sat ten minutes in the steam room, and then sat five minutes in the whirlpool. After the forty-five minutes, I felt relaxed and fit as a fiddle. After a good shower, I went home, fixed my hair, got dressed, and prepared breakfast for the family, and then, I went off to school. I always arrived in my classroom a few minutes before eight o'clock ready to go.

Usually, I had first year German for first period, a fairly big class of twenty-five students. Although usually motivated, sometimes it happened the kids appeared tired and didn't pay attention very well. Then I made them get out of their seats and do exercises with me. I gave the commands in German, and then we worked our bodies. I worked right with them. After a few minutes, the students seemed awake and alert. Afterwards, students usually said, "Mrs. Sterling, you have more energy than we have. You must have been swimming again." It's true; the morning swim helped my stress and energy level. This way I coped with my many preparations.

In the German classes, I had mostly boys and very few girls. In the French classes, I had just the opposite. With the French classes, I often went into Cajun country in Louisiana. We went to St. Martinsville to a French plantation, the Shadows. There, the students heard the real French, the 17th century French and could practice the language. We ate in the restaurants and the students understood and spoke French there as well.

We also went to New Orleans. There, the students always wanted to eat at Antoine's, the very famous restaurant. Before we left, I always told the students to exercise care at Antoine's because of the high cost of the food. On one trip, when we got there, Mr. Mouton, a father of two of my students went around and told the students to order anything they wanted on the menu. This came as a great surprise to the students and me. He paid the bill of over six hundred dollars! To this day, I always remember that trip with pleasure!

Off and on, funny little incidents happened. Around Christmas time we usually had an Advent wreath hanging in the classroom, and every morning my students and I sang German Christmas songs before class. In one of my classes, I had a student who played the guitar, and that year, we really had fun singing songs. As we sang away we didn't notice that a burning candle from the wreath fell in the paper basket that stood underneath. Suddenly, one of the students noticed smoke pouring out of the paper basket. He took it, opened the window, and threw it out at the moment when the principal and assistant principal walked by. They either didn't notice it for they walked on by or they figured it came from my class and assumed anything could go on. Upstairs, everybody had smelled the smoke, and other teachers almost called the fire trucks.

I taught 22 years in Austin High, all of them very busy. For this reason I hadn't much time to socialize with other teachers and didn't really make a lot of friends. Yet, those years at Austin High School still stand as the best time of my career.

Soon after we moved to Austin, Louis felt he might lose his job with the Job Corps in San Marcus. At the same time, because he did such a good job of counseling, the State of Texas offered him a job working with people who had their Master's Degrees and who wanted to work with handicapped people. He quit the Job Corps and accepted the state job. Now, he no longer had to travel to San Marcos. Instead, he traveled all over the state of Texas to hold workshops for those people. He taught rehabilitation and at the same time, wrote pamphlets and small books telling how to do rehabilitation work.

Louis had to build this program from scratch. The state Department of Mental Health and Mental Retardation had not had a program of this type, and they hired Louis to create it. Then, in 1966, he asked the Southwest Conference of the Methodist Church to reassign him. The Conference assigned him to a small church in Manor, just fifteen miles east of Austin. Every Sunday we all drove from south Austin to the little church in Manor for Louis to preach. He also visited the members of the congregation who were in the hospital in Austin.

While living in Austin, Louis joined the Masons. Soon after he joined the Shrine, I joined the LOS, or Ladies of the Shrine, about which Louis teased me, calling it the Ladies of the Night. Louis joined the Shrine Drum and Bugle Corps and played a bugle, and I joined the clown unit as a clown.

The members of the Drum and Bugle Corps, a very close knit group, saw each other often. Practically every weekend we went somewhere, and once a month we had parades. We went also to contests. We really enjoyed the work.

The LOS often made quilts and Afghans and had other projects. We auctioned those at the monthly dances, and the proceeds always went to the Children's Hospitals or the Burn Hospital in Galveston. Louis and I didn't miss any dances.

They often asked Louis to preach at the Shrine Temple, and he always had his heart in it. One cannot join the Masons unless one believes in a deity. The organization encourages strong faith and helping others. They have many charitable events and always seek to do something good. For these reasons, Louis felt the Masons a good organization and one we could enjoy socially. Louis and I benefited greatly from joining this wonderful organization.

Chapter 17

Living With My Three Boys
And Their Escapades

By the time we moved to Austin, my older children were entering their teenage years. I have found dealing with your own teenagers a difficult task. I have always enjoyed my teenage students, but the teen in a classroom is very different from your own at home.

My three boys were very disorderly. I always wanted them to lay out their clothes for the next day each night before they went to bed. I had learned to do this during the war when air raids became a regular event. We had to have clothes laid out so we could grab them and run to the shelter. I tried to establish the rule for my three sons. Either they forgot to do this, or they threw the clothes on the floor in some comer of the room. In the morning, they couldn't find them and ended up fighting about them. Almost every morning, they started a commotion I didn't like. One day, I'd had enough of it. I didn't tell the boys to lay out the clothes. While they slept, I put all the clothes in trash sacks and threw them out the window. The next morning the children stood in front of empty closets.

"Mother where are the clothes? They're not in the closets! We need our clothes! Tell us where they are!" they yelled from upstairs.

"On my back," I answered, using an old German expression.

"They're not on your back," they shouted.

"Then, look around and find them," I yelled.

"We will be too late to school," they whined.

"That is okay, too. Get detention," I answered.

Finally one of the boys must have looked out of the window and seen the bags in the yard. It dawned on them the clothes might be there. They ran into the yard and retrieved them. They knew why this had happened, and from then on, they usually laid the clothes out. The morning commotion stopped, mostly.

As the boys got older entering their teen years, Louis wanted to keep them with the family. He didn't want them hanging out with a crowd of friends or other teenagers from different parts of town. He firmly believed that children stay closer to home if the family provides interesting and exciting activities. Later we would start a couple of businesses to accomplish this, but at first Louis made sure that we saw movies together. Louis and the kids liked movies. We often went on Fridays to a drive-in theater and, often, looked at a Disney film. With the three boys, *Multi,* and me, it could have gotten quite expensive, but Louis, as a pastor, had a pass, and we usually went free.

Tahoe Trail, the street on which we lived, had just eleven houses. The only traffic consisted of the cars of the people who lived on the street, and they always drove carefully. Often, in the afternoon, the children gathered to play baseball, football, or basketball in the street. They got along well and had a good time.

One day, as my eight-year-old son, Marcus, and the kids played football, he ran as fast as he could after the ball. Always a little chubby, Marcus, concentrating on the ball, didn't see the neighbor's mailbox sitting on a steel rod. Suddenly, the kids heard a loud boom. The steel rod lay broken in two, and the mailbox wound up on the other side of the street. The children all ran to Marcus, fearing he'd gotten hurt. Mr. Albright, the neighbor and owner of the mailbox, heard the commotion and came out of his house.

"What happened to my mailbox?" he asked.

"I broke it," said Marcus with a little cry in his voice.

"Boy, you're too young to drive a car yet. Do your parents know that you took their car and drove it?" Mr. Albright asked.

"I didn't drive a car," Marcus answered.

"How did you knock the mailbox over and break the steel rod in two?"

"I ran after the football and didn't see the mailbox. I just flat ran over it," Marcus responded.

Then Mr. Albright said, "Boy, you're a powerful young man. What do they feed you at home?"

James and Andrew had come home and yelled, "Marcus just ran over Albright's mailbox!"

"What! My goodness, I hope he didn't hurt himself!" I gasped.

"He isn't hurt, only the mailbox," they answered back.

I ran out and went across the street to the Albrights'. Many of the neighbors stood in front of Mr. Albright's house and around the mailbox. I offered to have it fixed and wanted to pay for it, but Mr. Albright wouldn't hear of it. Everyone laughed and went back into their houses. Marcus had a hard time living that incident down.

When Marcus turned eleven or twelve years old, he wanted to earn some money and decided to sell Tyler roses. Poor little Marcus stood there in the heat and bad weather selling roses on a corner in Terrytown. When I saw other young people selling roses sitting in chairs, I brought him a chair. From then on, I had to lug that chair back and forth each time I took him to work or picked him up.

When he had roses left over, I would buy them. Then, when the weather looked rainy or stormy, I'd pick him up and take him home. I feared the Texas weather and didn't want my children to get caught in it. Marcus enjoyed selling those roses and did it for several months. I feel it cost me more than it was worth, and I drove many miles taking him to work and picking him up. Louis thought me silly. No wonder Marcus enjoyed the work!

As Andrew and James entered their teens, they developed a liking for danger: danger on highways, danger in the air, danger under the water, or danger in the snowy mountains. They regularly frightened their mother with their proposals and their activities.

Andrew enjoyed driving fast. He had a Rambler, a Volvo, and an Opel. They were by no means sports cars, but Andrew treated them like they were. Of course accidents happened. What a mess!

Andrew was working at Handy Andy. He worked very hard, saved his money, and bought a second hand Rambler. He also paid for the insurance. We couldn't afford to buy a car for each of the three children and pay their insurance. We also felt that earning it themselves seemed to make them feel good and just a bit independent.

Andrew drove too fast, and he also liked to stop short suddenly at red lights. That scared me, especially on wet roads. Since Andrew went to Austin High School, where I taught, we sometimes took my car and sometimes his. Every morning, we had a song and dance about his wanting to drive. Almost every morning, I gave in and let him drive and felt uncomfortable with his driving. For most of three years, I suffered his driving.

Then one afternoon, Andrew came home and told me he had had a little bump with his car. I felt Andrew was okay, and a little bump would not make a great deal of difference. Later, when Louis came home, he told me that Rambler was totaled! I almost panicked. Then Louis, who seldom raised his voice, told Andrew firmly that this could not continue, or Andrew could not drive any more. Since Louis still worked at Gary Job Corps and they had an auto mechanic program, the boys at the Job Corps had a good learning experience repairing the Rambler. We thought the problem was solved.

It was not too long after that the boys at the Job Corps were able to have another learning experience. Andrew had sold the Rambler and bought a Volvo. In the Volvo, Andrew had another wreck. This time he was taking one of my female German students home. He had her bring him home to tell me about the wreck, because he knew I would not hit the ceiling in front of one of *my* students. Later on, although mad at him, I'd cooled off enough to give thanks he hadn't hurt himself.

Another time he had one of *my* students bring him home after he had wrapped the Volvo around a tree. Again, I couldn't hit the ceiling. I just thanked the Lord my oldest son still had a chance to become an adult. I also prayed that would happen soon. Each time, Louis would remain calm.

He would only say, "I am so mad at him, I could squash a grape." That was as far as he would go.

Several years later, Andrew bought the small Opel Cadet. He was attending Southwestern University in Georgetown and had pledged Kappa Alpha Fraternity. One afternoon, Andrew and a fraternity brother had been tubing on the San Gabriel River near Georgetown. Realizing he was running late for work in Austin, Andrew drove quite fast on the gravel road back to Georgetown. The Opel Cadet, light and unsafe, couldn't handle a sharp turn, and it flipped on its side. Later, when I heard of it, I couldn't see how the two boys could have gotten out of the car unhurt, very scared but very thankful. They both knelt down at the side of the road and thanked the Lord. The hand of God had protected them.

Andrew had, of course, totaled another car! However, he still owed $600 on it. We insisted he pay it off. We took him out of Southwestern and enrolled him at the University of Texas, here in Austin. He went to school close enough to live at home and ride his 10-speed bike to work at K-Mart and to school. We felt we had to deal very hard with him to preserve his life.

Andrew wasn't the only teenager to give me heart failure. One day, James came home and told us he wanted to learn to fly! Not very enthused about the idea, Louis and I told him we not only couldn't, but wouldn't pay for flying lessons. We figured, with his job as an usher in the Southwood Theater paying a dollar an hour, James couldn't pay for them either. James, though, has a very strong will. I believe the German heritage settled in him. He saved his dollars, and when he had a hundred dollars, he took ten flying lessons. At 17 years of age, he received his license to fly small aircraft. I did hit the ceiling when I heard. At that time, I was afraid to fly at all, and especially, I feared the small airplanes. Louis, however, calmed me down, reminding me that if James was willing to save his own money and spend it for this, we must accept it. I did not have to like it, however.

Later, despite our reservations, we all took pride in James' accomplishment. His grandmother flew with him first. Then, my husband and both James' brothers flew with him. One time, James picked up Andrew and Marcus in Houston and flew them back to Austin. When I thought that all three of my boys were in that little plane and could all be killed, I prayed very hard. To this day, I have not flown with James. He and a friend plan to build a Piper Cub, but I don't plan to fly in it either.

I have worried more and prayed more for my second son, James, than either of the others because he always liked sports connected with the most danger. When he became manager of the Southwood Theater, he saved his money again and bought himself a motorcycle, a BMW 900. Now, I felt I had real reason to worry! James loved his *Beamer,* as he called it, and went all over the United States with it. I was always happy when I saw him driving into our driveway and knew he was safe and sound.

One day, he went flying with one of his friends. After they landed, he jumped on his Beamer and started for home at 75 miles per hour on Dessau Road, at that time a narrow, winding, two-lane gravel road, north of Austin.

Suddenly, a greyhound dog appeared on the road. James couldn't stop and couldn't get around it at that speed. The Beamer hit the poor dog and cut it in two. The back of his Beamer came up and threw James over the handlebars about twenty feet. It knocked him unconscious for a little while. When he woke up, he wasn't, at first, sure if he still lived, he told us later. James stood up, finding himself alive in one piece with tom clothes and bleeding all over. He walked to a nearby house down the road and asked if he could use the telephone. The lady of the house hesitated, but after James explained what had happened, she let him use the phone.

James called Marcus, who was then managing a theatre in south Austin. James told Marcus what had happened and asked Marcus to come get him. Marcus grabbed the moneybox so that nobody could steal it and drove as fast as he could to James on Dessau Road.

In the meantime, as soon as James left, the lady where he had made the phone call must have called the police. When Marcus arrived, James got in Marcus' car and told him the whole story.

Suddenly, the police arrived and walked around James' motorcycle asking each other, "Where's the body? Where's the body?"

James had a little fun and said in a deep voice, "Here's the body."

The police couldn't believe James had lived. The Lord had saved one of my boys, again.

The police urged the boys to see a doctor right away, and they did. They did not, however, call home to inform their mother that one of them had just been through a life and death experience! The doctor's examination, fortunately, showed that James had no internal injuries and no broken bones. He had only suffered road rash, deep scratches, and scrapes from sliding on the road. The doctor gave him peroxide and told him someone should carefully put it on the wounds.

James did not come home that night. He stayed at Marcus' apartment so Louis and I wouldn't know anything about the accident. The doctor's nurse called the next morning and gave the secret away. I nearly went out of my mind when I heard. When James came home, I, of course, was the one to treat his wounds. I admit I rubbed his road rash a bit hard so he'd remember the danger to himself and the worry he had caused me. To this day,

James has never ridden a motorcycle again, I don't think. He fixed up the wrecked Beamer and sold it. I thanked the Lord repeatedly.

Shortly before the motorcycle accident, James developed an interest in hang gliders. He and several friends decided to build one. They bought the material and put it behind the screen of the Southwood Theater. After the last show of the evening, the boys worked behind the screen. Since James was then manager of the Southwood, they could get away with that. It took several weeks to build this hang glider.

Then one morning, I came into James' room to wake him for church. Usually the first one up, it surprised me James wanted to sleep in. He told me he didn't feel well. He also had the covers pulled up tightly to his chin. Suddenly, I saw his suit all bunched up lying in a comer. As manager of the theater, he had to wear a suit all the time. I picked up the suit, and guess what I saw. The suit was very dirty and full of holes. Before I could ask questions, James told me what had happened.

The boys had finally finished the hang glider. It was time to try it out. Instead of trying it out in a park with relatively soft ground, the boys decided to try it out over the parking area of the Southwood Theater. James decided to go first in case something went wrong. They fastened the hang glider to a rope on the back of the motorcycle. One boy drove the motorcycle pulling James up in the hang glider. Then James turned the hang glider loose.

James had a great time gliding high over the parking lot until the something went wrong the boys hadn't anticipated. The wind changed. Suddenly, James crash landed on the pavement of the parking lot. Again, the hand of the Lord had protected one of my sons. Although all scratched up and bruised, James remained in one piece and not seriously hurt.

James often talked about parachuting, too. This really scared me, and I tried again and again to talk him out of it. Finally, I didn't hear anything about parachuting any more. Forgetting how stubborn James could be, I thought he'd forgotten it. Then, by accident, I found a certificate stating he'd made a successful parachute jump. I nearly fainted! When I talked to him about it, he admitted to one jump, but I believe he had made more jumps because he quickly broke up the conversation.

James also enjoyed scuba diving. I considered scuba diving very dangerous too and always prayed and worried about him. He dove in the San Marcus River near Austin, in the various lakes of the Texas Hill country, and in Cancun, Mexico. At first, he told me he was going snorkeling, which I considered less dangerous, but later he admitted that he was scuba diving.

He said, "But, Mother, I've taken classes, and I'll be going with a group, and I'll be safe."

I felt a little better about it, but I still worried each time he went. I'm surprised that I had time and energy to teach in addition to worrying about my three boys, especially the older ones, Andrew and James.

Marcus always seemed to have much milder interests, and I worried less about him as he entered his teens. Maybe, after worrying about the other two, I was hardened to the dangers. I believe Andrew's driving and James' adventures into flying and diving and cycling gave me more than my share of worry. I am glad we were able to live through those teen years and look back on them, now, with humor and joy.

Chapter 18

Businesses

One day, Louis saw a rental ad in the paper for a movie house in Round Rock. He investigated and rented the movie house. The place appeared in poor condition, but a tasteful coat of paint did wonders. James and Marcus sometimes stayed after midnight to help Louis with the renovating. They enjoyed it and learned to help Louis and work with him. Andrew, already at Southwestern University in Georgetown, didn't have time to help.

When the opening day came, there was such excitement in the air, and everyone had a job. *Mutti* sold the tickets, I sold drinks, candy and popcorn, and James and Marcus helped Louis show the films, a skill they soon learned and, later, took over from their father. Louis worked as the general flunky who oversaw everything. We had a very good time, but found it a lot of work. We opened the theater on Fridays, Saturdays, and Sundays. Louis worked during the week for the State at the Department of Mental Health and Mental Retardation. I taught five classes of foreign languages in Austin high school, and the boys of course attended school. We opened the show at 5:30 p.m. on Fridays. On Saturdays, the first show began at noon. On Sundays, Louis preached in Manor, and I taught Sunday school and gave the children's sermon. After church, we raced to Round Rock to open the movie house at 1:30 p.m. We certainly didn't worry about boredom during this time. We did this for almost two years.

Because we showed only good clean films, such as those produced by Disney, the theater stopped paying for itself. As a result, we had to cancel our lease. A new adventure in our lives had come to an end. In spite of a lot of work, we had enjoyed the movie house very much. The children had stayed close to Louis, *Mutti*, and me. They also learned the value of a dollar. Running the show went well at first, but toward the end, people wanted movies with more sex and violence. Louis wouldn't do that, so we just gave it up.

One day, soon after we closed the movie house, Louis said, "I think we should have another little business on the side." I had just found an ad for a donut machine in a magazine. The ad said you could take the donut machine in the back of a station wagon. I showed the ad to Louis, and he read it and thought the machine sounded like a good idea, so we bought it. It fit into the back of the Scout I drove at the time. We found little festivals, county fairs and some church fund-raisers, at different places in Texas and took the machine to these little gatherings.

Louis decided this business didn't work well out of the back of the Scout, and we needed to sell drinks as well. We bought a little trailer and pulled it behind the Scout. Soon we bought other machines and we sold slush, cold drinks, snow cones, and our donuts. Out of our one donut machine came quite a good business.

Then James, who enjoyed this donut business, met Mr. Thomas who owned the Thomas Carnival. Mr. Thomas belonged to the Masons, and Louis and James knew him. Mr. Thomas said he didn't have anything like our donut and drink trailer with his carnival. He suggested James bring his donut machine and go with the carnival. Each year from early spring to the middle of fall, it made a regular route through the country from Texas to as far north as Canada.

At the end of April 1981, James went off on the adventure with the Thomas Carnival. He took our trailer with the donut machine that made the cutest little donuts. One could smell them a mile away. The donuts smelled so enticing that every one wanted to buy some. Lines formed in front of the trailer, and James couldn't make the donuts and sell the drinks and donuts by himself anymore. He called home and asked me to come.

He said, "SOS, Mother. The people stand in lines and I can't do it all alone. Come help me."

It meant packing a suitcase and going. Just my cup of tea, because I had three months vacation from school during the summer. I needed another adventure.

I took the train and went to Chicago. There, I cried and wanted to go back home. While I changed trains, I went into a restaurant for lunch and people tried to run right over me. They pushed and shoved. Coming from Austin, Texas, I wasn't used to all this rush and hurry. It took too long for me to make up my mind, and the waitress pushed me to hurry. I went to the phone and called Louis and said I wanted to come home because everyone seemed so rude, and I felt fenced in. I missed Louis and wanted to get away from these rude people. He calmed me down and told me I would be alright, and I should go on and join James. So I did.

I arrived at the carnival in Duluth, Minnesota, on June 16, 1981, and James met me at the station. I felt emotionally and physically drained from the trip, but James wined and dined me and then took me to the concession trailer.

He said, "We're going to work, now."

The Carnival opened, and we worked as hard as we could. James made the donuts, and I sold them. We both fixed drinks and snow cones. Every so often we had specials. We offered several donuts and a free drink. We made up many different combinations. Boy, we sold donuts! People stood in long lines to buy them. What an experience! We made very good money, and we had fun!

From Duluth, we went first to Thunder Bay, Canada and then to Medicine Hat, and on to Red Deer, Alberta. We worked sixteen hours a day, and when I got out of the trailer at 2:00 a.m. in the morning, I could hardly move. I couldn't sleep at night being so keyed up from work. I took two extra-strength Tylenol to sleep.

I had never known any carnival people. Most were homeless people or seasonal workers who lived from hand to mouth and day to day. They had no concern for tomorrow and let tomorrow take care of itself. In fact, they didn't worry about anything. They treated me well and liked it when I listened to them. I heard many interesting stories about their experiences and their lives, often about living on the streets. I had never heard such stories and adventures before. The carnival people certainly lived a different life from mine.

When we left Medicine Hat, we had a head start. Our trailer closed up easily, and we wanted to see some of the country. The carnival people had to take down the equipment and followed later. We drove 800 miles on Highway One, the so-called Queen's Highway. Little more than a dirt road, the highway had few stopping places, making this a very lonely trip with few people, houses, or filling stations along the way. We had to take extra gas, water, and food along. James commented he liked to be alone, but found this isolation almost too much.

When we finally arrived in Calgary late at night, we rented a motel room and went to bed. The next morning, we received our place on the carnival grounds. We didn't have much to set up. We just needed to open the trailer and plug in the machines. We had cleaned everything before we left Thunder Bay. Since the rest of the Carnival wouldn't arrive for a few of days, we had some free time. We went to Banff, Lake Louise, and Emerald Lake and saw the beautiful alpine countryside. The carnival people called us the tourists. Every chance we got, we took off and went sight seeing. James and I both love to travel. We went on to Saskatchewan before leaving Canada.

From Canada we went to Billings, Montana where my husband met us. He took a little vacation while James and I worked. I loved having him there. Suddenly, Marcus and his girlfriend surprised us in Billings, so we had most of the family together again, briefly.

Our reunion did not last long, however. Marcus and his girlfriend went on by themselves. James had to drive the Scout and the trailer back home. Louis and I had, however, a leisurely trip back to Austin, Texas. We made many little side trips through Montana and on the rest of the way back. We returned one day before my school started. Through the hard work and the long hours, I lost weight and felt fit as a fiddle.

After this, James acquired some rides and a moonwalk and developed his own little routes in the area around Austin. He had a tea cup ride and a small roller coaster. He went to the Wurstfest in New Braunfels and to Fredericksburg. There, he booked additional rides from other carnivals. For fifteen years, James took his carnival all over central Texas. He, however, didn't take the donut machine with him. He had had enough of making donuts. We sold the machine soon afterwards.

Chapter 19

Karl

About 1982, Father James O'Connor, the Catholic Priest in Kyle, a small town near Austin, asked James to bring the carnival to the church's August festival. Every year the parish had a festival to make money for the Church. They always hired a carnival for the kids and young people.

James didn't know the parish people and didn't want them to handle the carnival money. For this reason he asked me, his mother, to come and help. Although still teaching in Austin High, after school, I drove to Kyle and helped with the money. James didn't have a booth for us to sell the tickets, so he used a card table. I had to sit on the moneybag. I enjoyed selling tickets and helping James very much. Louis came after work and ran one of the children's rides. He loved doing that and enjoyed the children.

That first evening, a young couple came hand-in-hand and wanted to climb Jacob's Ladders. They didn't pay and started to climb. If they had reached the top, they'd have won a Teddy Bear or another stuffed animal. I called them down and told them they had to pay. The young man looked at me and said, "I have to pay?" I answered, "Who do you think you are? If every one has this attitude the church will not get any money." James gave the church 30% of his intake. The couple left. After some time, the young man returned alone. He stood in front of me all dressed in white, Vienna written across his T-shirt. He said: "I know everything about you." "Big deal," I answered. I didn't like his attitude at all. For this reason I was pretty snippy to him. Normally, I treated customers with respect. Later on, he told me he liked the way I acted towards him. For this reason he came back to talk some more to me and get some more snippy answers.

Suddenly, he changed his attitude, introduced himself as Karl, and told me very politely he just had arrived from Vienna a few days ago. He then asked me if we could speak German to each other. I agreed gladly, and we both spoke our mother language. He also asked me if he could help me sell the tickets. I accepted his help gladly.

Later on, the Mexican Band the Church had hired played dance music, and Karl asked me to dance with him. This, of course, thrilled me. What fifty-year-old woman wouldn't enjoy dancing with a young man thirty years her junior? Then Karl, of course, asked my husband if he could dance with me, and Louis gave the green light.

The business had slowed down. I gave the tickets and money to James and went on the dance floor. Karl and I had a great time. Karl had finished seminary in Vienna, and Father Jim had met him there. Not yet a full-fledged priest, Karl had come to Kyle to help Father Jim in the Catholic Church there. Kyle offered him a good place to gain experience. The next day, both Karl and Father Jim told me that Father Jim had reprimanded him for dancing. We did not dance any more during the festival, but Karl continued to help me sell tickets.

The church festival lasted four days, and I looked forward to going back each day. Of course, I tried to look as pretty as possible. I was fifty years old, but no one could tell it. I always looked and acted younger. I am still a very vivacious and fun loving person who enjoys being on the go. The Lord has blessed me so far with a lot of energy, and often I can outdo a younger person.

My husband always said to me, "Stay as you are."

Karl and I had a good time those next three days of the festival selling tickets and conversing in German. After the festival ended, Father Jim asked me to take care of Karl. Father Jim was going to Munich for Oktoberfest and Karl had to take care of the Church by himself during Father Jim's absence, quite a task for a young seminarian. Father Jim hadn't given Karl very clear instructions about what to do, so Karl did as little as possible at the Church. At that time, I taught half days, so every afternoon, Karl drove over from Kyle and picked me up from school. We drove all over Central Texas.

Louis did his part and asked Karl to come for dinner as often as possible. Louis shouldn't have said that because Karl made time to come over every night. I enjoyed it very much, but I believe my husband and my sons got a little tired of Karl's constant visits. James didn't like it at all. Karl liked my quiche, and every time I made it, Louis and my sons all knew Karl wasn't far away. When Karl visited our home the first time, I thought he'd break his neck looking around. He couldn't get over the size of the house. He always marveled how Louis and I got along so well. Many times, he mentioned that he wished his parents lived so happily and peacefully.

Karl seemed like a fresh breeze that blew into my life. I loved Louis very deeply, but I also liked this young man with his playful ways. Of course, Louis with his conservative outlook talked to me and mentioned Karl was gay. My children had said this to me before Louis did. I laughed at them and accused them of being jealous because Karl and I had such a good time. Much later, I found out my husband and the kids had it right.

Later, Karl traveled to Austria and Germany with us when I took my students. He helped a great deal on that trip since he could also speak the language well. While in Austria, Karl's father insisted that he not return to America with us. His father wanted him to stay there and complete his ordination into the priesthood. He stayed.

On our second trip to Germany and Austria, Louis went with the students and me. I wanted to see Karl and called him to arrange a place to meet by accident, but, Louis caught all of my escapades. Louis said, "No, you are not going to see Karl this trip. Later you will see him, but not now." I didn't see Karl that trip nor for several years later. Only after Louis died, did I see Karl again.

Chapter 20

Odds and Ends

In addition to being a mother, housewife, and schoolteacher, I was a minister's wife. That meant I stayed very busy with church work, which I enjoyed very much. Louis served as pastor of the Manor Methodist Church for 12 years. We didn't live in Manor because the church had no parsonage. We lived in our own home in Austin and went every Sunday to Manor, a small congregation. During the week Louis worked for the State. He taught Master's Degree people how to counsel handicapped people. He also held workshops all over Texas. During this time Louis and I both stayed very busy.

While he worked for the state, Louis had a lovely secretary. Not only pretty, but also very nice, she had once been Miss Oregon, a wonderful accomplishment. One day, she came to Louis and asked him to perform her wedding ceremony. She had fallen in love with a young dentist. Her father was a dentist, too, and she had many friends in this practice. Louis, of course, happily agreed. She even invited the children and me. She then left her job because her husband had a job offer in West Texas. They moved there and we didn't hear much from them for a couple of years.

Then, one day a letter addressed to Louis arrived. She had separated from her husband and wanted counseling sessions from Louis. In fact, she wanted him to come to West Texas and give the sessions there. Louis told me very little about it. He kept the whole thing very confidential. I could understand that, but the letters kept coming quite frequently, too frequently to suit me.

One day a letter came from her again, and I decided to open it because my husband was considering going to West Texas to counsel her. I fixed a hot water kettle and steamed the letter open. Instead of finding a professional letter, I found what I considered a love letter. I wasn't surprised. Women have a feeling for such things. That he wanted to make such a long trip just for counseling made me even more suspicious. I trusted my husband but knew he was naïve. I confronted my husband with this counseling affair. He wasn't happy that I had opened the letter and argued there was nothing to it. Yet, he agreed to write her to tell her to find a counselor in West Texas. We never heard from her again. I nipped that situation in the bud.

In 1967, my husband bought a new Dodge station wagon because he wanted to take the family to visit his brother in California. For this reason we needed a bigger car and the Dodge gave us lots of room and comfort. I fell in love with it. I didn't like the brown color very much, but the other advantages outweighed the color. The kids liked the back seat that faced backward, and we liked the additional room the luggage rack provided. After we visited his brother in Orange County, California, we went up to San Francisco, a very beautiful city. With its big city atmosphere, it reminded me a bit of Berlin.

When we returned from our trip, Louis decided to sell the car because he thought it too big for running around town; it used too much gas and cost too much to operate. He put an ad in the newspaper and soon we had some people interested. One couple, especially, wanted it. While Louis and the man discussed the car, his wife and I had a nice conversation. I found out they lived in San Antonio, and they had three children who went to school there. I asked why they came to Austin to buy a car. The lady told me her mother lived in Austin, and while they visited, her husband had read the newspaper and seen the ad about the car. They decided to buy the car and gave my husband a three-hundred-dollar down payment. They promised to mail us the rest of the money the next day. Since my husband lived by the philosophy of give everybody the benefit of the doubt until proven otherwise, he gave them the car keys and let them drive off. Shocked, I told Louis he'd never see the rest of the money.

Folks have often made fun of me for being too talkative. This time it proved very useful. While I talked to the lady, I found out which schools the children attended. I didn't just find out the family's last name, but I learned the children's first names.

We waited three days for the rest of the car payment, but we didn't receive it. I got busy, called the schools in San Antonio, and found out the address of these people. Towards evening, Louis and I drove to San Antonio and found the address of these car thieves. Fortunately, they'd parked the car in front of the apartment house. Luckily, too, Louis had kept a key to the car. He opened the hood and took the distributor cap out. This way the car couldn't start. Then we went into the apartment house, up the stairs, and rang the doorbell. The lady of the house opened the door with her husband right behind her. We surprised them so they couldn't greet us. Louis showed them the distributor cap, and told them he wouldn't refund them the down payment, and we were there to pick up the car. They didn't say a word, and we knew they had intended to keep the car and not pay for it. We drove my wonderful car home. After this experience, we decided to keep it. I drove it for several years and enjoyed it very much.

On Tuesday, May 13, 1986 I had a great shock which I could hardly believe: my husband, Louis Sterling, died. He died from a massive heart attack. He had high blood pressure, and he'd had a slight heart attack two years before. At that time he had retired from his state job, and the doctors gave him a clean bill of health. On Friday, the week before, he substituted in an English class at Austin High. Some of my students came by my classroom to tell

214

me he'd substituted in their class and did an excellent job. On the next day, Wednesday, when the students and faculty of Austin High heard he had passed away, they were shocked.

In the funeral home, we made the visitation a celebration. We placed a tape recorder, a boom box, under the casket and played circus music. Louis loved circus music. Louis always said he wanted a happy funeral because he'd joined the Lord. The boys and I wanted to please him even in death. When people came for the viewing in the funeral home, the music made it an uplifting and happy occasion.

One man, a stranger, came to me and said, "Mrs. Sterling, if this man does not get to heaven, none of us has a chance."

The funeral home director, also a mason, said, "Gisela, I didn't know that Louis' death would do this to you."

I asked him what he meant. He said, "The circus music is not appropriate. What will people think?"

I said, "I don't care, but we're playing the circus music. Who is paying for the funeral? If you don't let me play this music, then you pay for the funeral." With me there, we played the circus music. After I left, I understand he played the sad stuff.

Louis' death seemed unreal to me. We buried him on May 15, 1986 at Forrest Oak Cemetery. Jack Hickcock, pastor of First United Methodist Church in Austin, preached the funeral in his church. The Masonic Lodge of the Ben Hur Temple held the graveside service.

I couldn't believe Louis had gone. I felt terribly alone. We had been married thirty-five years and had enjoyed a good marriage. We had also suffered and struggled together. Yet, we had each other. We had found a great deal of joy in our accomplishments with the churches and in raising three boys. Now, I felt absolutely lost. Again, I sat behind the old black fence and saw no way of breaking free. Louis, with his optimism and love and joy of God, could always lift my spirits. Now, I had no one to lean on and lift me free.

Chapter 21

Retirement, Vienna, and Karl Again

I couldn't stay in my surroundings without Louis. I was alone. I had the children, but they had their own lives and couldn't be with me very much. Marcus and his wife lived in Houston, and James lived in a mobile home on a five-acre lot in Creedmore about fifteen miles south of Austin. Andrew and his wife lived in Austin, but both worked and they had three children that kept them very busy. As a widow, I found it awkward to be with married friends. I didn't feel I had a friend to stand by me. Because Louis had the church and his other jobs, and he had wanted to be with the family whenever possible, we hadn't developed many close friendships. As a pastor, Louis didn't want to develop close friendships with members of his churches because he didn't want anyone to feel neglected. For these reasons, I felt I had no one to support me.

I'd never thought about retiring early from teaching, but after Louis' death, I considered it. When I found I'd make more in retirement than I made teaching, I decided to leave the classroom at the end of the school year on June 4, 1986.

After I had suffered alone during the summer, I couldn't stand living in our big house any more. I saw Louis everywhere. I had beautiful memories of him, but they hurt so very much. I thought of selling the house and going to Europe. Here in Austin, I held on to Louis and felt I still lived with him. I suffered constantly with memories everywhere. One day, I realized I hadn't told Karl about Louis' death, and so I called him in Vienna. When he suggested I come there for a while and learn to live with my loss, I thought it a good idea. When I called Karl a second time, he told me he couldn't spend as much time with me as he had in America, because he was no longer studying for the priesthood, but had a job teaching high school.

Before I put my thoughts into action, I spoke to the Lord. He was and is my friend and I trust Him. I prayed that he should put boulders in my way if this wasn't the right thing to do. I didn't want to make the wrong choice. With the Lord's help, I wanted to go to Vienna.

Moving to Europe meant I had to sell my house before I left. Besides, the 3,300 square feet proved way too big for me alone. I prayed to the Lord and asked for his guidance and put the house up for sale.

In the meantime, after the school year had started in the fall, Bob Enos, the new principal at Austin High, asked me to come back to teach German and French to finish out that year. They'd hired several different teachers who left after very short times. I told him I'd teach until the beginning of March because I'd decided to go to Vienna. Thus, I went back in the classroom during the winter.

By February, even though seven other people in the neighborhood had their houses up for sale, only I sold my house. I took it as a sign from the Lord he wanted me to leave for Vienna. I gave Mr. Enos my notice, and I bought my airline tickets for Austria. I gave most of the furniture to Andrew and Debbie, some to James, and sold the rest. This cleared the house, and I moved in with James until I left for Europe.

I left Austin on March 5, 1987. Karl couldn't meet me at the

217

airport because he had a class. His school taught skiing to their students, and he had to go skiing with them. I took Marcus and Wolfi, Louis' dog, with me. The ticket for the dog cost almost as much as the ticket for me. I didn't want to fly by myself with Wolfi, so I asked Marcus to go with me to help with the dog, and I paid for his ticket. We landed in Vienna on ice and snow. Coming from Texas, I wore summer clothes, skirt and blouse and light jacket, and open-toed, high-heeled sandals. I didn't even possess an overcoat. It was cold, and I was freezing!

After we arrived at Schwechart, the airport in Vienna, we waited for the baggage handlers to unload Wolfi, our beautiful German shepherd. All of a sudden, I heard my name called, asking me to come to the information desk. While Marcus waited for the dog, I went to the information desk.

There, Karl stood with a huge bouquet of flowers! He came to me and gave me a hug. Then he said, 'I'm happy to see you, and I'm very glad you're in Vienna."

I was glad too. My manner of dress shocked Karl. He thought I should've had better sense.

It surprised me to see him at the airport because I had thought he had to go on a ski trip with his school children. Most of the students, however, had fallen ill with the flu, and the school had canceled the trip. For this reason, Karl had time to meet us. Marcus joined us with the dog and the suitcases, and Karl drove us to Pension Felicitas, a small hotel in Vienna.

After we got settled, Karl took us, Marcus, Wolfi, and me, to the 13th District in order to view an apartment he had selected for me. Vienna's 13th District, the home of the wealthy, had parks, beautiful apartments, and large homes. This apartment, however, lay at the edge of the district, right by the railroad track. The Heart Association, the previous renter, had moved out and left it in bad condition, so it needed a lot of repair and renovation. The apartment, with plenty of room for me, had a large entrance room, a combination living and dining room, a bathroom, a separate toilet, a kitchen, and one bedroom.

The landlord agreed to split the cost for the repair work for the apartment with me. He paid for the more expensive things, and I paid for the less expensive items. The landlord paid for the floor work, a new hot water heater, and a new refrigerator. The walls, ceilings, and trim needed new paint. I selected the paint, the wallpaper, and the carpet, and paid for those items.

I chose a light gray wall-to-wall carpet for the whole apartment, more American in style than the usual Viennese area rugs. I had the walls in the living and dining rooms painted light pink and hung light pink curtains with floral designs. In the bedroom, I had walls of light gray with white voile curtains with light gray designs. The kitchen had white built-in cabinets. The entrance hall I had painted white, while the bathroom I had painted light yellow and I hung green curtains. They fitted very beautifully. Karl selected some of the curtains and did a good job. He had very good taste.

Then, I bought furniture from *Ikea*. In the bedroom, I had a big bed with a large headboard in blues and pinks and a large gray armoire. I like a big bed. In the dining area, I had a big white, square table with white chairs and pink seats that matched the wallpaper. I loved that table, too. The living room had two couches with flowers in gray and pink tones. Both couches converted to beds so one could sleep on them. You could open them up and put the bedding underneath. I also had a long, low white bookshelf and a television.

After I renovated and furnished the apartment, it looked beautiful. All my friends told me when they came to visit they felt happy and uplifted. They also liked my taste: the colors and furniture. Everything looked very feminine, very light, and very bright. I wanted it that way. My home in Texas, while beautifully furnished, had had a very masculine touch, because I lived together with four men, my husband and three sons. I wanted it different in Vienna.

219

While I had the work done, Marcus and I stayed in the two rooms we had rented at the Pension. We went into the mountains and saw beautiful views where we could see the castles in Vienna. Later, we went to the city's parks; in one we saw the statue of Johann Strauss. We also went to the cemetery to see the huge monuments of all the famous composers. We enjoyed the coffeehouses and ate delicious tarts and drank good wine. We went on the cog train to the top of the *Schneeberg* or Snow Mountain. Then, after two weeks, Marcus had to leave. We had a very sad good-bye because Marcus hated to leave me there alone.

I had made up my mind to stay in Europe and learn to live without Louis. Each summer I usually spent some time back in Austin with my children. I had a good friend in Karl. Although a schoolteacher with a busy schedule, he always made time when I needed him or when I wanted to go somewhere. I could depend on him. By making time for me, Karl gave me security. At first, I didn't know anyone else in Vienna and found a sense of safety in having such a close friend.

During long weekends or vacation time, Karl had another job as a tour guide. I always went with his tour groups. We went to Jordan, Rome, Morocco, and Ibizza. In Morocco we went to a fantastic restaurant and ate a seven-course dinner for hardly anything. I felt like we had been transported into a thousand and one nights. We found it so romantic! I often mentioned these trips to friends ahead of time, and we all went together with Karl. Since he knew his way around, I experienced many good restaurants, wonderful plays, great operas, and musicals.

In February 1988, I decided to attend the Vienna Opera Ball, and asked Karl to go with me. Since he had never gone and could hardly afford it on his teacher's salary, he jumped at the opportunity. I wanted to attend the ball with a good-looking man who knew his way around Austrian society. I offered to pay for everything, including his formal tails. Of course, when I did something, I wanted to do it first class. First, we had an excellent dinner in the very elegant Schwarzenberg Restaurant. We drank Khir Royal, a heavenly red Champaign and after dinner we had pictures taken. We left the Restaurant in a limousine that took us to the opera where the ball took place. When I heard the beautiful music and saw the well-dressed couples dancing, I said, "This is Vienna." I wanted to experience this event, and thankfully, I could. The ball cost me $3,000, but I don't regret a minute or a cent of it. It was a highlight of my life in Vienna! Karl and I danced till four o'clock in the morning. We had a wonderful time and just knew we'd never forget this ball as long as we lived.

On little weekend trips, which Karl and I made alone, he showed me lovely sights and gigantic vistas. We went into the mountains, and he took me on the cable car rides. We saw the Viennese forests. He showed me most of the nine states in Austria, and made them interesting, exciting, and informative trips.

On the organized trips, I met many people who today remain good friends. Traude and I met on a trip to Morocco. We both liked each other from the beginning and developed a close friendship. She invited me to her wedding and to her graduation when she received her Doctorate. After her wedding, she and her new husband moved to Hamburg, Germany. She had grown up in Vienna, Austria. She promised to stay in touch and never forget me. I thought it a nice promise, but I didn't believe it. I've always found distances broke up friendships, but not this one. She has kept her promise all these years. Every so often, she came back to Vienna to teach at the University. She always called, and we'd go to a coffee house or a *Heurigen*, a wine restaurant. She always tried to get me to visit her in Hamburg, and it finally happened in 2000. Before that, she and her husband had visited me here in Austin for a few days.

For three years, I traveled with Karl and enjoyed it. However, our weeklong trip to Ibizza changed our friendship. I found Ibizza a very interesting spot, but for the first time, I really felt used. Although Ibizza activities centered on the young, I enjoyed myself at first. Most days after breakfast, Karl and I went swimming, then lay in the sun a while. After an hour, he'd go to the nude beach. He always invited me to go too, but, of course, I declined.

We usually had lunch together, after which I went to my room and took a nap. In the evening, he picked me up for dinner. We always went to the finest restaurants. After dinner, we sometimes went dancing, and sometimes we went for a walk. Around 10:30 he usually took me to the hotel and left for a rendezvous with a new male friend he had met there. Sometimes, he wanted to leave at 9:00. That began to irritate me. I paid for the rental of the car. I paid for the room, the meals, and the flight. I felt he should spend the evenings with me when I wanted him to. By the end of the trip, we didn't speak to each other.

It didn't anger me that he wanted to go out with his male friend, but it angered me when he said, "People your age should be in bed by 9:00 p.m."

We had had misunderstandings in the past, but we had remained friends. After this trip we didn't speak for months.

Much later, we spent a week in Berlin together. He told me that he had the most wonderful time there with me. I had arranged the trip, and filled it with sightseeing, theater, concert, opera, operetta, and dance performances. Every night we went somewhere else. In Berlin, he didn't seem to have any male friends so he always spent the evenings with me. Karl had never been in Berlin, and through me, he saw a lot.

One day I met Karl's father, Ottokar Svoboda. Later, Ottokar told me that from the first day he met me, he liked me. I knew he had a wife, but I also knew the marriage had been on the rocks for thirty years. Karl had told me, unfortunately, his father and his mother didn't love each other any more, and even before his father met me, he had asked for a divorce. His father told me the same thing. Ottokar and I got to know each other better and seemed to enjoy each other more and more. We had so many things in common. We developed a wonderful relationship. He wanted to share the rest of his life with me, and that made me very happy. I didn't have to worry that I broke up his marriage. He had asked his wife for a divorce and, in fact, he asked her again in my presence, but she refused to give it to him. They were both Roman Catholic, but I believe she refused to divorce him for monetary, not religious reasons. He paid her 5,000 shillings or about 500 dollars a month, voluntarily. He wanted her to live comfortably because she didn't get very much pension. He didn't have to do this, but being a considerate person, he did.

I had enjoyed Karl's company for almost four years, but the thirty-year age difference between us began to bother me. I felt I had to look my best, dress very fashionably, and wear the newest clothes for Karl. He always made a point of complimenting me on my clothes. He always dressed in the latest fashion and I liked that about him. Yet, I grew tired of keeping up this costly, fashionable appearance. Finally, I told Karl we had to part company. Also, I found myself spending more time with Ottokar. Yet, when Karl called and asked me to go somewhere, I accepted. I wanted to break up the friendship, but he wouldn't hear of it. I started feeling fenced in by our relationship and felt I didn't have the strength to escape.

Ottokar helped me make my decision. He asked me to go to Greece with him. I had planned another trip with Karl and his tour group to Rome. I wanted to see Rome, so I went. After I returned, Ottokar came to my apartment. Angered I'd gone to Rome with Karl, he told me he'd gone to Greece with his mistress and had a wonderful trip. It made me angry that Ottokar had gone with his mistress, whom I knew, and I told him so. He flatly stated he hadn't wanted to go alone and since I didn't go with him, he took someone else. He also told me if we went out together, I had to stop going with his son, Karl. I had to make a decision.

I found it difficult to dissolve my friendship with Karl.

Ottokar said, later, "Karl and you have a connection of your souls. Yours is a Platonic love."

As a result, I felt I could not break up with Karl by myself. Our difference in age bothered me, and I liked Ottokar and wanted to go places with him. I had good reason to break up with Karl, but the problem seemed too great for me to solve alone. I had taken an active role in the Methodist Church in Vienna, so I shared my problem with my friends, the pastor and his wife. I told them when Karl asked me to go someplace with him, I didn't seem to have the strength to say "No!" to him. At the Church's altar, they and two others from the congregation put their hands on my head and prayed for me to get the strength to break off with Karl.

It worked. I told Karl our friendship had ended. I told him not to call me any more and to find another friend. Now, free from the fence I had created with Karl, I could spend time with Ottokar.

Chapter 22

Ottokar

Ottokar Svoboda knew I enjoyed surprises and traveling. His wife didn't like either. In fact, she didn't like to do anything with Ottokar. After Ottokar and I started going out together, he and his wife would come by on Sundays to my Methodist church after their Catholic service. They always wanted me to go with them on Sunday afternoon drives.

One Friday, she called me and asked, "Gisela, where are we going this Sunday?"

Ottokar and his wife didn't get along, and she wanted me with them so they wouldn't fight.

I enjoyed going with Ottokar. So many times Ottokar surprised me with tickets for the opera in Salzburg or Verona! We always stayed in four or five star hotels and ate in the best restaurants. In Verona, they performed the opera in open-air arenas under a star covered sky. The music, the stars, and the warmth of the summer night made it very romantic. I loved it. Ottokar took me all over Europe.

He never said, "Let's go to Italy or Spain."

He just suddenly arrived at the door and said, "I have tickets. Pack the suitcase," for wherever he thought I might like to go. He knew I liked these surprises. Two days later off we went to Grand Canaria or Southern Spain or Italy.

When we returned from our trips, he always brought things back for his wife, but she gave them away. When he finally realized she didn't appreciate his gifts, he stopped bringing remembrances back to her.

Ottokar and I made one trip to Madeira, the garden island of Portugal. We landed in Lisbon to change pilots. To land on Madeira we needed a special pilot because of the short landing strip surrounded by water on one side and mountains on the other. When a plane lands, it has to stop quickly, and when it leaves, it must climb quickly. I almost didn't go to Madeira because of this dangerous airport. We knew a plane had crashed into the ocean a few days before our trip.

Because he wanted to cure me of my fear, Ottokar always wanted us to do things connected with danger. He felt that if we did these things, I'd overcome my fear. He did a good job of it. I'm less afraid of things now. He always said, "If you have faith in God, you are never afraid." Ottokar never feared anything, not even death. He partially helped me escape the big old black fence of fear.

Madeira had the most beautiful flowers I ever saw. No wonder that Sisi, the Empress of Austria and Queen of Hungary, had spent a lot of time there. Her castle stood as a major tourist attraction, but we didn't know how to find it. Since all of Sisi's castles in Austria had pink exteriors and had a chapel, we looked till we found a building that looked right. I went in to see if it had a chapel, and found it did. Later, we found a guide who told us we'd found Sisi's castle. I love Sisi, my favorite of all the queens in Europe. I think I saw all of her castles in Europe while I lived there.

We also rode the famous chair rides down the mountain in Madeira. Before our ride, the operators told us the legend that the queen of Emperor Karl became very ill and needed to get to the hospital at the bottom of the mountain. To do this, her attendants placed her in a chair with runners and slid her down. Since then this sport has become a very famous attraction. We found it very exciting as you almost run into the walls and houses on either side of the road. One man pushes the chair down the mountain and another guides it from the front. The first time frightened me, but the second time I really enjoyed it. Ottokar had wanted to fly to Madeira especially for the chair rides, but we enjoyed the flowers and castles as well.

We also had a great time in Malaga, Spain, a quaint town with old buildings. Everybody went through the town in horse drawn coaches. I had never ridden in a horse drawn coach, so this represented a new and exciting experience for me.

One day, Ottokar appeared with tickets for a cruise. First we flew to Venice. Then, we cruised through the Mediterranean to the Greek island Corfu. There we stayed a week, and then, we went island hopping. We went to Crete, Rhodes, and Santorini as well as several other of the Greek islands. Simply beautiful! The most wonderful thing was that we loved each other and enjoyed each other very much. He never said a word that could hurt me.

We often traveled, and I loved it. When Ottokar said, "Pack the suitcase," I did. The Lord blessed me during this time with a fairy tale life. Ottokar did everything he could for me. In one word, he spoiled me. We lived together, very harmoniously, for 10 years.

I found Ottokar a fantastic man. He had married the first time in 1945. He told me later that during the wedding reception, he thought an angel touched him. A woman dressed like a gypsy suddenly appeared, and no one had seen her come. She asked to see Ottokar's palm and also his wife's. She wanted to read their fortunes. Ottokar didn't want to have this done as he didn't believe in fortune telling. He told his friends to feed her and give her something to drink and send her off. She refused food and drink, and she didn't go either. Finally, through the urging of the guests, Ottokar and his wife gave in.

For Ottokar, the Gypsy woman predicted a long trip, very far away. Ottokar asked, "Overseas?"

She shook her head, and said, "That will be later, much later." She told him of hardships he'd face and how he'd leave his home without saying good-bye to any of his family. She said he'd leave his father in anger and never see him again, predicting his death and burial four days before Ottokar returned.

Then she turned to his wife and told her future. The Gypsy woman predicted a good first year of marriage, but then she would divorce Ottokar, marry again and divorce a second time. Then the Gypsy grew angry and foretold of a third marriage. They never knew the reason for the Gypsy woman's anger. Of course, her anger might have stemmed from the fact Ottokar's wife later took her own life. After that, however, the angel in Gypsy clothes disappeared, and no one saw her go.

Her predictions all came true. The Russians took Ottokar to Siberia where he faced death, went through very hard times, and suffered greatly. He never saw his father again, returning, after ten years in a Russian prison, just four days after his father's funeral.

This happened because he tried to right a wrong done by Russian soldiers. After World War II, the Russian Army continued to occupy Austria. Because he spoke Russian well, the Austrian government had put Ottokar in the Austrian State Department in the Department of Foreign Affairs to deal with the Russian Military. He didn't like the job because he didn't like dealing with the Russians.

According to Ottokar, one day in 1946, he received a letter from a woman who told him three Russian soldiers had raped her. When he visited her in the hospital, she told him that some Austrians had tried to help her, but since the Russians had machine guns, the Austrians couldn't do anything. She said these witnesses had courage enough, however, to testify. After visiting the lady in the hospital and talking to the 32 witnesses, Ottokar took their statements. He then took the whole testimony to the Russian

228

authorities. After the Russian officers who dealt with Austrian relations read everything, they threw the papers in his face and said, "These were no Russians. These were Nazis in Russian Uniform." When the lady heard that, she said, "They were Russians. They spoke Russian, and they stank like Russians."

Ottokar's Austrian superiors told him, "Just write rapist unknown." They also told him he might otherwise have to dig potatoes in Siberia, but Ottokar stood firm. He'd have done the same thing had the rapists been Austrian. He wanted justice done.

One day, as he walked by the Parliament building in Vienna on his way to lunch, a black Limousine stopped by him. Being summer, Ottokar wore *lederhosen*, (leather shorts), with an Austrian jacket and tie. Suddenly, hands came out of the car, grabbed him, and pulled him into the limo. In the car, he recognized Russian officers.

At first, they took him to Russian headquarters in Vienna and questioned him day and night under a bright light. They asked him the same questions over and over again. This went on for days. He hated the bright light both day and night that constantly disturbed him and kept him awake The Russians wanted him to identify the rapists as Austrians in Russian uniform. After they saw they couldn't get him to cooperate, they flew him to Moscow, bound hand and foot. In Moscow they took him to the Kremlin and questioned him again the same way. Since he didn't cooperate, they sent him to Siberia by train. Still in his *lederhosen*, this made for a very long and cold trip. Later they gave him a flimsy prison uniform that provided no better protection against the Siberian cold. All this took place just one year after his marriage. He remembered the Gypsy's prediction of a long trip with hardships.

Through this all, he didn't care if they killed him or not. He almost couldn't bear the torture with the light and the cold and the lack of sleep. Ottokar, a very good Christian with a deep faith in God, relied on his faith for support through the many years of suffering.

He had one thing in his favor; he could speak and understand the Russian language. He could communicate with the guards and the political officers, the people to really fear. Even so, he sometimes gave them a piece of his mind. Surprisingly, one political officer didn't punish him for speaking up, for he respected Ottokar and only pretended to treat him roughly.

Ottokar couldn't stand a *spitzel*, an Austrian prisoner who went to the Russian officers and told things he heard from his fellow Austrians. The *spitzel* always came back grinning with extra bread and sugar.

When he saw this, Ottokar knew right away what had happened and he told the guy, "If you keep this up I will work you over one day."

A week or so passed, and the stool pigeon went again and came back with extra provisions. Because Ottokar knew he had talked and given information, he beat the guy to a pulp. After about an hour, this same political officer arrived, and Ottokar had to go to the office. He knew he might get solitary confinement, a horrible punishment. The political officer asked him why he had beaten this young man. Ottokar answered him by asking the officer to put himself in the prisoners' situation. Would he have liked a stool pigeon?

The officer understood and said to Ottokar, "We like the treason, but hate the traitor." Then he dismissed Ottokar, surprisingly, without punishment. Knowing the Russian language and dealing frankly with a political officer had helped him a great deal.

One officer always yelled at Ottokar and said, "Svoboda you can an make atomic bomb out of a can. You'll never be a communist!" Then one day he saw him and suddenly motioned Ottokar to come over to him and whispered, "Svoboda, my child died. Go to the next shack. There is a coffin there. Paint a cross on the inside of the lid."

This really surprised Ottokar. He asked what he should do if someone caught him doing this forbidden act.

The officer replied, "Just tell them they do it this way in your country."

The officer knew he could trust Ottokar not to say anything, otherwise the officer could've ended up in prison too.

His knowledge of Russian didn't always keep Ottokar out of trouble, however. For part of their imprisonment, the prisoners had to work in a rock quarry underground. They didn't have gloves or proper clothes and often cut their hands on the rocks. Finally, Ottokar refused to work. After he refused to work on the rocks for several days they placed him in confinement.

They put him alone in a small room with a concrete floor and walls. The room had no bed, no cot, not even a mat to sleep on. He had no coat or jacket, but only a light blanket and a prison uniform like a nightgown that came only to his knees. He had no socks or shoes to wear.

He used a hole in the middle of the floor for his waste. To keep from freezing to death Ottokar walked around and around the room in circles. He said this was the worst part of his ten years in Siberia.

It surprised Ottokar when they put another man in with him. At first, it made him happy because he had someone to talk to. Then, however, Ottokar asked the guy why they had put him in confinement. The guy said he enjoyed using women, but he also enjoyed cutting their throats and watching them bleed to death. They had put the guy in confinement for killing his wife in this manner after sex. Ottokar couldn't sleep after that, fearing the guy might attempt to sodomize him or cut his throat. Ottokar stayed in confinement for a week and rejoiced when they freed him. Despite the punishment, Ottokar didn't have to return to the quarries.

A lot of prisoners couldn't take the cold, the brutal treatment, and the starvation, and they died. Ottokar, young and with a will to live, didn't want to give the Russians the satisfaction of giving up, so he found things for the men in his barracks to do. One time,

Ottokar got hold of a Russian Bible and translated verses into German and distributed them to his German roommates. Some of the German prisoners didn't believe God was there in the camp or He wouldn't let such bad things happen, but Ottokar believed in God. He translated the verses to give everybody hope, and remind the prisoners that no matter how bad things got, the Lord stood by them.

One time, Ottokar found out women prisoners lived on the first floor beneath them. Through the water pipes he made contact with them, and then, all the men wrote notes to the women. When the political officers where not around they sent the letters on a line through the windows down to the women prisoners. Pretty soon every one had a lady to whom to write. This gave every one a little happiness and encouragement.

Eventually, in 1956, the Russians left Austria as a result of a peace agreement. The peace agreement called for the Austrians in Siberia to go home. The prisoners received clothes and provisions.

Before they left, the political officers and the guards grew friendly and treated them with great respect. Apparently, the guards feared the former prisoners might avenge the atrocities they had made the prisoners suffer. The former prisoners made the long trip from Siberia to Moscow, where they transferred to another train for Austria. Ottokar came back weak and sick, as did all the prisoners. He remembered his experiences well, but seldom spoke of them. He told me about his prison sufferings, but he never talked about them in public and generally didn't share them with others.

Ottokar hated the Russian military, but he loved the Russian language and their arts. Whenever Russian performers came to Vienna, Ottokar always went and often talked with the artists in Russian after the shows. Ottokar also liked to read Russian literature. He felt Pushkin, the Russian, matched the great German author, Goethe. He hated the cruelty of the Russian Army, but loved and used the language the rest of his life.

When Ottokar came home, he received the sad news his father had died four days before. Another revelation from the Gypsy angel had come true. Indeed, he had parted with his father in a misunderstanding as the angel had prophesied.

A few days later he wrote to his wife, then living in Berlin with her third husband. She had divorced Ottokar after three months when she couldn't contact him and didn't know his whereabouts. She married a second time, but finding this husband a drunkard, she divorced him. Later, she married a third time and had a very good marriage. In his letter, Ottokar told her he still loved her, forgave her everything, and wanted her back. She didn't know what to do. She opened the gas jets in her apartment and took her own life with Ottokar's letter in her hand. Her husband found her that way and wrote Ottokar about her death. She was thirty-eight years old and too young to die. Ottokar was very sad that he had to live through this tragedy too. The War caused many terrible and sad incidents.

A year later, Ottokar needed his suit mended. He went to a shop where the shopkeeper Johanna did reweaving in an artistic way. After Ottokar picked his suit up, they got into a conversation. They liked each other and met frequently. Soon, they began dating. After a year of courting, Ottokar and Johanna decided to marry. Married before, Johanna had a daughter by her former husband. Ottokar accepted the child, too. Ottokar looked for a good home where peace and tranquility dominated, and Johanna looked for financial security. They truly had a marriage of convenience.

Before they married, she got pregnant, and seven months after the wedding, she had Karl. After Karl's birth, she never had anything to do with Ottokar physically. I never saw them hug or kiss or even touch each other while I knew them. This was very bad for the marriage, and the rift and misunderstanding between them grew ever larger.

Later as a result of his difficulties with his wife, Ottokar met a widow fourteen years his senior with whom he got along well.

After a short time he took her as his mistress. She gave him what he needed, and he gave her a good life. They spent 30 years as lovers and companions.

When Ottokar and I began going out together, his mistress must have been 84 or 85. He still went out with her occasionally. He didn't want to just drop her coldly after thirty years, and I admired his loyalty. He continued to help her out from time to time but didn't tell me about it. It disturbed me he kept this from me. I had heard from friends about his relationship with her. I confronted Ottokar, but he didn't want to discuss it.

He said, "I don't want to talk about it. Let's let it rest."

I didn't let it rest and preached him several sermons about it. It didn't help. He didn't drop her at that time.

About the same time in 1990, my son James planned to marry on December 15th. I asked Ottokar to travel to America with me, and he decided to come along. He wanted to know about life in America and see if he could live here. It made me happy that he accompanied me, especially since I didn't like to travel alone to the States. Ottokar told his mistress he was going to America on business. I found out about it and wrote her a letter telling her the truth. That ended Ottokar's relationship with his mistress.

I behaved poorly, but I didn't care. Being close to Christmas I wrote the letter without signing it and gave it to a friend. I told my friend to send it to the mistress at Christmas. My friend mailed it so Ottokar's mistress received it as a Christmas present. I didn't care because he needed to end one affair or the other, either with her or with me.

Later, when we returned from the U.S., Ottokar went to see her, and she showed him the letter and refused to seem him again.

When he asked me about it I said, "How could I have sent it, I was in America."

Later, I told him the truth. He said, "You are not very Christian."

I told him, "You are not either with your lying."

Ottokar didn't say anything more, but neither did he see his mistress again.

When we arrived in Austin the children greeted me with joy. I loved seeing and being with them. Ottokar came as no surprise to them since they knew I had started dating Karl's father. At that time Ottokar and I didn't live together. Marcus and James liked Ottokar from the beginning and accepted him. Andrew, however, treated Ottokar very coolly and really never accepted him. He felt I shouldn't have had another man in my life after his father. Andrew also had difficulty with the fact Ottokar wasn't American and couldn't speak English well. The latter should not have caused a problem because all my three spoke fluent German. James and Marcus spoke German with Ottokar right away and made him feel comfortable, but Andrew remained withdrawn. Unfortunately, Andrew and Debbie had invited us to stay with them the four weeks we planned to be in the U.S. In reality, the invitation was nice, but because of Andrew's feelings, it proved uncomfortable, especially for Ottokar.

I wanted Ottokar to see more of America than just Austin, and we decided to fly to Florida. We went to Disney World and to the film studios. Ottokar and I enjoyed it very much. We also went to San Antonio, to Houston, and to Dallas. No matter what we did, we enjoyed just being together. Louis and I had the same type of relationship. Fortunately, I have had two good husbands with whom I could enjoy life.

My two youngest grandchildren Madison and Michaela enjoyed playing with Ottokar. He had great patience with them. We had a German board game, *Mensch ärgere dich nicht*, that they learned to play with Ottokar, and they had a lot of fun with it and learned to count in German. Our month in the U.S. went by very fast, and although I loved visiting with my children and their families, I wanted to go back to Vienna. My children didn't like to see me go, but I enjoyed Vienna, and Ottokar wanted to go home. With Ottokar there, I considered Vienna home too.

Back in Austria, Ottokar suddenly contacted the flu and became very ill. Several times he asked for me, and I went to his home. The last time, his wife practically begged me to take him home with me and to take care of him. She didn't want to do it. So I took Ottokar home with me. He had a very high fever, and I put him in my bed. I gave him hot lemonade and aspirin. I slept on a day bed in the other room. I woke up quite frequently during the night and went to his bed.

He perspired so terribly, soaking all the bedding and his pajamas. I had to change everything several times during the first night. In the morning, he felt much better, but I kept him in bed for a week. Once he'd recovered, he went to his apartment and got all his clothes. We had both made up our minds to live together, and it worked very well. We loved each other very much, and knew we would eventually get married. From the religious standpoint, it bothered me that I lived with a married man, even though I had nothing to do with the break up of his marriage. I went to my pastor at the Methodist church in Vienna and talked to him about it. He told me a marriage certificate didn't mean a thing if two people live unhappily together.

He said, "You are giving him a home and the love he needs."

I worried the Lord would be angry with me, but the pastor said, "The Lord understands, and He loves you."

I still worried so I went to a Catholic Priest. He knew Ottokar and knew Ottokar's wife, and he told me he rejoiced that Ottokar had finally taken the step to move away from his wife. He felt the same as the Methodist minister, and gave us the green light to live together. We lived together seven years and had gone together for three years before that. Ottokar told his friends those were the happiest years of his life.

Unfortunately, Ottokar had contacted Hepatitis C in the Russian prison camp. For many years the disease lay dormant, but then suddenly in 1997, it broke out again. I gave up my apartment in Vienna and we came back to America because he wanted to die here so he could stay with me even in death. In the cemetery we have three plots. My first husband, Louis, is buried in the left-hand plot. Ottokar wanted to be buried in the right-hand plot and have me buried in the middle.

My eldest son said, then, facetiously, they'd write on the gravestone, "Here lies our mother with her two lovers."

But Ottokar's wishes did not come to pass. Because Ottokar's medical insurance refused to pay here in the U.S., we had to go back to Vienna. There, I watched him slowly die for almost two years, for me a sad and hard endurance test. I took care of him in our apartment, and when he had to go to the hospital, I visited him twice a day and stayed with him when allowed. When he saw me coming into the hospital room he cried out, "Here comes my sunshine!"

After we got back to Austria, Ottokar's wife finally gave him a divorce. Ottokar agreed to give his wife a large portion of the sale of the apartment after he died. She also knew he hadn't long to live. Now, we could get married. We had wanted to do this for a long time. Since he was Catholic and the church didn't allow a church wedding, we stood before a Justice of the Peace or *Burgermeister* as it's called in Austria. We had several friends with us and all of us celebrated at a very nice restaurant after the ceremony. We didn't have a long marriage because his illness progressed so fast, but we had a happy one.

On February 8, 1999 Ottokar died. I had the funeral and burial in Vienna, his hometown. I sold the apartment and then came back to America. I hated to leave him there alone in the cemetery, but the U.S. is my home. I have three children and five grandchildren here, and I needed to come home to Texas.

Chapter 23

Back to Texas

On March 1, 1999, I moved into an apartment in Austin. During that summer, I kept my grandchildren. Marcus had divorced, and I kept his two girls, Madison and Michaela. From eight in the morning until about nine-thirty they watched children's programs on TV. At ten o'clock we had snack time. At ten-thirty, we'd go to the swimming pool at the city park at Walnut Creek in North Austin where the girls took swimming lessons. After lunch, they took a nap for a couple of hours, and I relaxed. I got the computer ready for stories and found coloring books and educational materials for them to do. At five-thirty or six, their mother came to pick them up. For two months, I kept the girls all day long five days a week and enjoyed it very much. In the fall, Madison went to kindergarten, and Michaela went to Debbie's preschool. Andrew's wife, Debbie, ran a very successful childcare business. The girls called it Debbie care. I now had my days free.

That fall of 1999, I felt very much alone. I phoned Max Seiler, Ottokar's cousin, and Guenter Beyer, his friend, in Berlin and invited them to come see me in Texas. Ottokar and I had visited them in Berlin while I lived in Austria. They agreed to come that September.

I asked a good friend, Warner Dahlberg, to help me entertain Max and Guenter during their visit. We had known each other a long time because we taught at Austin High School together. Back then, we had a very superficial acquaintance. As busy teachers we hardly spoke to each other. I once asked his advice when the German Club had to take a play to a contest. His youngest daughter took my German class. Warner always seemed so haughty, and I found it difficult to talk to him. Also, since he taught English, I felt very insecure about my German accent and English grammar with him and around the other English teachers. I didn't want anything to do with them for a long time, although later, I got to know Mary Adkins and Merle Jordan, with whom I enjoyed visiting. They treated me very nicely.

Warner and I met again when he sang with a choir visiting at my church, Covenant United Methodist Church. I didn't know he had gone to Germany with the Bethany United Methodist Church Choir, which had toured Germany. After I learned this, I decided to hear the concert. After the concert I spoke to him and wanted to invite him for a cup of tea because I lived almost across the street from the church. I complimented him on the two beautiful solos he sang. He expressed his regrets about Ottokar's death.

Then he said, "Now you're looking for the third husband."

That ticked me off so I turned around and walked away. He called me several weeks later to translate into German some thank you letters to German families with whom he and a friend had stayed while on the tour. I did the translations, and later asked him to help me entertain Ottokar's cousin Max and his friend Guenter when they visited. I asked him for suggestions about entertaining them. I didn't feel I could drive to places such as Houston and Fredericksburg around Texas. Since then, we have kept company and become good friends.

At first Warner hesitated to help me entertain them. First of all, he worried about the language barrier. Max spoke a little English but Guenter spoke none at all. Then, he had a time problem. Warner kept very busy with church work and volunteering to drive people to doctors' appointments.

In spite of his first reluctance, he helped me entertain my friends royally. He had great ideas about where to go and what to do. We drove to Houston where we saw the Renaissance Festival and NASA's Johnson Space Center. Then we drove into the Central Texas Hill Country to the German community of Fredericksburg and then to Warner's ranch where we spent the night. They had a wonderful visit they remember to this day. They liked Warner from the beginning, and he liked them too. They always ask about Warner when we visit by phone or letter. They still talk about that visit and how much fun they had.

At the beginning of December, I met an elderly German man named Paul who walked his dog every day. At the time, I kept Warner's dog, Lady, so I walked every day as well. Paul and I became friends, and he often spent time watching my TV.

He liked the large screen and always came over and turned the TV to his program. Then, he'd ask, "Isn't there anything to eat?"

I'd answer, "Who invited you?" but usually fixed something anyway.

For several months, almost every night he came and kept me company, though I often had the feeling he visited my TV rather than me. Then, when he asked me to loan him money, our friendship began to drift. Later, he suggested he might move in with me so he would not have to spend so much. He said otherwise he would have to change jobs and move to San Antonio because Austin was too expensive.

I told him, "Do what you have to do."

In March 2000, I saw him for the last time when he said, "Let's keep in touch."

I have never heard from him since. It was an interesting episode, and I enjoyed the diversion.

During the winter of 1999, Warner and I discussed going on a trip to Germany together. Not an easy decision for him to make, since he worried about what people might think. After all, two single people of the opposite sex going to Europe together. How shocking! I don't care what people think. Most people think the worst anyhow.

This friendship with Warner differed from others I've had. Warner made me feel we couldn't have a close relationship. At the beginning of our keeping company, he told me with brutal honesty that he couldn't give me any love. I didn't know what he meant. I thought it a strange thing to say. I felt rejected and hurt.

It really surprised me when he decided to go to Europe with me. The trip offered a good opportunity for him because I knew the languages of some of the countries, and I had lived in Europe a long time. He had a chance to visit his Swedish cousins whom he had never met before. I found it interesting and an adventure.

Friends in the church said to me, "Either you will hate each other when you return from the trip or you will have a closer friendship."

I believe we have a closer friendship. "When one has found a true and faithful friend one has found a treasure," someone has said. In spite of some little fights and disagreements, our friendship has endured.

Chapter 24

The World Traveling Day

March 31, 2000, the day we called world traveling day, Warner and I headed for Europe. I woke up bright and early ready to go. I had to leave the apartment at 7:30 a.m. because Andrew and I had to take Nathalie, my nine-year old granddaughter, to school, a job I normally did every day during the school year.

I stopped at the office to pay my apartment rent and to get my mail, and then, quickly drove to Andrew's house with my suitcase already in the trunk. Andrew had put it there for me the night before. I said my good-byes to Debbie, my daughter-in-law, Andrea my eldest granddaughter, and Nathan, my only grandson. Then we hurried off to Nathalie's school. I kissed her good-bye and Andrew and I left for the airport.

Warner had left for Houston a day before because he wanted to celebrate his grandson's first birthday on March 31st before we flew out. Warner had asked me to go with him, but I didn't want to disturb the family's festival, and I also wanted to spend time with my middle son, James, on his birthday, March 30th. For this reason I left by plane for Houston on March 31st.

The Lufthansa plane left Houston for Frankfurt, Germany at 3:30 p.m. Warner usually arrives late for everything, but he surprised me and arrived early! We met with a hug and checked in before we went upstairs to our gate and waited to board the plane. We flew tourist class but had good seats. I let Warner sit by the window because I don't care to look out. We had a smooth nine and a half-hour flight to Frankfurt. There we had a very rough landing, not because of the weather but because of the pilot. Warner said, "He's just a sporty German." I agreed.

After we went through Customs, we caught an electric cart to go to the gate for the Hamburg flight. There, we waited over an hour. Finally the time came to board the plane for the hour flight to Hamburg. Traude, my friend from Vienna, and her husband, Willy, met us.

After we got our luggage, Traude and Willy took us sightseeing through the cosmopolitan city of Hamburg. I had always wanted to see Hamburg. We had beautiful weather and saw that the flowers and trees had started budding despite it being late winter in Germany. We hadn't expected to see flowers so early.

Towards evening, they took us to dinner at an unusual and comfortable restaurant on the Elbe River. As each ship passed they were saluted with a ceremony that named their nationality and played their national anthem. We wondered where each ship was going or where it had been. We had an excellent fish dinner and a lot of fun as we watched the river and the ships out of the windows.

The fun stopped when we took Warner to the youth hostel where he planned to stay in Hamburg. Since he had forgotten to call in before 6:00 p.m., they rented the room to someone else. Now, we had to look for another place for Warner. The clerk at the hostel recommended the Fisherman's Hotel, and Willy found it just a few blocks away. It had reasonable rates, and Warner found it an interesting and enjoyable experience. I stayed with Traude and Willy in their apartment and enjoyed their guest bedroom.

While in Hamburg we went to the Baltic Sea and breathed its fresh air and went through interesting little villages with cozy and homey feelings. The village of Lubeck with its old buildings and narrow cobbled streets transported us back into the Middle Ages. The buildings, built next to each other without space between them, had sharply pointed roofs. Most had served as medieval homes as well as business buildings. Lubeck, in the northwestern part of Germany, once stood as a proud place of commerce.

We also toured the magnificent Hamburg harbor where we saw international ships loaded and unloaded. There we saw ships undergoing repair in dry docks and others under construction in covered sheds in this major shipbuilding center. The guide on the harbor tour pointed out all of the interesting sights and gave us a history of the harbor and told us of its importance.

We toured the lake in the middle of Hamburg where we saw the central business district and many of the foreign consulates. Traude and Willy lived at the north end of this lake on one of the small fingers. Then, we wandered through the city with its narrow covered streets for pedestrians with elegant shops on both sides. We rode to the top of the TV tower where we had wonderful views of the entire city of Hamburg and had coffee. When we got back down, we walked through a lovely early blooming garden. The garden with its walks, benches, and statues was very peaceful and pleasant. We had fantastic weather. Most of Germany normally stays quite cold in early April. We had good weather and the beginnings of spring blessed us everywhere we went.

While in Germany, I decided to visit Werner Gosau and his wife in Glueckstadt, a village down the river from Hamburg. He had invited me several times when we spoke over the phone. I had met him in Austin the year before. About every two years, singers or band players from Germany visited the *Saengerrunde* in Austin, a club of Germans and German descendants and their families who enjoy singing German songs. The German visitors usually stayed a week in Austin, performed for our club, and then traveled to other central Texas *Saengerrunde*. These German visitors had to have accommodations, and every time a group visited, I threw my name into the pot. I always enjoyed having someone from my homeland stay with me. The last time I could accommodate only one person because I only had a two-bedroom apartment.

I received Werner Gosau as a guest and I enjoyed his visit very much. We went to the singing and band performances, and on free days we drove through Austin and the Hill Country. On the last Saturday of their visit we had a dance. I took enough pills to keep my arthritis from bothering me, and we danced every dance until the party ended. Werner's wife stayed in Germany because she had traveled to the U. S. before and didn't want to make the trip again.

Warner and I went by train to this little northern German town of Glueckstadt. Werner Gosau and his wife picked us up from the train station. They showed us their Lutheran church, a tall and large building in the middle of town. Then we went to the marketplace with its many stands selling flowers, vegetables and fruits, seeds, cheeses, and meats. I bought *Matjes* Herring at a fish stand to take along with me to eat later. I can't find them in Texas, so it really excited me to find them to take back to Traude's in Hamburg. Unlike most stores that stayed open to six, the market in Gluckstadt closed at noon.

After our market shopping we went to a very old and very quaint restaurant. We ate upstairs, climbing a set of very narrow stairs at the back of the building. The upper room had heavy old beams supported by large wooden columns. The building, famous for its food and age, sagged on one side and the floor slanted a little. I ate, of course, *Matjes* Herrings.

After lunch we walked a little more around the town. Werner took us to the city hall or *Rathaus* and showed us historical maps of the city. Gluckstadt had served as a fortress that protected Germany from attacks up the Elbe River by the Swedes. Then, we went shopping at a small gift shop where I found a teddy bear. Afterward, Werner and Eva took us to the canal built by Emperor Kaiser William to connect the Elbe River with the North Sea. We

245

watched ships going through the canal, and its western locks, and then, we crossed it on a ferry and visited the museum where we saw pictures of the building of the canal. On the way back to Glueckstadt we drove over a very large and beautiful bridge, then through the smelly fields. Being spring, German farmers were fertilizing their fields with manure from their barns. Truthfully speaking, it stunk to high heaven everywhere. We had a very interesting and educational trip.

Back in Gluckstadt, we went to the Gosau's lovely home. They lived in a row house connected to other houses on either side and had a small very nicely kept back yard. We had coffee and tea and different delicious tarts from the bakery. After visiting and dinner, Warner and I wanted to go back to Hamburg by train, but Werner offered to take us by car. That way he met our friends Willy and Traude who invited him into their home. Then, we had a lovely evening with good conversation, good snacks and good wine.

On April 6th we said good-bye to Traude and Willy and headed to Copenhagen, Denmark by train. The youth hostel where we had our reservation, sat out in the sticks with no buildings in sight except for a large convention center about two blocks away. Despite the isolation we found the hostel a very nice accommodation, clean and comfortable and almost new.

After checking in, we caught a bus downtown, where we looked for a restaurant. We found a small place where we had lunch and met some Swedes who had come down for the day. They said they did this quite often to get away from the dreary winter. We had a nice meal and enjoyed visiting with the Swedes who really had fun. They left the cold winter in Sweden to warm up in Copenhagen. They warmed up all right. I wanted to have some spirits too, but Warner kept me from them. He probably feared he might have to carry me to the bus afterwards. With Germans one never knows! Warner pointed out that this cozy little restaurant was a real pub, where people drank and had a good old drunken time.

We left the pub and went to the Tivoli Gardens on the way back to catch the bus. Unfortunately, the Gardens didn't open during the winter season. We could only look through the fence. We lost our way and ended up on the wrong side of the Tivoli Gardens. We had to walk and walk and walk in order to reach the bus. We didn't get to walk through the Gardens, but we did have a long and pleasant walk around them.

The next morning, I visited with an elderly lady from Norway. She urged me to see an orchid show at the nearby convention center. I told Warner, and we walked to the convention center and spent the morning seeing the most beautiful orchids. Warner took a lot of lovely pictures and we ate at the show as well. Then, because I was so tired, we spent the afternoon napping in the hostel. That evening Warner washed our clothes in the hostel laundry room.

On Saturday morning, April 8th, we had a strange experience. About 10 o'clock, we caught the bus to the downtown square of Copenhagen to find everything very quiet on this very beautiful Saturday morning. No one walked the streets, the busses traveled empty, and the shops remained closed. I wanted to go to a beauty shop to have my hair done, but with no shops open, I thought I'd have to give up the idea. Just then I saw a nice lady standing on the corner. I asked her in English why everything was closed.

She understood me and said, "The businesses are not closed all day. They just open later between eleven and twelve o'clock."

Sure enough, at 11:00 a.m. everyone came out of their houses to enjoy the first sun's rays, and the stores opened. I made an appointment at a beauty shop to have my hair done later in the afternoon.

We walked all around the square in Copenhagen. Again, as in Hamburg, we made a harbor tour and saw the famous Little Mermaid. We went to a church that reminded us a little of our painted churches here in Texas. They were preparing for a funeral and were placing flowers on the floor around a white coffin. I

247

asked if a child were being buried since the coffin was white, but the florist told me that everyone in Denmark is buried in a white coffin, and flowers are always placed on the floor around the coffin.

Later, we sat by the canal in a nice sidewalk restaurant, drank coffee, and then had lunch. This beautiful, sunny, and quiet morning, the banks of the canal soon filled with people as they enjoyed the outdoors and the warm sun. They crowded the tables in front of the restaurant and walked the quay. It seemed all of Copenhagen was out enjoying the sun with us. A group of young Swedes sitting next to us, supposed to be at a Y.M.C.A. convention, had escaped to enjoy the sun. They soon took off their coats and seemed comfortable in their shirtsleeves, but Warner and I found it comfortable with our coats on.

While I got my hair done, Warner discovered an amber museum. He came by the beauty parlor to let me know to meet him there. When I caught up with him, I bought a ring and matching earrings with oval amber stones in silver settings. Warner bought amber for his children, but nothing for himself.

After that buying spree, we went to a modern art museum. I could easily have missed that. Modern Art frustrates me because I can't tell what it represents. I always like to read something into the painting. Warner told me not to do that and just enjoy it. I tried, but I didn't have much success.

We went back to the Youth Hostel fairly early so we could pack our things for Sweden. We boarded the train in Copenhagen early and headed for Jonköping, Sweden or *Yongshipping* as it sounded to us. There, Warner planned to meet cousins he had never seen before. When we arrived at the station, we met Sven-Olof, one of Warner's cousins, waving a Swedish flag, blue with a yellow cross. He came quickly towards us, apparently recognizing the American in us. We greeted each other, put our luggage in the car, and then went off to a wonderful lunch.

Afterwards, Sven-Olof took us to our hotel. Even though the

Swedish hotel was brand new, I liked the Youth Hostel in Copenhagen better. I found the heavy, thick, metal doors almost impossible for me to open. The small computer outside the door that unlocked the door didn't work for me at all. Without Warner's help, I might have ended up sleeping in the hallway. The light in the fiberglass, self-contained bathroom units went off if you sat there too long. The lights, the doors, and the computers, gave me fits.

About two hours later, Magnus and May, other cousins of Warner's, arrived to pick us up for a family gathering. We met everyone at Sven-Olof's and Eva's beautiful home. After the greeting and welcoming, we sat in the dining room around a big table and had a delicious quiche dinner Eva prepared. After dinner we shared good conversation and spent a lovely evening in the warmth and love with Warner's cousins.

The next day Sven-Olof met us early, and we went from one end of Jonköping to the other. We saw the beautiful library where Eva worked, we saw the university and the teacher's college where Sven-Olof had worked as a teacher and administrator, and we visited Covenant Church, a large, beautiful modern building decorated in light colored wood, in which Sven-Olof and Eva worshipped. The sanctuary invites the visitor to sit down in a pew to meditate and pray. He proudly showed it to us. It also had a nice coffee shop where we drank coffee, for Europeans can't live without coffee or tea. I found the coffee very strong and thought of our German expression, "The spoon almost stands straight in the cup."

We saw many beautiful sights in Jonköping. I particularly liked the *Stadtpark* with its lovely view of the town and lakes. We had both lunch and dinner overlooking the water.

Two of Warner's cousins took us into the country to see his grandfather's birthplace in a small, recently renovated, three-room cottage. This lovely cottage overlooked beautiful fields and woods. We also saw the church where Warner's grandfather was baptized.

His grandfather immigrated to America at the age of eighteen.

The following morning, Sven-Olof took us for a last sightseeing tour of the area outside Jonköping. We visited a park atop a high hill with a lovely view of the village below and a well-known arch built to remember the visit of a Swedish king. Then, we had to say good-bye to our gracious host, Sven-Olof. We boarded a bus that took us to catch a train en route to Stockholm.

We had a lovely trip to Stockholm through beautiful countryside filled with lakes, and arrived at 3:30 in the afternoon. In Stockholm, Warner's cousin Agne Werneskög, whom he did not know, didn't meet us as planned. Warner looked all over and had him paged twice, but we didn't find him. Finally, he appeared. He had expected us an hour later. Agne felt terrible we had to wait for him.

He drove us around Stockholm, a city built on a group of islands, to give us an idea of the city. Then, he took us to the youth hostel. The hostel, a remodeled prison, had cell-like rooms so small one could hardly turn around. Warner and I planned to spend a night there together because we could find nowhere else to stay. I couldn't imagine two people in one of these and being so fenced in. I told Agne and Warner that I couldn't stay there and would rather go to a reasonable hotel. Agne laughed and understood. He then offered us their summerhouse.

So Agne took us to their summerhouse on a lake about thirty kilometers outside of Stockholm where we stayed. Warner had a big room and I did too. Comfortable and cozy, I enjoyed it very much. We named it the Palace.

The next morning, after breakfast, Agne took us to downtown Stockholm to his office, and we arranged to meet him later to go back to the Palace. We took a Royal Canal tour, saw the beautiful homes of the rich, and went to the Grand Hotel where we had Kahlua and coffee and whipped cream. I must say it lifted our spirits. We entered the hotel by walking past the bar which I thought was a café. Warner said it was a bar and showed me the piano with pads and bar stools around it. As we went out, we passed the bar again, and I finally believed him.

Around noon, we went to St. Joseph's Church to listen to Agne's friend, the organist, in a wonderful Bach Concert. After the concert, we caught a taxi and went to see the great ship Vasa. The sailing ship, constructed for the Swedish king, sank in the harbor before its maiden voyage. It was top heavy and flooded when water ran into its open gun ports. We walked all over the museum, took pictures, and bought souvenirs. At four, we went to Agne's office, had coffee, and then went back to the Palace where Warner and I had supper, washed laundry and played UNO. Agne had a meeting and came in very late.

The next day when Agne took us to Stockholm, he told us we should visit the Royal Palace, so we did. Then we went to see Old Town near the Royal Palace. We strolled slowly through it and landed in a quaint coffee shop where Warner had apple cake with vanilla sauce and I had cheesecake with whipped cream. Of course, we took pictures of Old Town and bought some souvenirs.

Around 12:30 we met Agne and Brigitta, Agne's wife, for lunch. We had a wonderful, tasty seafood lunch in the restaurant on the 6th floor of the best department store in Sweden.

Then Agne and Brigitta drove us around Stockholm. We saw their beautiful former home and more lovely places of the rich. Later on, we went to their apartment for coffee and princess cake.

In the evening, we went to The Tower with them, where the family prepared for Agne's sixtieth birthday. I found The Tower quite interesting. It's built like a medieval fortress tower, with a turret and crenellated wall around the top. The man who began building it could not finish it because he died. His two daughters lived there and finally finished it. When they died they willed it to the city which uses it for parties and city functions.

Our last day in Stockholm, we had a good lunch in Agne's favorite Italian restaurant near his office. Then we went to Milles Gardens. There we saw and admired Strindberg's sculpture and paintings and an exhibition of Eckström's paintings. I found Eckström's paintings more fitting to my mood and mentality than Strindberg's, which are too dark for my taste.

After the museum we drove to the Polish Ferry. Practically the last passengers who arrived, it took a long time to get our tickets as they wouldn't accept my credit card, and we had to use Warner's. Then, on the ferry, it took a long time to get the keys for our room. Neither of us spoke Polish and we didn't always understand what to do. To us, they seemed disorganized, but finally we got our rooms, had supper, and went to bed.

The next morning we got up at 8:00 a.m. and had a very good breakfast. The Ferry landed at 11:30 a.m. in Gdansk, Poland, and it took quite a while until we could disembark. We needed to get a taxi to the railroad station. The taxi drivers all wanted to exchange money for us, but since we had enough German Marks for Berlin, we didn't need Polish currency. When we told the drivers we did not need to exchange, they left us sitting high and dry. Finally we caught a taxi that took us to the station and took our Swedish Kronen. We thought we had to pick up tickets for our reserved seats on the train. After standing in line for twenty minutes, we finally found we didn't need additional tickets. Then, we waited one hour and thirty minutes for the train to Berlin.

It proved a real ordeal to get on the train. I had my purse zipped closed under my arm, and I tried to board the train. After I got on, I turned around and I saw Warner in the narrow aisle with my large suitcase between two struggling Poles. They pushed him from one side to the other. A Polish woman stood to the side yelling and waving. Suddenly, one of the Poles jumped my large suitcase and both of the Poles left hurriedly. Finally, Warner maneuvered himself into the compartment. Once we got the suitcases on the overhead rack and took our seats, we could relax and enjoy ourselves.

After a while, I felt quite hungry and mentioned it to Warner. When the food cart came through the train with sandwiches and other goodies, we started selecting things. As we got ready to pay, Warner couldn't find his billfold or I mine. Warner took it very calmly, but I got somewhat excited. I hate not having money, especially in a foreign country. Suddenly, I felt fenced in again. I got nervous and angry. We suddenly realized those two Poles staged the struggle in which Warner got caught to steal our billfolds. I couldn't understand how someone could steal my billfold out of a zipped-up purse that I held under my arm, but they had. Those thieves were very skillful. I hated to come penniless to Berlin. What a deal!

We arrived in my beloved hometown, worn out and not in a good mood. We went to Karin and Guenter Koesling's apartment near downtown Berlin on the Spree Canal in former East Berlin where we ate supper. We told our story about the theft and a little later I went to bed. Max, Guenter, and Warner left for Zehlendorf to Max's apartment. Max had invited Warner to stay with him, and had made the arrangements for me to stay with Karin, Max's niece, and Guenter.

The next morning when Warner came to the Koesling's apartment, he asked first thing, "Did you pray for the Polish thieves?"

Of course I said, "No." I didn't even think of praying for them. I felt like slapping them, but not praying for them.

Warner kept on and said praying for them would make me feel better. Of course, the Bible speaks of praying for one's enemies. I told Warner he was a much better person than I. Warner, of course, had prayed for them several times. Little by little I brought myself to pray for them. Indeed, it made me feel better. Warner was right. In fact, I got most of what I lost when I received my travelers checks back. Later, after we returned to Texas, Warner received his billfold in the mail. A Polish postal worker sent it back with everything except his credit cards and the cash.

Berlin's old greatness has returned. On Sunday, April 16, I went by taxi to Zehlendorf where Max lives and where I grew up.

When I told the taxi driver I had grown up in Berlin, he drove me around the city. I rode from one end of Berlin to the other, and I saw its new greatness. Enormous things have been done in the years since the Berlin Wall fell. In Berlin, the old connects to the new in perfect harmony. Where old buildings still stood with their beautiful artistic decorations, they have added new buildings in beautiful simplicity. What a great idea!

When I arrived at Max's place, Warner had gone to the little church that goes back to the time of Frederic the Great. Now an interdenominational and international church with the service in English, Warner had a wonderful experience. He felt very welcome and even met a young lady there who grew up in Austin, Texas.

In the afternoon, we went to an extravaganza in the *Friedrichsstadt Palace* near the center of Berlin not far from the main U-Bahn station for the city. We saw an elaborate show called *The Elements*, where the sections represented the four elements, fire, water, air, and earth. It had lots of colored lights, lasers, spotlights, special effects, and extensive dancing and acrobatics. Some dancers performed underwater in a special tank that rose up out of the stage, and some displayed their talents dancing on special platforms. The show stunned us with its excitement, color, and activity

Afterwards, we walked around Unter den Linden, the large parade street of the Nazis. Later, we caught a bus to the home of the Koeslings'. There, we enjoyed the rest of the evening with them, seated around their table having drinks and snacks and discussing the day.

The next day, Max drove us to downtown Berlin to get my traveler's checks replaced. Warner had canceled his credit cards by telephone. He had travelers' checks in his suitcase, so both of us had money to finish our trip. The robbery cost us really very little, fortunately, and we had a good story to tell when we got home.

After I got my money, we went to the big *Kaufhaus des*

Westens or *KA DE WE,* one of the largest department stores in Europe. We bought several things, but primarily we looked for beer glasses for *Weiss Bier* to take home for Warner's son-in-law. From the department store, we went by Valet Taxi, a bicycle taxi with a seat for two attached to the front of a bicycle, to the Memorial church, *Kaiser Wilhelm Gedächtniskirche.* The new church stands beside the bombed out tower of the old church which Berliners now call the *Hohle Zahn* or hollow tooth. The Germans have left the bombed out tower as a reminder that a war like World War II should never happen again. We went into the new church, very plain but quite beautiful inside. Shaped like an octagonal cylinder, Berliners call it the *Puder Quaste* or powder case. The tall bell tower beside the new church they call the *Lippenstift* or lipstick. The walls of the church, inside and out, have no decoration except for embedded irregularly shaped stained glass, mostly in blue. The pieces of broken stained glass together with the bombed out tower represent the broken Berlin, the broken country, and the broken people after the war. From the outside, the glass appears as holes in the walls, but from the inside, colored light from the stained glass surrounds you. It's a very moving sight.

Every day, we had different things planned. We went to a Mozart Opera, made a boat tour on the Spree River, and went inside the *Berliner Dom,* or the main church of Berlin where we listened to the powerful organ. Traveling on the Spree River we found spring had arrived as the trees blossomed and the first flowers bloomed. The sun shone brightly and we felt warm and comfortable under its rays. It so enchanted Warner he wrote this little poem.

A Greeting to Spring

While traveling to Hamburg and Berlin
We see the unfolding of spring.
Forsythia, Narcissi, and Tulips
Sweeten and bless our fling.

The sun, the weather is warming.
By its warmth the buds are swelling.
As trees are greening and opening,
We're surrounded by life's indwelling.

What joy to experience spring
In Germany on our fling.

Unfortunately, with the unfolding of spring we had to say good-bye to Berlin. The next morning, Warner and I flew back to America. Our trip to Europe remains a most enjoyable experience that we will always fondly remember. We got along well, and found no faults with one another.

Every so often Warner says, "I held my tongue and behaved myself."

I think he just says that in jest. Throughout the trip, people and even friends thought us lovers or a married couple. Warner had anticipated that. Even Eva, Warner's cousin in Jonköping, wanted to know our status. She seemed surprised to find us just good friends. Then she said, "It is wonderful to have a good and true friend. Lovers go, but a friend stays." I truly hope so. Warner and I enjoyed each other. I believe our friendship grew deeper and closer.

Chapter 25

Another Time of Testing

When I came back from Europe on April 21, 2000, my feet really hurt. I had bad bunions on the sides of my feet, and my toes piled on top of each other. For many years, I had worn very beautiful, but very pointed and very high-heeled shoes, and now I suffered for it. I wanted the bunions cut off and the hammer-toes straightened.

I found an orthopedist, Dr. Chenault. When I first saw him, he said, "Well, I can recommend extra large shoes, or surgery. When I look at you I suspect you won't go for extra large shoes. I have a feeling you will want the operation."

I trusted this understanding, good-humored doctor from the beginning. Each time I went to see him, we joked. I asked him if he believed in Christ and if he prayed. He assured me that he did and that he prayed before he operated. He arranged for foot surgery on May 25.

Suddenly, I developed high blood pressure, not dangerously high, but high enough to put off the surgery. I felt fenced in without any control of my own troubles. I had no answers. A few days later, I realized the problem! I had made all the arrangements by myself. I had not even asked the Lord for guidance. I had acted as if the Lord were not even there. He was on the job and showed me. He put a little pebble in my way to teach me patience. I had to wait. I hate to wait! He wanted me to pray and ask him to tell me when I should have this operation.

Finally, on June 21st, my surgeon's nurse called me and told me the operation would happen on June 23, 2000. I knew the Lord had arranged it that way. I knew also, that Doctor Chenault was a very good foot surgeon and a firm believer in God. I no longer felt trapped, but felt confident to go in for surgery on my feet.

The surgery, very delicate and complicated, lasted three and a half hours. Dr. Chenault cut my bunions off and broke three hammer-toes on each foot. He set them straight and put pins in each toe to keep it in place. Then, I had to stay two days in the hospital. After that, for three months I had to walk on my heels with a walker.

For those three months, I couldn't drive. Any time I had to go to the grocery store or anywhere else, I had to ask someone to help me. I hated to bother people. My children did drive me some, but most of the time I found it very difficult to wait for one of them. Fortunately, the Lord had sent Warner, my good friend, who was there for me when I needed him. He drove me to and from the hospital for my surgery and then visited me there. He also took me many other places as well.

Later, on July 4th, I needed groceries, and my youngest son, Marcus, took me to the grocery store. I grabbed an electric shopping cart and drove around the store to pick up what I needed. As I sped around a stack of boxes, I hit a counter full force and banged the pin sticking out of the middle toe of my right foot! Ouch, it hurt! I drove the pin into my toe almost all the way. One could hardly see it. I celebrated the Fourth of July at the home of my middle son, James, in great pain.

The next morning, with my toe all red and swollen, I went to the emergency room at St. David's Hospital. The doctors feared I might have an infection. In fact, I did; I had a staph infection in that toe. The doctor put me on antibiotics in the vein and put me in the hospital for several days. They insisted on waiting until my doctor, Dr. Chenault, returned from Europe to do anything else. After a few days, Doctor Chenault arrived, put me under anesthetic, and removed all the pins. Then, he told me I could drive! Warner wrote a poem to celebrate my freedom from imprisonment with my toes.

Finally Free

Hooray, Hooray!
It happened today!
The doctor was neat;
He OK'ed the feet!
Now, Gisela can drive;
The time did arrive!
She thought that she'd never
Be able to sever
Herself from her room.
She feared her doom:
Not ever to roam
A block from her home.
Her feet had been cut
And put in a rut
Of "clunky" blue shoes
She wanted to lose.
"They're ugly!" she said
"And I'd rather wear red!"
She wanted some style,
But had lived quite a while
In dirty blue shoes
That she'd never choose.
Now, happy the day
She'll go out to play.
Her Ford she'll drive!

She feels she's alive!
She's no longer trapped,
Her joy always sapped
By doctor's denying
Her Ford for driving.
Oh, wonderful day
When Gisela can play!
We hope she'll care
Her feet to spare
And always keep
Her lovely feet!

Hooray, hooray!
It happened today!
Now, Gisela is free,
As all can see!
She's happy to be
Able to flee
Her stuffy old house
As free as a mouse
To do as she pleases.
The doctor's releases
We celebrate now!

And How!

A few weeks later, as my eldest son, Andrew, tried to fix my computer, he stepped back and stepped on the same middle toe on the right foot! During the evening, my foot hurt, and I could hardly walk. I called my good and faithful friend Warner. He came over, sat on the floor, and rubbed my toe for a few minutes. After he left, the toe did not hurt so badly any more.

The next day, however, I woke up with a big pustule on my bluish right toe. I didn't want to call my friend Warner again. I knew he had to teach Sunday School and go to church. I called my eldest son's house and my grandson answered. I told Nathan the situation, and he jumped in the car and took me to Saint David's Emergency Room. The doctor spoke angrily when he saw my toe and told me very firmly I could've not only lost the toe, but my whole foot! He opened the pustule and gave me antibiotics and sent me up for another week in the hospital. I told him what my friend had done the day before. The doctor said had Warner not massaged the toe, the staph infection wouldn't have come out, but gone through the body. I feel the Lord sent him to me and caused him to massage the toe. I feel he saved my life. After a week, Warner picked me up from the hospital.

Soon after that, in October of 2000, I walked the *Walk to Emmaus*, a wonderfully spiritual weekend. I knew I had Jesus with me very close.

Everywhere we went, the helpers told me that my "chariot" awaited, and I was driven from one place to another. The walk with Jesus to Emmaus was filled with laughter, happiness and joyful tears. It was a highlight of my life. I came back home closer to Jesus and to others, and I now have a desire to serve the Lord more.

Wednesday, November 1, 2000 came with another challenge. I had done the laundry of a grumpy old man from church because his washer had broken down. It was 10:30 in the morning, and as I drove down the road to return it, I smelled something burning. I thought something electrical had caught fire. Fortunately, I drove into a Texaco station on the corner and asked three young men filling a van if they had time to look under my hood. They were very nice and did so. They thought that the electrical fan that cools the motor no longer worked. They advised me to drive the car to Friendly Car Care back up the road. The young men thought that the mechanics there would take care of me and not cheat me, since I am an elderly lady and by myself.

Of course, I first called my son Andrew, but then, I

remembered that I had road service with my insurance company. I called them. Road service sent a tow truck that came and loaded my car. I also called Debbie, Andrew's wife. She sent Andrea, my granddaughter, and we drove to Friendly Car Care behind that tow truck. While they examined my car, Andrea and I had lunch in the Black-eyed Pea Restaurant down on the next corner.

After we finished, the mechanic still hadn't found the problem so Andrea took me home. An hour later, the mechanic called me and told me that the electric fan under the hood was jammed. I told them to unjam it. They laughed and told me that it had to be replaced for only $383. Then, they informed me that the radiator was very dirty and needed flushing. I got away for only $445. Just a small matter! I don't know why, but every time I think I'm ahead with my money, the Lord throws some pebbles my way. I had the car fixed and the Friendly Car people promised that I could pick it up by 6:30. They kept their word, and Andrew drove me out to pick it up.

I still had Wesley's laundry in my car. He needed it, and I wanted to get rid of it. I headed over to Wesley's, but when I stopped at a light, all the electricity in the car went off and I had no power. I tried to get out of the car, but I couldn't even open the doors or windows. What they designed as a safety device became a death trap.

I knocked on the window, made all sorts of noises, waved my hands, and made faces. No one saw me except one young man. He probably thought me deranged. Minutes felt like hours. After the young man saw that I couldn't move when the light turned green, he finally realized I wasn't deranged, but had car trouble. He tried to open the door but couldn't. He quickly called the police on his cell phone. I didn't have a cell phone at that time, but I got one soon after this. Finally, a policewoman came and pushed me to a filling station on the other side of the road. Then, suddenly, the power came on again and the doors and windows opened! Was I glad!

First, I got out of the car. Then, I called my son and told him what had happened.

He said to me, "Mother I just left you five minutes ago, and you're trouble again."

Andrew came to the filling station. I drove his car, and he drove my car almost home. Suddenly, the power went out again! Fortunately, it happened on a little hill in the apartment complex, and Andrew let the car roll elegantly down into my parking place. Then, the car doors opened! Andrew said the electrical cords of the replaced fan had probably gotten wet, and that had made the car stop. He felt if the electrical cords dried out, the car would work. I was so very glad the car had stopped with Andrew, and he could not think it was just his mother's crazy imagination. Twice in one day, I had had car trouble. I wondered why God tested me this way.

The next morning the car started but I worried about driving it. With all three of my sons busy, I called my friend Warner. Warner offered to drive behind me to take the car back to the Friendly Car Care. We left the car there, and went about the business of taking the laundry to Wesley. Wesley got his laundry, and Warner took Wesley's picture for the church directory. Afterward, we had lunch in the Black-eyed Pea, and then we went to the homes of some other elderly people whose pictures Warner also needed for the church directory. The lady at the last house invited us for coffee and cake.

Finally, we went for the car. They couldn't find anything wrong. They didn't charge me any more for examining it, and I took the car and drove it home. Warner followed behind to make sure I got home safely. Apparently, when the system dried, the problems ended. I know the Lord tests us sometimes to build up our faith in Him. I figure I must've passed.

Since I live alone, my computer helps to pass the time, but it did, however, get me into trouble.

One day, my son Marcus said to me, "Mother you're always

alone on weekends. You don't hear very much from us, your children, and your friends don't call or do things with you either. Why don't I fix it so you can get into the chat boxes? You can find friends and also have interesting conversations. The time passes away and you won't feel so alone during the weekend."

I thought it a good idea and encouraged Marcus to do that for me. One Saturday afternoon I finally got into the chat box.

I said for the fun of it, "Is anybody out there who wants to talk to a lady from Germany?"

At once a message popped up. It read, "I am a man 73 years old, three times divorced, looking for a nice female partner. Please write to me."

I thought if he's 73 years old, he doesn't want to write to a 75-year old lady. He probably wants a 55-year old e-mail partner, so I didn't write back. I got a little more into that chat box and found most of the conversations boring and sometimes stupid. I then got into some European chat boxes that I enjoyed more. I have not, though, continued to use the chat boxes.

I did, however, find that I had made a connection. After two weeks, the 73-year old man appeared again, and this time with my e-mail address. He wondered why I had not written to him and asked me, please, to write. I wrote back to him that he probably wanted a young woman and not someone two years older than he. He assured me it wasn't like that and told me he had married younger women and that all these marriages ended in divorce. We started sending e-mail to each other, regularly. Everett wrote, sometimes two and three e-mails a day. Since I like e-mail so much, I looked forward to hearing from him and enjoyed writing him.

We started writing the beginning of December, and by the end of January, he talked about coming to Austin to meet me. Curious, I wrote him that I'd like to have him come. Towards the middle of February, Everett wrote he wanted to visit very much, but he needed some money to come. He asked if I could loan him

$300.00. I wrote back to him that I wasn't a bank, but a little later, I bought a plane ticket for him from Southwest Airlines. This ticket was non-transferable and couldn't be returned for cash. Since he didn't have money for traveling, the plane ticket didn't help much, and he didn't come to see me. I canceled the ticket, but held it until the expiration date in January 2002. I thought I might use it myself for something.

On April 26, 2001, I made another trip to Europe. Bertie, a friend from Austin High, had researched her German heritage. She wanted to go to Germany and do more research there, so we had arranged to go and sightsee in Germany. We even hoped to see the Fiords of Norway.

Everett didn't like it at all. He told me it'd hurt our friendship and correspondence. I told him the lady I stayed with in Berlin had a computer. I gave him her e-mail address, and when I arrived I already had an e-mail from Everett. He e-mailed me daily in Berlin which surprised me. I didn't respond every day as I had too much to see. We had a pleasant trip, but one that ended in a tragedy. It became another major test of my endurance of pain and of my faith. But that all came later.

First, Andrew, my oldest son, informed me that Nathan, my grandson, would go with me on this trip even though he still had classes in high school. Andrew arranged for Nathan to leave school early and do his school work while on the trip. Since Andrew did not ask me, first, it shocked me, but I still looked forward to spending some time with my grandson Nathan.

We flew on United to Dulles Airport in Washington D.C. and, then, Lufthansa to Berlin. We had a very good flight, the first for Nathan. My friends Max and Guenter met us at Tegel, the airport in Berlin. An hour later, we picked up Bertie at Templehof, a different airport in Berlin.

We stayed at Guenter and Karin Kösling's apartment. Karin and Güenter live in a big, but old-fashioned apartment, with a very large combined living and dining room. The tiny office, Karin's little paradise, sat next to the living room. They also had a very small kitchen with a breakfast table much too small for five people. The apartment had two good-sized bedrooms, and Bertie and I stayed together in the guest bedroom. Nathan stayed upstairs in an apartment with Karin and Güenter's close friend.

Nathan and I took many sightseeing walks. I had trouble walking long stretches because of pains in my back and hip. When we had to take long walks, Karin loaned me some crutches that wrapped around the elbow. This way, I could walk straight and with less pain. I also could keep up with the others. I almost bought crutches like that, but my pride didn't let me do it.

After two weeks in Berlin, we finally made it to the archives. They had been closed and opened only one day a week. Güenter and I helped Bertie look for material about her ancestors, but we couldn't find anything. The archivists suggested she might find information at a church. She couldn't find records at the church with so many records lost or burned during the war. The German archivists told Bertie she could probably find more in Salt Lake City in the U.S.! They'd sent many of their records there. She traveled all the way to Germany just to learn she could probably find more in our own country.

After four weeks in Berlin, we flew to visit Vienna, Austria for twelve days. We had to find a place to stay because I had sold the apartment in which I lived with Ottokar. Finally, we found a very nice apartment in the Jewish district. Our Landlord, a Hungarian, was very nice and accommodating. The apartment had one room on the bottom floor with a loft. The loft had an ornately decorated railing and a big bed and a large armoire. Despite the small apartment, the high ceiling gave us a sense of space, and one didn't feel confined. A very narrow circular iron stair led to the loft. Nathan wanted to occupy the loft, which he enjoyed very much. We could speak to him and also see him when he stood near the railing.

We ladies stayed downstairs. The apartment had a small

kitchenette where we enjoyed preparing simple meals. Most the time we prepared lunch and snacks. Eating in the apartment proved convenient and pleasant and also saved a lot of money. Our rent included breakfast served at a neighboring house every morning. We had to go down the street for that, and then, usually we ate dinner out. On the first floor of the apartment, we had a big table, a big French bed like a Hollywood bed, several chairs, a television, and a phone. Since we had no closet and the armoire was up in the loft, we girls hung our clothes on the rail of the circular staircase.

The apartment had an excellent location with a big market, shops, and the post office very near. The streetcars and subway also ran close by, a wonderful arrangement indeed.

In Vienna, we saw the beautiful, majestic castle Schoenbrunn with its magnificent park. We visited the Hofburg, now the seat of government. We went to Strauss and Mozart concerts, visited the coffeehouses with their delicious tarts and cakes, and saw the famous Hundert Wasser House with its buckled floors, crooked walls, and crooked, odd shaped doors, some large and others small. The windows varied; some of them quite large and others almost tiny, none of them alike or straight. The surrounding small village had unusual gift shops and crooked buildings. Even the winding walks make one uneasy with their uneven surfaces. It made our heads swim. We really exercised care to prevent falling. The most amusing part of this journey for me was to watch Nathan. He excitedly hopped and skipped around seeing every shop.

We couldn't leave Vienna without seeing the top of a mountain so we visited the Vienna Houseberg, a mountain very close to the city. When we reached the mountaintop, we had a splendid view of the sun shining through a clear sky. We visited the chapel which the Austrian queen Sisi had built atop the mountain, and walked around, stepped on a field of snow, and had a good hot lunch in the restaurant on top of the mountain. The Texans, Bertie and Nathan, grew quite excited about the snow.

While in Vienna, we also took a trip to Budapest, basically to get an impression of the city and also the country. Since we did not have much time, we took a taxi and hired a tour guide to take us all over the city. Toward evening, we went back to Vienna by train. Nathan found this especially interesting since he'd never ridden a train before. We really made the most of our twelve days in Vienna.

When we left Berlin for Vienna, Everett didn't hear from me for twelve days. When I returned to Berlin, I had ten e-mail messages from him. Wow! I thought he must be really interested in me. This flattered me and made me feel good.

Back in Berlin, we went back to the archives for Bertie's genealogy. During our trip to Vienna, Guenter found several other places for her to look. We went to those places, but unfortunately, found nothing.

In the beginning of June, my friend Bertie had to leave before her free ticket expired. We really had wanted to travel to Norway, but found it impossible to get bus, train, or ship to Norway. The Germans had booked every passage. Norway is a very popular and expensive country. Germans, however, with lots of time and money, go there for vacation.

Nathan and I now toured by ourselves. As the weather turned rainy and cold, Nathan decided to write his journal for school, and I read some books. We had the heaters on until the sixteenth of June. It was quite cold, especially for us Texans. Because we went during the early summer, we didn't bring warm clothes along. Suddenly, Nathan and I had had enough of Europe, and we wanted to come home. Before we went to the travel agency, I wanted to look at the e-mails to see if a family member had written to us.

Sure enough, Andrew had written, "I'm coming to visit Berlin on June twentieth."

Andrew didn't ask if he could, he simply said he was doing it. That meant we had to stay fourteen more days until Andrew arrived. We did not know whether to laugh or cry. We waited. Nathan came down and stayed with me in the Kössel's guest bedroom. That left the room upstairs vacant for Andrew.

Andrew had first visited Berlin at age five-and-a-half, and later, he learned to speak German fluently from his grandmother and great grandmother. Now, after forty years, he gladly came back. An excellent photographer, he came prepared to take many pictures, and he found Berlin a picture haven.

One evening at sunset, as we crossed a bridge, Andrew photographed the *Berliner Dom* with the sunset behind it. The sun made everything gold and very beautiful. Then he began taking other pictures of the river Spree and of the park nearby with the surrounding houses with small shops on the lower floors.

The temperature had really dropped that evening, and I grew very tired. I started out to go to Karin's place, and Andrew and Nathan trailed behind taking pictures.

As they caught up with me as I walked along the street, I suddenly fell on my right side and back. It shocked me so much I called out: "That is it, Andrew! Now you can put me six feet under!"

I had such terrible pain I began to cry. I really thought every bone in my body had broken. People stopped on the side of the road and wanted to take me to the hospital.

People said, "You can't walk. Come on, we will take you to the hospital."

While I lay there on the hard pavement, I suddenly felt that someone urged me to get up and walk. It must have been the Lord. Andrew and Nathan helped me get up. I took one step at a time, and when I felt that I could walk, I kept on until we reached Karin's apartment.

Karin called the doctor who lives in the next house. She came and examined me. She told me that I had not broken anything. My body looked, however, like a rainbow. The Dr. prescribed ice and a healing cream. The next day, Max brought a wheel chair and put me into it against my will. I couldn't walk, so I could either stay home or ride in the wheel chair. Nathan didn't mind wheeling me around. I didn't want to stay home, so I went everywhere in the wheel chair. I had to leave my pride at home. Soon, I got better, and by the time we left for Austin, Texas, I could walk again. Finally, on July fifth, Andrew, Nathan, and I left Berlin and flew home feeling the Lord had tested me again.

When I got back, Everett and I continued our exchange of e-mails. Now, he began talking about California and invited me to come to visit him. California and the San Fernando Valley interested me, and I wanted to visit him, but we had not set a date. My children didn't approve at all.

About four weeks after I got back to Austin, Everett wanted to come to see me. I agreed and it certainly made a better impression on my children. My children worried about my traveling to visit Everett. They didn't want me to go to see a complete stranger. All three of my sons said, "No, you must not go." They didn't worry about our writing back and forth. They didn't see that as dangerous.

Yet, I was determined to go to California, and I called Southwest Airlines and validated the ticket I had bought earlier. Before I was to leave, however, Everett called and we exchanged telephone numbers. He said that he could not get to the airport and asked that I send him a money order for one hundred dollars for him to get a cab to the airport. I sent the money order, but I have since found out I sent the money order to his office address. I have never had his home address, just those of his office and his e-mail.

When Everett called over the phone, he sounded very gentlemanly, soft spoken and polite. But when he wrote, he seemed like a different person as he was often rude. When he asked for money, I couldn't believe this soft-spoken gentleman had such nerve.

I believe he didn't give me his home address because he still lived with his common-law wife. He had told me she had taken care of him when he had a heart attack and also when he had a quadruple by-pass operation. He said they lived in her house and had lived there together long enough that she was legally his wife. He told me, however, they lived separately in different parts of the house. He wrote he wanted to get rid of her, but she had gotten a lawyer, and he had to pay her alimony for three years. This was one of the reasons he said he needed money from me. He told me he didn't get very much pension. He said he worked with real estate and he sold houses. He never wrote he sold a house, but that he was always close to it. Then, he'd write something happened, and the house did not sell. Much of what he told me didn't add up, but his e-mails usually caused me to wonder what he'd say next. I got some fun out of the e-mails.

Everett planned to arrive in Austin on September 4th. He told me his flight got into Austin at 9:30 p.m. I had sent him the hundred dollars to get to the airport in California. Marcus planned to go to the airport with me to pick him up. My sons refused to let me go meet a stranger alone.

Marcus said, "Mother, if he doesn't look alright, we will just leave him there."

A few days before the 4th, Everett wrote me that his niece had fallen very ill and lay in a coma.

I thought, in a few days she dies, and he has a good way out of the visit. Sure enough, on Sunday, September 2nd, he called to say the niece had died at 5:00 a.m. He apologized because he couldn't come, and he asked for another hundred dollars because he had used seventy dollars of the first one hundred dollars to send roses to the funeral of his niece. He couldn't come to visit because he needed to stay there for his family. It wasn't a very plausible excuse.

I felt very strongly, however, he'd lied to me, and I'd had enough. I knew he'd never come to meet me. He only wanted money and he tried to draw as much out of me as I'd let him. He had the nerve to ask me for another hundred dollars saying he had sent seventy dollars worth of roses to his niece's funeral! Now he said he didn't have enough money to get to Burbank airport to fly to Austin! He asked if he could use the Southwest Airlines ticket if he identified himself at the airport.

I said, "No."

He has never asked for money again, and I never used the ticket to fly to California..

In another e-mail, Everett tried to sell me a house for $189,000, and he told me he'd make 3% commission off of it from me. I told him in my next e-mail I'd love to have the house as my summer home. Right away he bit and told me in his next e-mail I should come to California and see it. After I read this, I clicked block sender on my computer and Everett disappeared. I canceled the airline ticket. The next day he called me twice and left messages on my answering machine. Meanwhile, he might have caught on that I had had enough of this foolishness. After nine months of e-mail, sometimes fun, sometimes boring, sometimes exciting, sometimes frustrating, the episode with Everett finally ended.

Once I had overcome the jet lag from the flight from Berlin, I decided to look at my bank account. I didn't get a surprise; I got a shock! I had overdrawn my account by over five hundred dollars. It shocked me so I couldn't think straight. First of all I had to stop some checks. This cost me seventy-five dollars. I got the checks stopped and the five hundred dollars paid. My bills were all paid, but I didn't have a penny to spend for groceries.

Since World War II when we lost all our money, I have never experienced a situation like this. What to do? I always call my friend Warner when I'm in trouble. He always knows what to do and has always given me the right advice. I called him and told him what a mess I had made of my bank account. Right away, he asked me if I needed money.

For the fun of it, I told him, "Yes, a lot."

He said, "I can't give you a lot, but I can loan you two hundred dollars. I just put it in savings the other day."

I hated to borrow it from him, but he told me, "It's okay."

Two hours later, he appeared at my apartment with two hundred dollars cash. It overwhelmed me. This, I call real friendship. He sure came through for me when I needed it. I told our friend Mary about it, and she gave me the nickname *pauper*. From the two hundred dollars I had to pay for something which came up unexpectedly. Anyhow I had to live on fifty-three dollars grocery money the whole month!

I learned a lot during my pauper days. First of all, I learned I had very dear friends. Secondly, I learned that when I can't pay for dinner my kids can. What a surprise! In the past, I had had to pay when the family went out for dinner. I also learned we're very blessed and have more than we need. One can live on a lot less.

Most importantly, I learned to never short-change the Lord. I wondered why I got myself in such a financial mess, and I remembered. I had cut my tithe money in half and had taken the other half with me. After all, I planned to go to church every Sunday and give the tithe then, but it didn't work out as I had hoped. Nathan and I had devotionals, but I didn't make it to church to give the other half of the tithe money. Half of the tithe money ended up spent, but not for God. I know the Lord didn't like that, and I received a very hard lesson.

Dear Lord, I'm so sad I wasn't faithful to you. Please forgive me for that. You are so faithful and steadfast to me, and you have blessed me so greatly.

It is good talking to the Lord daily. I do that, but not with long prayers. I talk to the Lord as my friend, my best friend, and I tell Him everything on my heart. Some people say beautiful prayers, but I can't do that. I just talk to the Lord with short prayers all day long. The only unfortunate thing is that I cannot see Jesus or touch Him. He has treated me so well and blessed me so much that I often feel like hugging him. He has often lifted me from behind the big black fences of my life. He would lift me from behind those fences many more times.

In the fall of 2001, I felt I needed to see a doctor. I didn't want to drive to far South Austin to see the doctor I had seen for 39 years. I asked around in church, and a good friend Ralph told me the name of a Christian doctor at an Emmaus prayer meeting. I wrote down the name and telephone number and made an appointment the next day.

Doctor Butler asked me how he could help me. I told him that I needed a good check up and received one. He sent me for my first ever mammogram. It came back positive. I had breast cancer. When Doctor Butler told me that, the tears flowed. The doctor took my hands and began to pray for me. I felt better but still couldn't stop crying.

When I told Warner, he sent me to our good friend Mary, who lived near the doctor's office, and told me that he'd be on his way. In a little while he was there. Then both Mary and Warner took me to lunch. We visited about many things, and I felt much better. Later they went with me to see the surgeon.

The surgeon arranged a lumpectomy and radiation treatments. Both went well and I had little trouble with them. I am now a cancer survivor and have had no more trouble from it. The Lord took me from behind that big fence again.

Two days before Christmas 2001, I suddenly couldn't walk, and this scared me very much. I felt fenced in again by my health and felt like dying. I even thought of taking a few pills. The cold and rainy weather made me think my arthritis caused the pain. The pains were terrible and I couldn't sit or lie down comfortably. I had a miserable Christmas. I had pain around the clock that no painkillers helped. Again, I was behind the big black fence!

Doctor Chenault, my orthopedist, told me that my right hip was completely worn out and I needed a hip replacement. This didn't surprise me. Now, unfortunately, I could not have the surgery right away because I had to finish the radiation treatments. Before I could have the surgery, almost three months, I was pain ridden in the worst way, could not drive a car, and had to walk on a walker.

I could hardly lie still on the cot for the radiation, and I had to lie very still. One day, I started praying and asked Jesus to lie next to me. Then, even the technician noticed that I could lie still. The pain didn't leave entirely but I could stand it. From then on, I prayed every day, and from then on, I could lie still until my last treatment, which I had on my seventy-seventh birthday, February twenty-first. What a wonderful birthday gift! I had it all behind me. I did well, was neither sick nor tired. I just flew through it. The whole time I suffered from my hip pain, but, now, I could have that fixed.

On Sunday the 10th of March, I went into the hospital. I could hardly wait for the operation. I could barely stand the severe pain. Two cancer operations, thirty-five radiation treatments, and now a hip replacement!

"Isn't it a little much?" I asked the Lord. Then I remembered that he does not put more on us than we can bear. The 11th of March came, and Dr. Chenault and his team took only a little over two hours to perform the operation. He said it was "a piece of cake."

The terrible pains had left, but the aftermath of the operation was still somewhat painful. After three days, I went from the hospital to rehabilitation. Soon someone came to take my vital signs, and then I wanted to take a little nap before supper. Taking a nap! Who ever heard of that in rehab! Instead, they got me out of the bed slowly, and I had to walk! On my right leg, on which I had the operation, I could only bear down 25 percent. In other words, I had to go on my toes with my walker. After I made a couple of rounds of the hall, the therapist brought me back to my room. That walking hurt!

Here we had roommates. I was in room 214 B, and when I first entered the room, I saw an elderly lady in a wheel chair. I greeted her and introduced myself. No answer. She sat in that chair looking at the wall. I thought, "What's wrong with her! Silence can be real good for a day, but soon it gets old!" I would have no one to converse with.

A little while later, I was pushed into the dining room. There were no chairs. We all sat in our wheel chairs. It was most uncomfortable for me; I hated those wheel chairs. I did not want to get used to them; I wanted to walk again. I did not want to remain behind the big black fence. In the dining room, I saw so many handicapped people, especially the stroke victims. With just a hip replacement I could count my blessings. How often do we take our health for granted, and how often do we neglect to count our blessings.

After supper, they put me back to bed because I had had the operation just three days before. They wheeled my roommate into the room too, and suddenly, she introduced herself and started a conversation. She told me she was 93 years old and very hard of hearing. I had thought she had mental problems, but she was sharp as a tack. She was an old maid with a dry sense of humor. We laughed and shared together a lot in those few days. She made me feel better, and I think I helped her as well.

On March 21st Dr. Chenalut released me from rehab and I went home. I have since had both knees replaced and now walk every morning and evening with my dog. I believe God tested me again and once again released me from behind my big black fence.

To withstand the tests in life, I have discovered that one must have faith in Jesus Christ, and remain steadfast in that faith and have perseverance and endurance. Many times, I had to endure hunger, sleepless nights, and fear because of the Nazis and the bombing. I had to flee from the Russians and overcome the fear of war. Very often, I felt locked in behind the big black fence.

America and the love of Louis, my husband, gave me security, and my children and grandchildren have given me great pleasure. With that husband, I found a faith that continues to give me peace and assurance. I have found many friends who have strengthened that faith with love and support. I have found that my faith has helped to strengthen the faith of others. In this strength, I have felt free.

From time to time, however, I still find myself feeling I'm back behind that fence. When I feel that way, the Grace, Peace, and Love of Jesus Christ always set me free again. Through my faith and the support and love of my family and my friends, I'm ever reminded I can always rely on God, and He will release me from behind my big old black fences, whatever they are and whenever they come.

Printed in the United States
42523LVS00008B/124-135